SRA Reading Mastery

Signature Edition

Answer Key
Grade 2

Siegfried Engelmann
Susan Hanner

SRA

Columbus, OH

SRAonline.com

 SRA

Send all inquiries to this address:
SRA/McGraw-Hill
8787 Orion Place
Columbus, OH 43240-4027

ISBN: 978-0-07-612549-4
MHID: 0-07-612549-1

16 17 18 19 20 GPC 24 23 22 21 20

The *McGraw·Hill* Companies

1

Name _____

Skill Items

1. **Finish the rule** that Tom's brother told Tom. "I keep the frog in the box that is <u>striped</u> _____."

2. Is this box striped? <u>yes</u>

3. So is the frog in this box? <u>yes</u>

4. Is this box striped? <u>no</u>

5. So is the frog in this box? <u>no</u>

6. Use the rule and **underline** the box that has a frog in it.

---

7. **Every big box has kittens in it.**

Cross out every box with kittens in it.

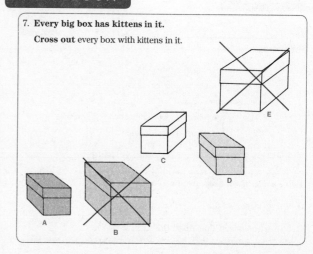

GO TO PART E IN YOUR TEXTBOOK.

Trees are living things. So trees make baby trees.
Are fish living things? So what do fish make?
Are spiders living things? So what do spiders make?
Remember the rule: All living things make babies.

C Number your paper from 1 through 13.

1. What do all living things need? <u>water</u>
2. What do all living things make? <u>babies</u>
3. Do all living things grow? <u>yes</u>
4. Are flies living things? <u>yes</u>

5. Write the letters of **3** things you know about flies.
   a. Flies need water.   d. Flies need ants.
   b. Flies need sugar.   e. Flies make babies.
   c. Flies grow.   <u>a, c, e</u>

6. Are dogs living things? <u>yes</u>
7. So you know that dogs need ▨. <u>water</u>
8. And you know that dogs make ▨. <u>babies</u>
9. Are chairs living things? <u>no</u>
10. Do chairs need water? <u>no</u>

E Story Items

11. What's the title of today's story?
   • The Tiger and the Dog
   • The Tiger and the Frog
   • The Dog and the Frog
12. Name **2** pets that Tom's brother had. <u>tiger, frog</u>
13. Did Tom open the right box? <u>no</u>

3

WORKBOOK

Name _____
Skill Items

1. Find out who has a moop that eats glass.

   Here's the rule: **All mean moops eat glass.**

   • Jean's moop is mean.   • Jack's moop is not mean.

   • Meg's moop is mean.   • Tom's moop is not mean.

   • Fran's moop is not mean.

   Who has a moop that eats glass? Jean   Meg

   Here's a rule: **Tim's frogs are spotted.**

   2. Is frog A spotted? no

   3. So is frog A one of Tim's frogs? no

   4. Is frog B spotted? yes

   5. So is frog B one of Tim's frogs? yes

   6. Use the rule and **underline** Tim's frogs.

Lesson 2   3

WORKBOOK

Review Items

7. What do all living things need?

   water

8. What do all living things make?

   babies

9. Do all living things grow?

   yes

10. Are ants living things?

    yes

11. **Underline** things you know about ants.

    • Ants make babies.

    • Ants need sugar.

    • Ants need houses.

    • Ants grow.

    • Ants need water.

    GO TO PART E IN YOUR TEXTBOOK.

4   Lesson 2

TEXTBOOK

C **Number your paper from 1 through 9.**

1. Write the letter of each make-believe animal. A, C, D

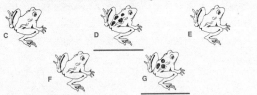

D **Bob and Don Find Moops**

Don and Bob lived near a strange forest. There were many strange animals in the forest. One strange animal was a moop. Moops were little animals with long hair. They made very good pets.

8   Lesson 2

TEXTBOOK

Don kept his moop for years. Don had a lot of fun with his moop. But Bob did not have fun with his moop. He never found his moop. All he could see was a room full of hair.

THE END

E **Story Items**

2. What is the title of today's story?

   • Moops Find Bob and Don

   • Bob and Don Find Moops

   • Bob and Don Find Mops

10   Lesson 2

4

TEXTBOOK

3. Write the 2 missing words.   **hair**
The wise old man said, "The more you cut its ▓▓▓, the ▓▓▓ its hair grows."   **faster**
4. Who did not listen to the wise old man?   **Bob**
5. What happened to the moop's hair when Bob cut it?
6. Did Bob have fun with his moop?   **no**
7. Are moops **real** or **make-believe**?   **make-believe**

8. One of the pictures shows Don's moop in a room. Write the letter of that picture.   **D**
9. One of the pictures shows Bob's moop in a room. Write the letter of that picture.   **C**

5. Idea: It grew back.

Lesson 2   11

WORKBOOK

Name _____

Skill Items

Use the rules and see which frogs are Mike's and which frogs are Jean's.
Here are the rules:

- **Jean's frogs are spotted.**   • **Mike's frogs are not spotted.**

1. Is this frog spotted?   **no**
2. So who does this frog belong to?   **Mike**   A
3. How do you know this frog doesn't belong to Jean?
Idea: It's not spotted.

4. Is this frog spotted?   **yes**   B
5. So who does this frog belong to?   **Jean**
6. How do you know this frog doesn't belong to Mike?
Idea: It's spotted.

7. **Make a box around** Jean's frogs.
8. **Underline** Mike's frogs.

© SRA/McGraw-Hill. All rights reserved.   *Lesson 3   5*

WORKBOOK

9. Find out who is smart.

Rule: **The people with hats are smart.**
- Kim has a hat.
- Pete has a hat.
- Tom does not have a hat.
- Jane has a hat.
- Ron does not have a hat.

Who is smart?   **Kim   Pete   Jane**

Review Items

10. Are snakes living things?   **yes**
11. **Underline 3** things you know about snakes.
- Snakes need ants.   • <u>Snakes need water.</u>
- <u>Snakes grow.</u>   • <u>Snakes make babies.</u>
- Snakes need cake.

12. **Underline** the pictures of animals that are make-believe.

GO TO PART E IN YOUR TEXTBOOK.

6   Lesson 3   © SRA/McGraw-Hill. All rights reserved.

TEXTBOOK

Small trees begin to grow before big trees grow. Small trees grow first because their roots are not very deep in the ground. Their roots are in warmer ground. So their roots warm up before the roots of big trees warm up.

PICTURE 2

C **Number your paper from 1 through 17.**
1. What part of a tree is under the ground?   **roots**
2. Roots keep the tree from ▓▓▓.   **falling over**
3. Roots carry ▓▓▓ to all parts of the tree.   **water**
4. Could trees live if they didn't have roots?   **no**
5. When do trees begin to grow?   **in the spring**
   • in the winter   • in the spring

14   Lesson 3

5

6. Trees begin to grow when their roots get [____]. warm

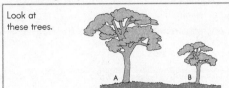

Look at these trees.

7. Write the letter of the tree that has deeper roots. A
8. Write the letter of the tree that begins to grow first every year. B

9. Which letter in the picture below shows where the ground gets warm first? E
10. Which letter shows where the ground gets warm last? T

Lesson 3   15

E Story Items

11. What's the title of today's story?
    • Don Washes the Moop
    • Don Washes the White Spot
    • Don Spots the White Moop
12. Did Don like white coats? no
13. The old man said, "The more you wash this spot, the [____] it will get." bigger
14. What color was the coat that the old man gave Don? blue
15. What happened to the spot when Don washed it?
16. What color was the coat after Don washed it? white
17. Write the letter of the picture that shows a forest. C

15. It got bigger.

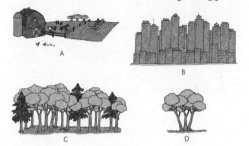

18   *Lesson 3*

4

Name _____

Skill Items

1. **The bigger the forest tree is, the meaner it is.** 3 of the trees in the picture are very mean. **Make a box around those trees.**

A   B   C   D   E   F

2. Find out which dogs just ate a cake. Here's the rule:

Every sitting dog just ate a cake.

    • A black dog is sitting.
    • A spotted dog is running.
    • A brown dog is lying down.
    • A gray dog is sitting.
    • A white dog is standing.

Which dogs just ate a cake? black dog, gray dog

Lesson 4   7

Review Items

3. Roots keep a tree from falling over _____.
4. Roots carry water _____ to all parts of the tree.
5. When do trees begin to grow?
    • in the winter   • in the spring
6. Trees begin to grow when their roots get warm _____.

7. Which letter shows where the ground gets warm last? R
8. Which letter shows where the ground gets warm first? D

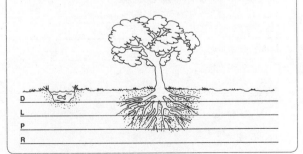

GO TO PART E IN YOUR TEXTBOOK.

8   *Lesson 4*

The pictures below show a twig of an apple tree in the spring, the summer, the fall, and the winter.

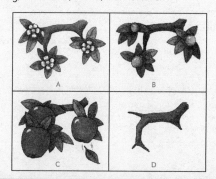

C Number your paper from 1 through 17.
1. What color are the flowers that apple trees make?
   • red   • <u>white</u>   • blue
2. When do those flowers come out?
   • fall   • summer   • <u>spring</u>
3. What grows in each place where there was a flower?
   (little) apple

4. Which has a tall straight trunk, a forest tree or an apple tree?
   • <u>forest tree</u>   • apple tree
5. Which has larger branches, a forest tree or an apple tree?
   • forest tree   • <u>apple tree</u>

D   The Little Apple Tree

Tina was an apple tree. She loved to hold her leaves out to the sun. She loved to make green leaves and pretty white flowers in the spring. She loved to make big red apples in the fall. And she loved to have a great big sleep every winter.

But Tina didn't get to do all the things she loved to do. She didn't live in a nice grove of apple trees. She lived in a forest with big mean trees that didn't care about her. Those big trees took all of the sunshine they could reach. And they didn't leave much for Tina. They dropped leaves and bark and seeds and branches all over little Tina.

The biggest tree said, "Ho, ho. She really doesn't want us to do **this.**" That tree dropped the biggest branch it had. That branch crashed down on top of Tina. It cracked two of Tina's branches.

The big trees howled and said, "That was good. We really dropped some big ones on that apple tree. Ho, ho."
MORE NEXT TIME

E Story Items
6. What's the title of today's story?
   • The Mean Trees
   • <u>The Little Apple Tree</u>
   • How Apples Grow
7. How many apple trees were near Tina?
   • 26   • <u>none</u>   • one
8. Who kept the wind and the sunlight away from Tina?
   • the wind   • the rain   • <u>the tall trees</u>

For items 9 through 12, read each thing that Tina did. Then write the season that tells when she did it.
   • winter   • spring   • summer   • fall
9. Made big red apples   fall
10. Made leaves and white flowers   spring
11. Made little apples where each flower was   summer
12. Went to sleep   winter

13. Write 3 things the big trees dropped on Tina.
   • <u>bark</u>   • apples   • bottles   • boxes
   • <u>branches</u>   • <u>leaves</u>   • cans

The pictures show the same twig in 4 seasons. **Write the name of the season for each twig.**

14.	15.	16.	17.

fall   winter   summer   spring

WORKBOOK

5

Name ____________________

Skill Item

1. **The bigger the wind, the faster it moves the forest fire.** The arrows in each picture show a wind. **Circle the 3 pictures that will make fires that move fastest.** (Accept circled cloud, arrows and/ or fire C, E, and G)

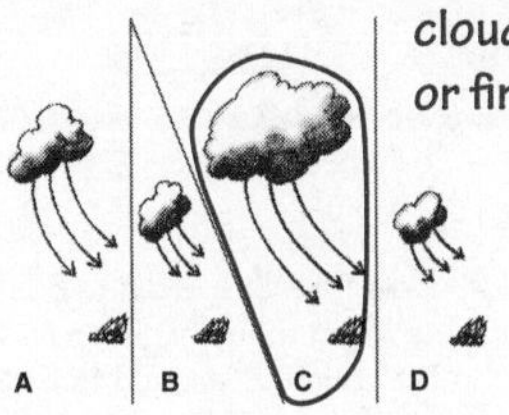

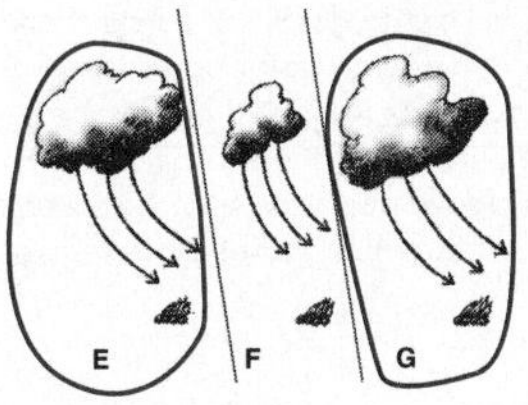

WORKBOOK

Review Items

2. What color are the flowers that apple trees make? white
3. When do those flowers come out? spring
4. What grows in each place where there was a flower? (small) apple
5. Which has larger branches, an apple tree or a forest tree?
   - forest tree
   - apple tree
6. Which has a tall straight trunk, an apple tree or a forest tree?
   - forest tree
   - apple tree

The pictures show the same twig in 4 seasons. Write the name of the season below each twig.

7. 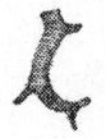 winter

8. 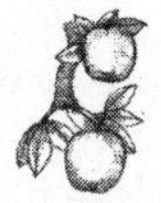 fall

9. 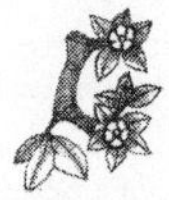 spring

10. 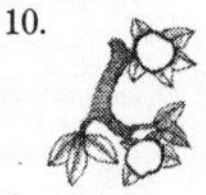 summer

GO TO PART E IN YOUR TEXTBOOK.

TEXTBOOK

C **Number your paper from 1 through 15.**

1. In which season is the danger of forest fires greatest?
   - winter • spring • summer • fall
2. In the fall, are the leaves on trees dead or alive?
   - dead • alive
3. Are dead leaves wet or dry?
   - wet • dry
4. In summer, are the leaves on trees dead or alive?
   - dead • alive
5. Are those leaves wet or dry?
   - wet • dry
6. A forest fire may burn for ____.
   - minutes • weeks • hours
7. A forest fire kills both ____ and ____.
   - plants • animals • fish • whales
8. About how many years could it take for the forest to grow back?
   - 100 years • 20 years • 200 years

TEXTBOOK

E **Story Items**

9. Did Tina feel happy or sad?
   - happy • sad
10. What did the big trees do to knock off her apples?
    - dropped boxes on her
    - yelled at her
    - dropped branches
11. How many apples did she have left at the end of the game?
    - 26 • 3 • 1
12. The big trees didn't knock off the rest of her apples because they didn't have any more ____.
    - time • money • things to drop
13. Who came to the forest at the end of the game?
    - an apple tree • a bear • campers
14. What did the campers make?
    - a fire • a house • a hut
15. The big trees saw something the campers did not see. What was that?
    - Tina • a glowing fire • a hot rock

Name _____

Skill Items

The more sunlight the tree gets, the faster the tree grows. The trees in the picture are the same age.

1. **Circle** the one tree that got the most sunlight.

2. **Cross out** the one tree that got the least sunlight.

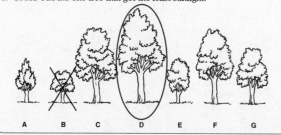

A   B   C   D   E   F   G

You measure your weight in pounds.

3. What one word tells what you do to find out how heavy or long something is? **measure**

4. What one word tells how many pounds something is? **weight**

5. What one word names the unit you use to measure weight? **pounds**

Review Items

6. **Draw lines to connect the season with the thing that Tina did in that season.**

Made little apples where each flower was •   • winter
Made big red apples •   • spring
Went to sleep •   • summer
Made leaves and white flowers •   • fall

7. In which season is the danger of forest fires greatest? **fall**

8. In the fall, are the leaves on trees **dead** or **alive**? **dead**

9. In the summer, are the leaves on trees **dead** or **alive**? **alive**

10. Are those leaves **wet** or **dry**? **wet**

GO TO PART D IN YOUR TEXTBOOK.

D Number your paper from 1 through 17.

Some of these parts belong to a **cow**. Some of them belong to a **camel**. And some belong to a **pig**. Write the name of the animal that has the part shown in each picture.

 1. cow   2. camel   3. pig

 4. camel   5. pig   6. camel

7. Which is bigger, a camel or a pig? **camel**

8. Which has a longer tail, a camel or a pig? **camel**

E Story Items

9. The big trees didn't drop something on the campers because they didn't have any more ▓▓▓.
   • time   • money   • things to drop

---

10. The big trees wanted someone to help them. Who was that?
    • a big tree   • a farmer   • Tina

11. The big trees told Tina that they would be good to her for ▓▓▓ years.
    • 30   • 100   • 500

12. How many apples did Tina have before she dropped some? **3**

13. How many apples did she drop? **3**

14. What did one camper see when he was picking up an apple?
    • the campfire   • Tina   • the tall trees

15. Did the campers put out the fire? **yes**

16. Do the big trees still do mean things to Tina? **no**

17. Write the letters for the 2 things the big trees do to make sure that Tina gets lots of sunshine.
    a. move their branches so Tina gets sunlight
    b. make shadows
    c. drop bark and branches
    d. bend to the side

WORKBOOK

Name _____

Skill Items

> The bigger the camel, the more water it can drink.

1. **Circle** the one camel that can drink the most water.

2. **Cross out** the one camel that can drink the least water.

A   B   C   D   E   F

Review Items

3. In the summer, are the leaves on trees **alive** or **dead**? <u>alive</u>

4. Are those leaves **dry** or **wet**? <u>wet</u>

5. A forest fire may burn for ▮▮▮.

   • minutes   • hours   • <u>weeks</u>

6. A forest fire kills both ▮▮▮ and ▮▮▮.

   • <u>animals</u>   • sharks   • <u>plants</u>   • whales

7. About how many years could it take for the forest to grow back?

   • 100 years   • 20 years   • <u>200 years</u>

WORKBOOK

Some of these parts belong to a **cow**. Some of them belong to a **camel**. And some belong to a **pig**.

Write the name of the animal that has the part shown in each picture.

8. <u>pig</u>   9. <u>camel</u>   10. <u>camel</u>

11. <u>cow</u>   12. <u>pig</u>   13. <u>camel</u>

▮▮▮▮ GO TO PART D IN YOUR TEXTBOOK. ▮▮▮▮

TEXTBOOK

D Number your paper from 1 through 12.

1. Camel hooves keep camels from sinking in sand. How are camel hooves different from pig hooves?
   • They are sharper and smaller.
   • <u>They are wider and flatter.</u>
   • They are harder and longer.

2. Are camels used more in **wet places** or **dry places**?
   • wet places   • <u>dry places</u>

3. Camels can go for ▮▮▮ days without drinking water. *10*

4. How many pounds of water can a 1 thousand-pound camel drink at one time? ▮▮▮ pounds. *250*

E Story Items

5. What's the title of this story?
   • The Cow and the Horse
   • How Animals are Different
   • <u>The Camel and the Pig</u>

6. Which animal believed that tall was better?
   • pig   • cow   • <u>camel</u>

TEXTBOOK

7. Which animal believed that short was better?
   • <u>pig</u>   • cow   • camel

8. Which animal got tired of the yelling and shouting?
   • pig   • <u>cow</u>   • camel

9. What did the camel agree to give up if she was not right?
   • hooves   • <u>hump</u>   • head

10. What did the pig agree to give up if she was not right?
    • teeth   • <u>nose</u>   • <u>tail</u>

11. Which animal was able to eat at the garden?
    • <u>camel</u>   • pig   • cow

12. Why was she able to eat from the garden?
    • She could open the gate.
    • She could jump over the fence.
    • <u>She could reach over the fence.</u>

10

WORKBOOK

Name _____

Skill Items

The bigger the pig, the more it sleeps.

1. **Circle** the one pig that sleeps the most.

2. **Make a box around** the one pig that sleeps the least.

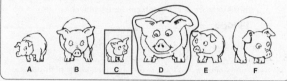

A   B   C   D   E   F

Underline everything the cow said in each item.

Sample: "You both look better," the cow said, "and I'm glad you're not fighting."

3. "Well," the cow said, "the pig showed that short is better."

4. "You agreed to give up your hump," the cow said, "so give it up."

5. The cow said, "The camel showed that tall is better."

6. "Take back the things you gave up," the cow said, "but don't yell and fight."

Lesson 8   **15**

WORKBOOK

Review Items

The pictures show the same twig in 4 seasons. Write the name of the season below each twig.

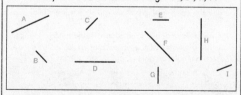

7. spring   8. fall   9. winter   10. summer

11. Which is smaller, a pig or a camel? **pig** _____

12. Which has a shorter tail, a pig or a camel? **pig** _____

13. Camels can go for **10** _____ days without drinking water.

14. How many pounds of water can a 1 thousand-pound camel drink at one time? **250** _____

GO TO PART D IN YOUR TEXTBOOK.

16   Lesson 8

TEXTBOOK

D Number your paper from 1 through 12.

1. Which is longer, an inch or a centimeter?
   • an inch   • a centimeter

2. Some of the lines in the box are one inch long. Some of the lines are one centimeter long. **Write the letter of every line that is one inch long.** A, D, F, H

   A   C   E   F   H   B   D   G   I

3. Write the letter of every line that is one centimeter long. B, C, E, G, I

E Story Items

4. What did the camel agree to give up if she was not right?
   • hump   • hooves   • head

5. What did the pig agree to give up if she was not right?
   • teeth   • tail   • nose

Lesson 8   **49**

TEXTBOOK

6. Who ate at the first garden?
   • camel   • cow   • pig

7. Who ate at the next garden?
   • camel   • cow   • pig

8. How did the pig get food from this garden?
   • jumped over the wall
   • went through a hole
   • opened the gate

9. Which parts did the pig give to the camel?
   • hump   • nose
   • feet   • tail

10. Which part did the camel give to the pig?
    • hump   • nose
    • feet   • tail

11. Which animals promised not to argue about tall and short?
    • goat   • cow   • toad   • pig
    • horse   • fish   • dog   • camel

12. Did they keep their promise? **no**

50   Lesson 8

11

WORKBOOK

Name _____
Skill Items

Here's a rule: **Everybody on the construction team helps make pictures.**

1. The paint is on the construction team. So what else do you know about the paint? <u>The paint helps make pictures.</u>

2. The pencil is on the construction team. So what else do you know about the pencil? <u>The pencil helps make pictures.</u>

Underline everything Joe said in each item.

3. "<u>Well</u>," Joe said, "<u>I'm tired of making red lines.</u>"

4. Joe said, "<u>Our team works hard.</u>"

5. "<u>Very soon</u>," Joe said, "<u>I must do something else.</u>"

6. "<u>What job can I get?</u>" Joe asked.

7. "<u>Can you tell me</u>," Joe asked, "<u>how to find a new job?</u>"

They waded into the stream to remove tadpoles.

8. What one word tells about taking things from the stream?
<u>remove</u>

9. What one word names baby frogs or toads? <u>tadpoles</u>

10. What one word tells about walking in water that is not very deep? <u>waded</u>

© SRA/McGraw-Hill. All rights reserved.   Lesson 9   17

WORKBOOK

Review Items

11. Camel hooves keep camels from sinking in sand. How are camel hooves different from pig hooves?

- They are sharper and smaller.
- <u>They are wider and flatter.</u>
- They are harder and longer.

12. Are camels used more in **wet places** or **dry places**?
<u>dry places</u>

13. Which is longer, a centimeter or an inch? <u>an inch</u>

14. Some of the lines in the box are one inch long. Some of the lines are one centimeter long. **Circle** every line that is one inch long.

15. **Write the letter** of every line that is one centimeter long.
<u>A, B, E, H, I</u>

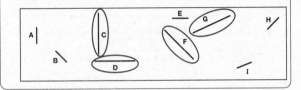

GO TO PART D IN YOUR TEXTBOOK.

18   Lesson 9   © SRA/McGraw-Hill. All rights reserved.

TEXTBOOK

D Number your paper from 1 through 15.

1. Felt is a kind of ▨▨▨. *cloth*

2. Most felt-tipped pens do not have an eraser because ink is ▨▨▨.

- wet
- hard to erase
- red

3. Which letter shows the ink? *C*
4. Which letter shows the shaft? *B*
5. Which letter shows the felt tip? *E*
6. The pen in the picture does not have an eraser. Write the letter that shows where an eraser would go on the pen. *A*

E Story Items

7. What color ink did Joe Williams have? *red*
8. What kind of tip did Joe Williams have?
9. What kind of job did Joe have?

- <u>making red lines</u>
- making erasers
- making blue lines

8. Idea: *felt or felt-tipped*

Lesson 9   55

TEXTBOOK

10. Write the names of 3 other members of the construction team.

- cans
- <u>pencils</u>
- drills
- <u>erasers</u>
- <u>brushes</u>
- baskets

11. Where did Joe live?
12. His wife was named ▨▨▨. *Mary*
13. Did she think that Joe could get a new job? *no*

14. One of the things in the picture could be Joe's wife. Write the letter of the object that could be Joe's wife.

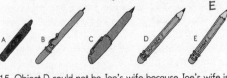

E

15. Object D could not be Joe's wife because Joe's wife is ▨▨▨. *a number-1 pencil*

11. Ideas: in a desk; in an apartment

56   Lesson 9

12

TEST 1   10

Number your paper from 1 through 24.
1. Are flies living things? *yes*
2. **Write the letters of 3** things you know about flies.
   a. Flies need ants.   d. Flies grow.
   b. Flies need sugar.   e. Flies make babies.
   c. Flies need water.
3. Roots keep a tree from ▓▓▓. *falling over*
4. Roots carry ▓▓▓ to all parts of the tree. *water*
5. When do trees begin to grow?
   • in the spring   • in the winter
6. Trees begin to grow when their roots get ▓▓▓. *warm*

7. What color are the flowers that apple trees make? *white*
8. When do those flowers come out? *spring*
9. What grows in each place where there was a flower?
                                        (small) apple

10. In summer, are the leaves on trees dead or alive? *alive*
11. Are those leaves wet or dry? *wet*

---

12. Which is bigger, a camel or a pig? *camel*
13. Which has a longer tail, a camel or a pig? *camel*
14. Camels can go for ▓▓▓ days without drinking water.
15. How many pounds of water can a 1 thousand-pound camel drink at one time? *250*
16. Which is longer, a centimeter or an inch? *inch*
17. Some of the lines in the box are one inch long. Some of the lines are one centimeter long. **Write the letter of every line that is one inch long.** *A, B, D, G, H*

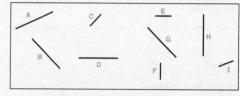

14. Camels can go for ⟨10⟩ days without drinking water.

Skill Items

For each item, write the underlined word or words from the sentences in the box.

> You measure your weight in pounds.
> They waded into the stream to remove tadpoles.

18. What word names baby frogs or toads? *tadpoles*
19. What word names the unit you use to measure weight? *pounds*
20. What word tells how many pounds something is?
21. What word tells about taking things from the stream?
22. What word tells about walking in water that is not very deep? *waded*
23. What word tells what you do to find out how heavy or long something is? *measure*

24. **The more sunlight apple trees get, the more apples they make.** Write the letter of each tree that got lots of sunlight. *B, D, E*

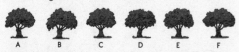

▬▬▬▬ **END OF TEST 1** ▬▬▬▬

20. weight
21. remove

11

Name _____

Ⓐ

1. Some of the lines in the box are one inch long. Some of the lines are one centimeter long. **Circle every line that is one centimeter long.**

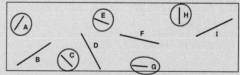

2. Write the letter of every line that is one inch long.
   B, D, F, I

Ⓑ **Story Items**
3. What color ink did Joe Williams have? *red*
4. Who made marks on Joe? *Mary/his wife*
5. Did Joe get a new job? *yes*
6. On his new job, Joe was a ▓▓▓.
   • round ruler   • number-1 pencil   • flat ruler

7. How far apart were Joe's marks? *1 centimeter*
8. **Circle** the line that shows how far apart Joe's marks were.

   ⎯⎯ A   ⎯⎯ B   ⎯ Ⓒ ⎯   ⎯⎯⎯ D

WORKBOOK

9. **Make an X** on the picture that shows what Joe may have looked like after he got his new job.

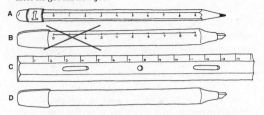

10. Object D couldn't be Joe because it does not have marks (on it) _____

Skill Items

Underline everything Joe said in each item.

11. "Doing the same thing every day," Joe said, "is very boring."

12. "I've got an idea," Joe said loudly. "And it's a good one."

13. Joe said, "Make marks on me. Make marks all down my side."

14. "Make marks," Joe told Mary, "that are one centimeter apart."

Here's a rule: **All the flat rulers work on Saturday.**

15. Pete is a flat ruler. So what else do you know about Pete?
Pete works on Saturday.

16. Jane is a flat ruler. So what else do you know about Jane?
Jane works on Saturday.

━━━━━━━━━━━ GO TO PART D IN YOUR TEXTBOOK. ━━━━━━━━━━━

20   Lesson 11

TEXTBOOK

D Number your paper from 1 through 16.
Story Items

1. One of the things in the picture could be Joe's wife. Write the letter of the object that could be Joe's wife. C

2. Object B could not be Joe's wife because Joe's wife is ▨▨. a number-1 pencil

Here's the rule: **The faster Mary dances, the shorter her lines.**

3. Write the letter of the lines Mary made when she danced the fastest. D

4. Write the letter of the lines Mary made when she danced the slowest. A

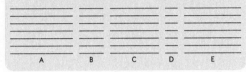

64   Lesson 11

TEXTBOOK

Skill Items

Use the words in the box to write complete sentences.

remove	weight	sing	waded
measure	tadpoles	pounds	circus

5. They ▨▨ into the stream to ▨▨ ▨▨.

6. You ▨▨ your ▨▨ in ▨▨.

Review Items

7. Which has a tall straight trunk, an apple tree or a forest tree?
   • apple tree   • forest tree

8. Which has smaller branches, an apple tree or a forest tree?
   • apple tree   • forest tree

9. A forest fire may burn for ▨▨.
   • hours   • minutes   • weeks

10. A forest fire kills both ▨▨ and ▨▨.
    • plants   • whales   • fish   • animals

11. About how many years could it take for the forest to grow back?
    • 20 years   • 200 years   • 100 years

5. They waded into the stream to remove tadpoles.

6. You measure your weight in pounds.

Lesson 11   65

TEXTBOOK

12. Camel hooves keep camels from sinking in sand. How are camel hooves different from pig hooves?
    • They are harder and longer.
    • They are sharper and smaller.
    • They are wider and flatter.

For items 13 through 16, read each thing that Tina did. Then write the season that tells when she did it.
    • summer   • fall   • spring   • winter

13. Made leaves and white flowers   spring

14. Went to sleep   winter

15. Made big red apples   fall

16. Made little apples where each flower was   summer

66   Lesson 11

14

Name _____

A

1. A spider is not an insect because it doesn't have the right number of legs. Look at the picture of a spider. How many legs does a spider have? **8**

2. How many legs does an insect have? **6**
3. How many legs does a flea have? **6**
4. If a fly is an insect, what else do you know about a fly?
   It has 6 legs.

B Story Items

5. In what year was Aunt Fanny's Flea Circus formed?
   • <u>1993</u>　• 1999　• 1949

6. In what year did Aunt Fanny and the fleas start to fight?
   • 1993　• <u>1999</u>　• 1949

7. **Underline** the names of 3 fleas that were in the circus.

   • <u>Carl Goodscratch</u>　• <u>Martha Jumpjump</u>　• Aunt Fanny
   • Harry Hurt　• <u>Henry Ouch</u>　• Fran the Flea

　Lesson 12　**21**

---

8. Draw a line from each flea's name to the objects the flea used in its act.

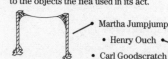
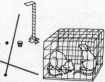

　　• Martha Jumpjump
　　• Henry Ouch
　　• Carl Goodscratch

9. The fleas were mad at Aunt Fanny because she hogged all the **fame** _____ and all the **money** _____

10. She made them live in a **little box** _____
11. She fed them dry **bread** _____
12. Where did Aunt Fanny live?
    • in New York　• <u>in expensive apartments</u>　• in a circus tent
13. **Circle** the picture of the object where the fleas lived.

A　　B　　C　　D　　E

Skill Items

14. **Underline** everything the fleas said.

    "No," all the other fleas agreed. "Things must change."

Here's a rule: **Every person loved the flea circus.**

15. Tom is a person. So what else do you know about Tom?
    Tom loved the flea circus.
16. Jean is a person. So what else do you know about Jean?
    Jean loved the flea circus.

━━━━━━━━━━━ GO TO PART D IN YOUR TEXTBOOK. ━━━━━━━━━━━

D Number your paper from 1 through 16.

Review Items

1. What do all living things need?　**water**
2. What do all living things make?　**babies**
3. Do all living things grow?　**yes**

4. Which letter shows where the ground gets warm first? **D**
5. Which letter shows where the ground gets warm last? **C**

Lesson 12　**71**

The pictures show the same twig in 4 seasons. Write the name of the season for each twig.

6. **fall**　7. **spring**　8. **summer**　9. **winter**

10. In the fall, are the leaves on trees **dead** or **alive**?　**dead**
11. Camels can go for ▮▮▮ days without drinking water.　**10**
12. How many pounds of water can a 1 thousand-pound camel drink at one time?　**250**

13. Which letter shows the felt tip? **N**
14. Which letter shows the ink? **S**
15. Which letter shows the shaft? **T**
16. Write the letter that shows where an eraser would go on a pen. **R**

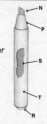

72　Lesson 12

13

Name _____

A

1. **Underline** the 4 names that tell about time.

   • meter   • <u>hour</u>   • centimeter   • inch

   • <u>minute</u>   • <u>second</u>   • <u>week</u>

B

2. Were the fleas in Aunt Fanny's flea circus **real fleas** or **make-believe fleas**? <u>make-believe fleas</u>

3. How do you know?

   • They do tricks.   • They are in a flea circus.   • <u>They talk.</u>

4. Where do the fleas in flea circuses usually come from?

   • Rome   • <u>Russia</u>   • Canada

5. What's the first thing that fleas must be taught?

   <u>Idea: to walk instead of hop</u>

6. **Underline** 2 other things that fleas have been taught to do.

   • <u>pull a cart</u>   • <u>walk on a high wire</u>   • eat dry bread

   • bark   • stand on their head

C Story Items

7. In what year was Aunt Fanny's Flea Circus formed? <u>1993</u>

8. In what year did Aunt Fanny and the fleas start to fight? <u>1999</u>

9. The fleas were mad at Aunt Fanny because she hogged all the <u>fame</u> and all the <u>money</u>.

10. She made them live in a <u>little box</u>

---

11. She fed them dry <u>bread</u>

Pick the right answers for items 12 through 15.

   • pull a cart   • fell off the high wire   • sit on a horse
   • bite Aunt Fanny   • skip rope on a high wire   • hopped around
   • swim in a tea cup   • make rats do tricks

12. What trick did Aunt Fanny want Martha to do? <u>skip rope on a high wire</u>

13. What trick did Martha do? <u>fell off the high wire</u>

14. What trick did Aunt Fanny want Henry Ouch to do? <u>make rats do tricks</u>

15. What trick did Henry do? <u>hopped around</u>

The picture shows what each flea did. Write the name for each flea.

   • Martha Jumpjump   • Henry Ouch   • Carl Goodscratch

   16. <u>Carl Goodscratch</u>

17. <u>Martha Jumpjump</u>

18. <u>Henry Ouch</u>

19. Which flea tried to get Aunt Fanny to change her ways? <u>Carl Goodscratch</u>

20. **Circle** the picture that shows how Aunt Fanny probably looked after Martha fell off the wire.

GO TO PART E IN YOUR TEXTBOOK.

The next act was Henry Ouch. He got in the cage with three rats. But he didn't make the rats do tricks. He hopped around the cage while the rats went to sleep. "Boooo," the crowd yelled.

MORE NEXT TIME

E Number your paper from 1 through 12.

Skill Items

Here are titles for different stories:
   a. 100 Ways to Cook Turkey
   b. Why Smoking Will Hurt You
   c. A Funny Story

1. One story tells about reading something that makes you laugh. Write the letter of that title. <u>c</u>

2. One story tells about something that is bad for you. Write the letter of that title. <u>b</u>

3. One story tells about how to make different meals out of one thing. Write the letter of that title. <u>a</u>

Here's a rule: **All the people got mad and booed.**

4. Tim is a person. So what else do you know about Tim?

5. Liz is a person. So what else do you know about Liz?

The fly boasted about escaping from the spider.

6. What word tells about getting away from something?

7. What word means **bragged**? <u>boasted</u>

Review Items

8. Which is longer, a centimeter or an inch? <u>inch</u>

9. How many legs does an insect have? <u>6</u>

10. How many legs does a spider have? <u>8</u>

11. How many legs does a flea have? <u>6</u>

12. If a beetle is an insect, what else do you know about a beetle? <u>A beetle has 6 legs.</u>

4. <u>Tim got mad and booed.</u>

5. <u>Liz got mad and booed.</u>

6. <u>escaping</u>

16

WORKBOOK

Name _____

A

1. Which is longer, a centimeter or a meter?

    • centimeter   • <u>meter</u>

2. How many centimeters long is a meter?

    • <u>100 centimeters</u> • 36 centimeters • 48 centimeters • 10 centimeters

---

B

3. Write **north, south, east,** and **west** in the right boxes.

4. Touch the **X.** An arrow goes from the **X.**
   Which direction is that arrow going? **west**

5. Touch the **Y.** An arrow goes from the **Y.**
   Which direction is that arrow going? **north**

6. Touch the **B.** An arrow goes from the **B.**
   Which direction is that arrow going? **south**

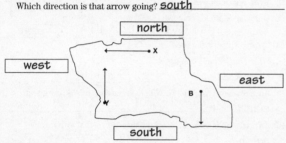

north

west

east

B

south

Lesson 14   25

WORKBOOK

C Story Items

7. The fleas were mad at Aunt Fanny because she hogged
   all the **fame** _____ and all the **money** _____

8. She fed them dry **bread** _____

The picture shows what each flea did. Write the name for each flea.

9. **Carl (Goodscratch)**

10. **Henry (Ouch)**

11. **Martha (Jumpjump)**

12. Did Aunt Fanny change her ways? **yes**

13. Which flea made Aunt Fanny say she would change?
    Carl (Goodscratch)

14. **Underline 2** reasons why Aunt Fanny is happy now.

    • <u>The acts are better.</u>   • She lives in a dog house.
    • <u>The fleas work harder.</u>   • The fleas bite dogs.

15. Where do the fleas live now? **in a (big fancy) dog house**

16. Where did they used to live? **in a little box**

17. **Underline 2** reasons why the fleas are happy now.

    • They are scared.   • <u>They live in a nice place.</u>
    • They have lots of dogs.   • <u>They have lots of money.</u>

Skill Items

18. **Underline** everything Aunt Fanny said.

    "<u>Ladies and gentlemen,</u>" Aunt Fanny said, "<u>you will see the greatest</u>
    <u>flea show in the world.</u>"

    ━━━━━━━━ GO TO PART E IN YOUR TEXTBOOK. ━━━━━━━━

26   Lesson 14

TEXTBOOK

E Number your paper from 1 through 14.

Skill Items

Here are titles for different stories:
   a. Jane Goes on a Train   c. My Dog Likes Cats
   b. The Hot Summer   d. The Best Meal

1. One story tells about eating good food. Write the
   letter of that title. **d**

2. One story tells about somebody taking a trip. Write
   the letter of that title. **a**

3. One story tells about a time of year when people go
   swimming a lot. Write the letter of that title. **b**

4. One story tells about pets. Write the letter of that
   title. **c**

Use the words in the box to write complete sentences.

escaping	covering	visited	remove
rough	first	waded	tadpoles	boasted

5. They ▨▨ into the stream to ▨▨ ▨▨.
6. The fly ▨▨ about ▨▨ from the spider.

---

5. They |waded| into the stream to |remove| |tadpoles|.
6. The |fly| boasted about |escaping| from the spider.

Lesson 14   81

TEXTBOOK

Review Items

7. In the summer, are the leaves on trees **dead** or **alive?**
8. Are those leaves **wet** or **dry?** **wet**

9. How many legs does an insect have? **6**
10. How many legs does a spider have? **8**
11. If a bee is an insect, what else do you know about a
    bee? **It has 6 legs.**
12. Where do the fleas in flea circuses usually come
    from?
13. What's the first thing that fleas must be taught?
14. Write the 4 names that tell about time.

    • centimeter   • |hour| • inch   • |minute|
    • |week| • |second| • meter

   7. **alive**
   12. **Russia**
   13. **to walk**

82   Lesson 14

17

Name _____

15

Ⓐ

Some things happen as tadpoles grow.

1. **Circle** what happens first.

2. **Underline** what happens last.

- Their tail disappears.
- They grow front legs.
- They turn red.
- (They grow back legs.)

3. **Make a box** around the animals that live on the land.

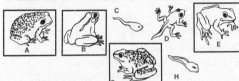

Ⓑ Story Items

4. What kind of animal was Goad? **toad**

5. Name the lake that Goad lived near. **Four Mile Lake**

6. Why did the lake have that name?

- It was 10 miles long.
- It was 4 years old.
- It was 4 miles long.

7. Was Goad **fast** or **slow** on land? **fast**

8. Was Goad **fast** or **slow** in the water? **slow**

9. **Underline** 2 reasons people wanted to catch Goad.

- to get wet
- to get rich
- to get tricked
- to have a great circus act

Lesson 15 27

---

10. **Make a box** around the animal that could be Goad.

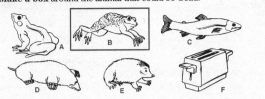

11. Hunters from a zoo said 2 of the things below. **Underline** those 2 things.

a. "I'd sure like to catch that toad."

b. "Let's shoot it."

c. "That toad would make a good dinner."

d. "We must not hurt that toad."

Review Items

12. Write **north, south, east,** and **west** in the right boxes.

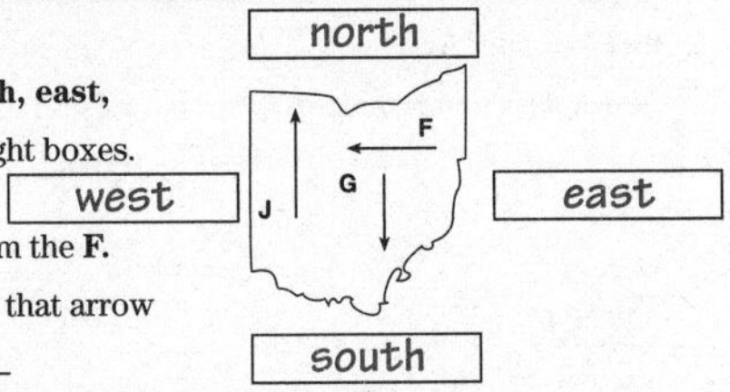

13. An arrow goes from the **F.** Which direction is that arrow going? **west**

(map with labels: north, west, J, F, G, east, south)

14. An arrow goes from the **G.** Which direction is that arrow going? **south**

15. An arrow goes from the **J.** Which direction is that arrow going? **north**

▮▮▮ GO TO PART D IN YOUR TEXTBOOK. ▮▮▮

28 Lesson 15

---

knew that if they had Goad, they could put on a show that would bring thousands of people to the circus. Hunters from zoos knew that people would come from all over to visit any zoo that had a toad like Goad. Some hunters came because they wanted to become rich. Goad was worth thousands of dollars to anybody who could catch her. But nobody was able to catch her.

MORE NEXT TIME

Ⓓ Number your paper from 1 through 16.

Skill Items

Rule: **Frogs have smooth skin.**
1. The rule tells something about any ▨▨▨. **frog(s)**

Rule: **Birds have two feet.**
2. The rule tells something about any ▨▨▨. **bird(s)**
3. Is a robin a bird? **yes**
4. Does the rule tell about a robin? **yes**
5. Does the rule tell about an ape? **no**

Lesson 15 87

Rule: **The largest mountains were covered with snow.**

6. What's the only thing that rule tells about?
- any mountain
- the largest mountains
- any frog

7. Does the rule tell about Happy Valley? **no**

8. Write the letter of each picture the rule tells about. **A, D**

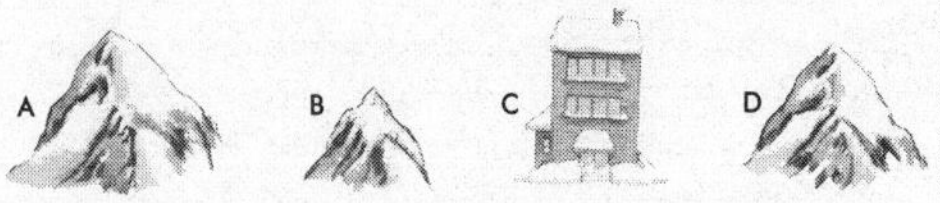

Here are titles for different stories:
a. Liz Goes to the Zoo   b. A Pretty New Hat
c. The Green Dog

9. One story tells about someone who went to look at animals. Write the letter of that title. **a**

10. One story tells about a funny-looking animal. Write the letter of that title. **c**

11. One story tells about something you put on your head. Write the letter of that title. **b**

88 Lesson 15

Review Items
12. Which is longer, a centimeter or an inch? inch

13. Some of the lines in the box are one inch long. Some of the lines are one centimeter long. Write the letter of every line that is one inch long. A, C, D, E, F, H
14. Write the letter of every line that is one centimeter long. B, G, I

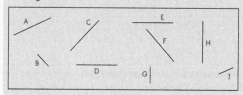

15. Where do the fleas in flea circuses usually come from?
16. What's the first thing that fleas must be taught?

15. Russia
16. how to walk

Lesson 15   **89**

Name _____

16

A

1. At each dot, draw an arrow to show which way the string will move when the girl pulls it.

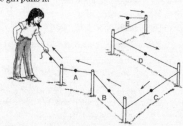

B

2. Which animal has smooth skin?   • toad   • <u>frog</u>
3. Which animal can jump farther?   • toad   • <u>frog</u>
4. Do any frogs have teeth? yes
5. **Make a box around** the toads in the picture.

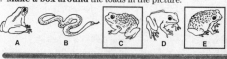

A   B   C   D   E   F

C   Story Items

6. Goad was hard to catch because she was very ▨▨.
   • old and slow   • fast and old   • <u>smart and fast</u>

Lesson 16   **29**

---

7. What did the hunters from Alaska use when they tried to catch Goad?
   • a fish   • a box   • 12 dogs   • <u>a big net</u>
8. Goad fooled the hunters from Alaska by making herself look like a ▨▨.
   • toad   • net   • <u>rock</u>
9. What part of Goad is white?
   • nose   • <u>belly</u>   • back
10. **Underline** the picture of Goad using her first trick.

Review Items

11. Write **north**, **south**, **east**, and **west** in the right boxes.

north

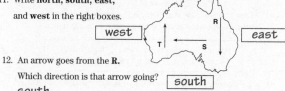

west   east

south

12. An arrow goes from the **R**. Which direction is that arrow going?
    south
13. An arrow goes from the **S**. Which direction is that arrow going?
    west
14. An arrow goes from the **T**. Which direction is that arrow going?
    north

▬▬▬▬ GO TO PART D IN YOUR TEXTBOOK. ▬▬▬▬

30   *Lesson 16*

D   Number your paper from 1 through 16.
Skill Items

Write the word from the box that means the same thing as the underlined part of each sentence.

weight	measure	leaves	paws
grove	family	hooves	evening

1. The deer ran into the <u>small group of trees</u> to hide.
2. The horse's <u>feet</u> were covered with mud. hooves
3. She used a ruler to <u>see</u> how long the rope was.

4. Look at object A, object B, and object C. Write at least **2** ways all 3 objects are the same.   (Accept 2 or 3.)

Object A   Object B   Object C

• They are all big.   • They are striped.
• They are pink.   • They are circles.
• They are not round.

1. grove
3. measure

Lesson 16   **93**

19

TEXTBOOK

5. propped up; 12. Russia; 13. how to walk

The workers propped up the cage with steel bars.
5. What 2 words refer to supporting something?
6. What word names a strong metal? *steel*
7. What objects were made of a strong metal? *bars*
8. What object was propped up? *cage*

Review Items
9. Which is longer, an inch or a centimeter? *inch*

10. Some of the lines in the box are one inch long. Some of the lines are one centimeter long. Write the letter of every line that is one centimeter long. *A, F, G, H*
11. Write the letter of every line that is one inch long.

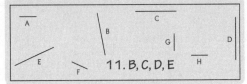

11. B, C, D, E

12. Where do the fleas in flea circuses usually come from?
13. What's the first thing that fleas must be taught?

14. What color are the flowers that apple trees make?
15. When do those flowers come out? *spring*
16. What grows in each place where there was a flower?

14. white; 16. little apple

94   Lesson 16

WORKBOOK

17

Name _____

A

1. **Underline** the 4 names that tell about length. Remember, those names tell how far apart things are.
   - hour   • year   • <u>centimeter</u>   • minute   • <u>meter</u>
   - <u>mile</u>   • second   • week   • <u>inch</u>   • day

2. Write the letter of the box that has names for time. *A*
3. Length tells how far apart things are. Write the letter of the box that has names for length. *B*

   A | hour minute second year week month |
   B | inch meter mile centimeter |

B

4. A toad catches flies with its ▓▓▓.   • legs   • <u>tongue</u>   • feet
5. Why do flies stick to a toad's tongue?
   - because the tongue is wet   • because the tongue is dry
   - <u>because the tongue is sticky</u>

C   **Story Items**

Underline **make-believe** after each statement that could not be true.
6. A toad was as big as a pillow. **make-believe**
7. A toad could hop. **make-believe**
8. A toad ate flies. **make-believe**
9. A toad is smarter than a person. **make-believe**

© SRA/McGraw-Hill. All rights reserved.   Lesson 17   31

WORKBOOK

Here's a picture of a food trap. The arrow at **A** shows the way the fly will move when the toad grabs it.

10. **Draw an arrow** to show which way the string will move at **B**.
11. **Draw an arrow** to show which way the pole will move at **C**.

Review Item

12. At each dot, draw an arrow to show which way the string will move when the girl pulls it.

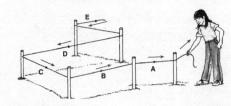

GO TO PART E IN YOUR TEXTBOOK.

32   Lesson 17   © SRA/McGraw-Hill. All rights reserved.

TEXTBOOK

E   Number your paper from 1 through 17.
Skill Items

Rule: Dogs have four legs. *C, E, F*
1. Write the letter of each object the rule tells about.

Write the word or words from the box that mean the same thing as the underlined part of each sentence.

| danger | million | a meter | half | bark |
| great | during | ruler | measure | an inch |

2. The <u>tree's covering</u> was full of holes. *bark*
3. She went on a <u>wonderful</u> trip. *great*
4. The string was <u>100 centimeters</u> long. *a meter*

Lesson 17   99

20

Here are titles for different stories:
   a. The Prancing Bear   b. The Fly That Couldn't Fly
             c. How to Grow Roses
5. One story tells about an insect that was different. Write the letter of that title. *b*
6. One story tells about a large animal that walked on its tiptoes. Write the letter of that title. *a*
7. One story tells about pretty plants. Write the letter of that title. *c*

Use the words in the box to write complete sentences.

steel	third	down	boasted	decided
	propped	gulp	escaping	up

8. The fly ▓▓▓ about ▓▓▓ from the spider.
9. The workers ▓▓▓ ▓▓▓ the cage with ▓▓▓ bars.

Story Item
10. People in Toadsville said that Goad had escaped from over five hundred food traps. But Goad had really escaped from ▓▓▓ food traps. *4 hundred*

8. The fly [boasted] about [escaping] from the spider.
9. The workers [propped up] the cage with [steel] bars.

100   Lesson 17

Review Items

11. Some things happen as tadpoles grow. Write the letter that tells what happens first. *a*
   a. They grow back legs.   c. Their tail disappears.
   b. They turn blue.   d. They grow front legs.
12. Write the letter that tells what happens last. *c*

13. Write the letter of each toad in the picture. *B, D, F*

A   B   C

D   E   F

For items 14 through 17, read each thing that Tina did. Then write the season that tells when she did it.
   • winter   • spring   • summer   • fall
14. Made little apples where each flower was   *summer*
15. Went to sleep   *winter*
16. Made big red apples   *fall*
17. Made leaves and white flowers   *spring*

Lesson 17   101

18

Name _____

A

1. **Circle** the moles.

A   B   C
D   E   F

B

2. What's the opposite direction of north? south
3. What's the opposite direction of south? north

C   Story Items

Here are Goad's four tricks for escaping from hunters:
   • eat the trap   • blow the trap away
   • look like a rock   • dig

4. Goad's first trick was to look like a rock
5. Goad's second trick was to dig
6. Goad's third trick was to eat the trap
7. Goad's fourth trick was to blow the trap away

Lesson 18   33

8. A mole's legs work like shovels _____.

9. The man from England put his steel trap on a rock. He put it there so that Goad could not ▓▓▓.

   • see it   • <u>dig under it</u>   • smell it

10. What did the man from England put in his trap?

   • 60 black flies   • 70 blue flies   • <u>60 blue flies</u>

Review Items

11. Which animal has smooth skin, a toad or a frog? frog
12. Which animal can jump farther, a toad or a frog? frog
13. Do any frogs have teeth? yes
14. A toad catches flies with its ▓▓▓.

   • <u>tongue</u>   • feet   • legs

15. Why do flies stick to a toad's tongue?

   • because the tongue is dry
   • <u>because the tongue is sticky</u>
   • because the tongue is dirty

▓▓▓▓ GO TO PART E IN YOUR TEXTBOOK. ▓▓▓▓

34   Lesson 18

There is no toad in the world that can stay away from sixty blue flies. So before very long, out popped Goad. Her tongue came out. In one gulp, she had swallowed half of the flies. She was ready for her second gulp, when BONG.

MORE NEXT TIME

E Number your paper from 1 through 12.

Skill Items

> **Rule: Tadpoles have a tail.**
> 1. Milly is a tadpole. So what does the rule tell you about Milly?
>   • She has a tail.   • nothing
> 2. A cat is not a tadpole. So what does the rule tell you about a cat?
>   • It has a tail.   • nothing   • It is a tadpole.

> **Rule: Cats have eyes.**
> 3. A robin is not a cat. So what does the rule tell you about a robin? **nothing**
> 4. A manx is a cat. So what does the rule tell you about a manx? **Write the complete sentence:** A manx ▤.

4. A manx has eyes .

106   *Lesson 18*

---

5. Look at object **A** and object **B**. Write 3 ways the objects are the same.

Object A   Object B

① They are both ▤.
② They both have ▤.
③ ▤.

> Write the word from the box that means the same thing as the underlined part of each sentence.
>
> | England | station | famous | steel |
> |---------|---------|--------|-------|
> | breath | bark | Alaska | |

6. The tree's covering was burned by the forest fire.
7. This book is well-known. **famous**
8. Jill wanted to take a trip to the largest state. **Alaska**

5-1. dogs; or standing
5-2. 4 legs; or tails, ears, paws, more than one color
5-3. (Accept reasonable 3rd sentence.)
6. bark

Lesson 18   107

Review Items

9. Write the letters of the 4 names that tell about length. (Remember, those names tell how far apart things are.) **d, g, h, j**

a. minute	f. week
b. hour	g. mile
c. day	h. meter
d. centimeter	i. year
e. second	j. inch

10. The names in one box tell about time. Write the letter of that box. **B**
11. The names in one box tell about length. Write the letter of that box. **A**

> A | centimeter   inch   meter   mile |
> B | week   year   second   month   minute   hour |

12. Two things move in opposite directions. One moves toward the front of the room. The other moves toward the ▤. **back (of the room)**

108   *Lesson 18*

Name _____

A

1.

Here's what you see through the circles made by your hands.   Draw what you would see through strong binoculars.

2.

Here's what you see through strong binoculars.   Draw what you would see through the circles made by your hands.

B

3. Names that tell how fast things move have ▤.
   • one part   • two parts

4. Names that tell how far apart they are have ▤.
   • one part   • two parts

5. Here's the rule: **Names that tell how fast things move have two parts.**
   Circle the 4 names that tell how fast things move.
   • (centimeters per week)   • (inches per day)   • (meters per hour)
   • feet   • day   • meters
   • hours   • (feet per minute)   • inches

Lesson 19   **35**

WORKBOOK

C Skill Items

Underline everything the man from England said in each item.

6. "No toad can eat through this trap," he said.

7. "If I put the trap on hard rock," he said," no toad can dig under it."

Hunters were stationed at opposite ends of the field.

8. What word tells they were not at the same end of the field? **opposite**

9. What word tells that the hunters had to stay where they were placed? **stationed**

Review Item

10. Draw an arrow at **B** and an arrow at **C** to show which way the string will move when the toad moves the blue fly.

GO TO PART E IN YOUR TEXTBOOK.

TEXTBOOK

Last summer, a group of wild hunters had the chance that everybody dreams about. They spotted Goad swimming in the middle of the lake. And they were ready for action. These wild hunters were part of the famous Brown family. The Brown family was made up of 40 people. Fifteen of them were on vacation at Four Mile Lake, and they decided to spend all their time looking for Goad.

MORE NEXT TIME

E Number your paper from 1 through 18.

Skill Items

> Rule: **Trees have leaves.**
> 1. A maple is a tree. So what else do you know about a maple? **It has leaves.**
> 2. A bush is not a tree. So what else do you know about a bush? **nothing**
> 3. A weed is not a tree. So what else do you know about a weed? **nothing**

TEXTBOOK

Story Items

4. What is Goad's only weakness?
   - She sleeps too much.
   - <u>She has a short tongue.</u>
   - She cannot swim fast.

5. People hoped they could be around when Goad was swimming in the lake because ▇▇▇
   - <u>she would be easy to hear.</u>
   - she would be easy to catch.
   - she would be easy to smell.

6. There were 40 people in the Brown family. How many of them were going to try to catch Goad?
   - 39   • 15   • 12

> Here are Goad's four tricks for escaping from hunters:
> - blow the trap away
> - dig
> - look like a rock
> - eat the trap
> 7. Goad's first trick was to ▇▇▇.
> 8. Goad's second trick was to ▇▇▇.
> 9. Goad's third trick was to ▇▇▇.
> 10. Goad's fourth trick was to ▇▇▇.

11. How did Goad get away from the famous steel trap?
    Idea: She blew it away.

7. **look like a rock**
8. **dig**
9. **eat the trap**
10. **blow the trap away**

TEXTBOOK

Skill Item

12. Look at object **A** and object **B**. Write 3 ways the objects are the same.

Object A   Object B

1 They are both ▇▇▇.
2 They both can hold ▇▇▇.
3 ▇▇▇

Review Items

13. Which is longer, a centimeter or a meter? **meter**

14. How many centimeters long is a meter? **100 centimeters**

> 15. Write the letter of each statement that could not be true. **a, d**
> a. A toad could fly.
> b. A toad could swim.
> c. A toad was as big as a baseball.
> d. A toad was as big as a house.

12-1. cups or They are both empty.

12-2. water or drinks, etc.

12-3. (Accept reasonable 3rd sentence.)

16. The names in one box tell about time. Write the letter of that box. **B**
17. The names in one box tell about length. Write the letter of that box. **A**

| A | centimeter | inch | meter | mile |
| B | week | year | second | month | minute | hour |

18. Write the letter of each mole in the picture below. **A, H**

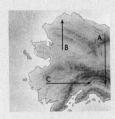

Number your paper from 1 through 22.

1. How many legs does an insect have? **6**
2. How many legs does a spider have? **8**
3. If a beetle is an insect, what else do you know about a beetle? **A beetle has 6 legs.**
4. Write the letters of the 4 names that tell about time.
   a. meter   b. second   c. week   d. hour
      e. inch   f. centimeter   g. minute
5. Which is longer, a centimeter or a meter? **meter**
6. How many centimeters long is a meter?

7. Write the letter of each toad in the picture. **B**
8. Write the letter of each mole in the picture. **C, D**

9. Which animal has smooth skin, a frog or a toad? **frog**
10. Which animal can jump farther, a frog or a toad? **frog**
11. Do any frogs have teeth? **yes**

4. b, c, d, g; 6. 100 centimeters

---

12. The names in one box tell about time. Write the letter of that box. **B**
13. The names in one box tell about length. Write the letter of that box. **A**

| A | centimeter | inch | meter | mile |
| B | week | year | second | month | minute | hour |

14. An arrow goes from A. Which direction is that arrow going? **south**
15. An arrow goes from B. Which direction is that arrow going? **north**
16. An arrow goes from C. Which direction is that arrow going? **east**

Skill Items

For each item, write the underlined word or words for the sentences in the box below.

> The fly <u>boasted</u> about <u>escaping</u> from the spider.
> The workers <u>propped up</u> the cage with <u>steel</u> bars.

17. What word names a strong metal? **steel**
18. What word means **bragged**? **boasted**
19. What word tells about getting away from something?
20. What 2 words refer to supporting something?

> **Rule: Cars use gas.**
21. What's the only thing that rule tells about? **cars**
22. Write the letter of each object the rule tells about. **B, C**

=== END OF TEST 2 ===

19. **escaping**
20. **propped up**

WORKBOOK

Name _____

A

1. When wouldn't a fox bother a rabbit?
   * • <u>during a fire</u> • during summer • during meal time

B

2. The arrow in each picture shows which way the wind is blowing. Start at the dot and draw the smoke in each picture.

 Wind
 Wind
 Wind

C Story Items

3. What is Goad's only weakness?
   * • She eats too much. • <u>She cannot swim fast.</u>
   * • She cannot hop fast.

4. Why did people use binoculars to look for Goad?
   * • They had bad eyes. • <u>They could see Goad far away.</u>
   * • They could see other people.

5. How many Browns went to Four Mile Lake?
   15

6. What did the grandmother do most of the time?
   * • <u>yell</u> • sleep • laugh

WORKBOOK

7. **Underline** the names of 2 members of the Brown family.
   * • Bobby • Bernie • <u>Billy</u> • Mary
   * • <u>Doris</u> • Luke • <u>Mike</u> • Moe (any two)

8. Did the people in Toadsville know the Browns' plan for catching Goad? no

9. The Browns wanted to make Goad think that there was a
   fire

10. What did the Browns burn to make the smoke?
    * • tires • <u>torches</u> • trees

Review Item

11.

Here's what you see through the circles made by your hands.

Draw what you would see through strong binoculars.

GO TO PART E IN YOUR TEXTBOOK.

TEXTBOOK

E Number your paper from 1 through 15.

Skill Items

Rule: Birds have feathers.

1. A robin is a bird. So what does that tell you about a robin? It has feathers.
2. A tiger is not a bird. So what does the rule tell you about a tiger? nothing
3. A jay is a bird. So what does the rule tell you about a jay? It has feathers.

Use the words in the box to write complete sentences.

| trouble | solid | stationed | happened | steel |
| propped | paddles | opposite | up | |

4. The workers ▓▓ ▓▓ the cage with ▓▓ bars.
5. Hunters were ▓▓ at ▓▓ ends of the field.

4. The workers [propped] [up] the cage with [steel] bars.
5. Hunters were [stationed] at [opposite] ends of the field.

TEXTBOOK

Review Items

6. What color are flowers that apple trees make?
7. What grows in each place where there was a flower?

8. What do all living things need? water
9. What do all living things make? babies
10. Do all living things grow? yes

11. Roots keep a tree from ▓▓. falling over
12. Roots carry ▓▓ to all parts of the tree. water
13. When do trees begin to grow?
    * • in the winter • <u>in the spring</u>
14. Trees begin to grow when their roots get ▓▓.
15. In which season is the danger of forest fires greatest?
    fall

6. white
7. an apple
14. warm

Name _____

22

A

1. Names that tell how <u>fast</u> things move have two parts.

Here are names that tell how fast things move.

- **Underline** the part of each name that tells about length.
- **Circle** the part of each name that tells about time.

2. <u>miles</u> per (second)   4. <u>meters</u> per (minute)
3. <u>feet</u> per (minute)   5. <u>inches</u> per (year)

B

6. Which arrow shows the direction the air leaves the balloon? <u>B</u>

7. Which arrow shows the direction the balloon will move? <u>A</u>

A B

8. Which arrow shows the direction the air will leave the jet engines? <u>D</u>

9. Which arrow shows the direction the jet will move? <u>T</u>

D   T

© SRA/McGraw-Hill. All rights reserved.   Lesson 22   **39**

C **Story Items**

10. When the Brown family tricked Goad, what did Goad think was coming down the hill?
    - <u>a fire</u>   • the Browns   • blue flies

11. What was really coming down the hill?
    - a fire   • <u>the Browns</u>   • blue flies

12. What did Goad do when she smelled the smoke?
    - sneezed   • <u>jumped in the lake</u>   • hopped up the hill

13. Air rushes out of Goad this way ←——. **Draw an arrow** to show which way Goad will move. ——→

14. How do people know how Goad got away from the Browns?
    - <u>They saw snapshots.</u>   • They saw movies.
    - • They saw TV.

15. What was Goad doing in the second snapshot?
    - turning over   • flying away   • <u>getting bigger</u>

16. What was Goad doing in the third snapshot?
    - turning over   • <u>flying away</u>   • getting bigger

17. The picture shows Goad filled up with air. Arrow A shows air leaving Goad this way ——→. Write the letter of the arrow that shows the way Goad will move. <u>G</u>

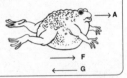

→ A
→ F
← G

━━━━━ GO TO PART E IN YOUR TEXTBOOK. ━━━━━

40   Lesson 22   © SRA/McGraw-Hill. All rights reserved.

---

4. Ideas (any 2): They're both dogs; they both have 4 legs/(straight) tail/spots, etc.]

E Number your paper from 1 through 16.

Skill Items

Write the word from the box that means the same thing as the underlined part of each sentence.

| human | remove | horse | motion |
| boasting | outsmart | escape | expensive |

1. That <u>person</u> can run very fast. **human**
2. He was <u>bragging</u> about how fast he is. **boasting**
3. Goad used her fourth trick to <u>get away</u> from the Browns. **escape**

4. Look at object A and object B. Write 2 ways both objects are the same.

Object A   Object B

Review Items

5. Are camels used more in [dry places] or wet places?
6. Which animal has smooth skin, a [frog] or a toad?
7. Which animal can jump farther, a toad or a [frog]?

Lesson 22   **133**

Some things happen as tadpoles grow.
8. Write the letter of the first change. **c**
9. Write the letter of the last change. **b**
   a. They grow front legs.   c. They grow back legs.
   b. Their tail disappears.   d. They grow a tongue.

10. The names in one box tell about time. Write the letter of that box. **A**
11. The names in one box tell about length. Write the letter of that box. **B**

| A | hour second year minute week month |
| B | inch meter mile centimeter |

12. Which has a tall straight trunk, a forest tree or an apple tree?   • [forest tree]   • apple tree
13. Which has larger branches, a forest tree or an apple tree?   • forest tree   • [apple tree]

14. Camel hooves keep camels from sinking in sand. How are camel hooves different from pig hooves?
    - They are harder and longer.
    - <u>They are sharper and smaller.</u>
    - [They are wider and flatter.]

15. Where do the fleas in flea circuses usually come from? **Russia**
16. What's the first thing that fleas must be taught? **to walk (not hop)**

134   Lesson 22

26

Name _____

23

A

- Things that are this far apart ←——→ on the map are 1 mile apart.
- Things that are this far apart ←————————→ are 2 miles apart.

1. Write **1** in the circle if the line stands for 1 mile.

2. Write **2** in the circle if the line stands for 2 miles.

3. How far is it from the hill to the lake?
   - 1 mile   • **2 miles**

4. How far is it from the school to the hill?
   - **1 mile**   • 2 miles

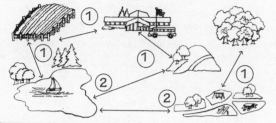

5. A mile is a little more than ▦▦▦ feet.
   - 5 hundred   • 1 thousand
   - **5 thousand**

Lesson 23   41

B

Review Items

6. **Underline** the moles.

7. **Circle** the frogs.

8. **Cross out** the toads.

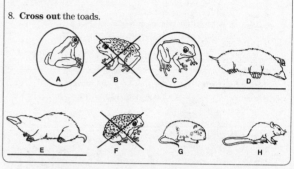

Here are names that tell how fast things move.

9. feet per hour   11. centimeters per day

10. inches per week   12. yards per minute

- **Underline** the part of each name that tells about length.
- **Circle** the part of each name that tells about time.

▭▭▭▭▭▭▭ GO TO PART D IN YOUR TEXTBOOK. ▭▭▭▭▭▭▭

42   Lesson 23

D Number your paper from 1 through 21.

Story Items

1. A boy from New York took three snapshots of Goad getting away from the Browns. What was Goad doing in the second snapshot? **getting bigger**

2. What was Goad doing in the third snapshot? **flying away**

3. Did the Browns catch Goad? **no**

4. What happened right after the grandmother smiled?
   - Everybody else started yelling.
   - Three Browns started crying.
   - Everybody else started laughing.

5. Why were so many other people around the lake?
   - to see the Browns catch Goad
   - to watch the sun set
   - to see the fire

6. Write 2 things that the people ate at the picnic.
   - corn   • cake   • pie   • salad
   - chicken   • hamburgers   • hot dogs

7. Air rushes out of Goad this way ↙. Draw an arrow to show which way Goad will move. ↗

8. Air rushes out of Goad this way ↘. Draw an arrow to show which way Goad will move. ↙

Lesson 23   139

---

12. Ideas (Any 2): They're all moles; they all have legs like shovels; they're all brown; they all have tiny eyes; etc.

Skill Items

Here's a rule: **Moles have legs like shovels.**

9. A rat is not a mole. So what does the rule tell you about a rat? **nothing**

10. Joe is a mole. So what does the rule tell you about Joe? **He has legs like shovels.**

11. Jan is not a mole. So what does the rule tell you about Jan? **nothing**

12. Look at object A, object B, and object C. Write **2** ways all 3 objects are the same.

Object A   Object B   Object C

Review Items

13. In which season is the danger of forest fires greatest? **fall**

14. Would a pig or a camel sink deeper in sand?

15. A forest fire may burn for ▦▦▦.
   - weeks   • minutes   • hours

140   Lesson 23

16. Write the letter of each statement that is make-believe. *a, b*
    a. A dog can jump twenty feet high.
    b. An apple tree can talk.
    c. A forest fire can kill animals.
    d. A frog catches bugs with its tongue.

17. Which arrow shows the way the air will leave Goad's mouth? **T**
18. Which arrow shows the way Goad will move? **R**

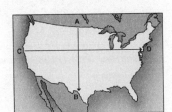

R   T

19. The names in box A tell about ▨.
    • length   • time   • how fast things move
20. The names in box B tell about ▨.
    • length   • time   • how fast things move
21. The names in box C tell about ▨.
    • length   • time   • how fast things move

A	• miles per day • feet per minute • meters per second • meters per hour
B	yard inch meter centimeter mile
C	minute year hour second week month

━━━━━━ END OF LESSON 23 INDEPENDENT WORK ━━━━━━

24

Name _____

A

1. What part of the world is shown on the map?
    • Africa   • United States   • Holland

2. The map shows how far apart some places are. One line shows 13 hundred miles. The other line shows 25 hundred miles. How far is it from A to B?
    • 15 hundred miles
    • 13 hundred miles
    • 25 hundred miles

3. How far is it from C to D?
    • 15 hundred miles
    • 13 hundred miles
    • 25 hundred miles

B Story Items

4. On the way to school, the children raced. Which child won the race?
    • Lisa   • Jack

5. Who was out of breath?   • Lisa   • Jack

6. How far did they race on their way to school?
    • less than one mile   • one mile
    • more than one mile

7. On Saturday, the children had another race. How long was that race?
    • less than one mile   • one mile
    • more than one mile

8. Who was ahead right after the race started?
    • Lisa   • Jack

9. Who was ahead when Jack could read the signs over the bridge?
    • Lisa   • Jack

10. Who won the race?
    • Lisa   • Jack

11. How far ahead was the winner at the end of the race?
    • one thousand feet   • one hundred feet
    • one mile

12. What did Jack decide to do after losing the race?
    • sleep more in the morning   • run in the morning
    • read every morning

C Review Item

13.

B

B

Here's what you see through the circles made by your hands.

Draw what you would see through strong binoculars.

━━━━━━ GO TO PART D IN YOUR TEXTBOOK. ━━━━━━

TEXTBOOK

D **Number your paper from 1 through 15.**

Skill Items

1. Here's a rule: **The short girls run every morning.** Write the letters of the girls who run every morning. B, E, F

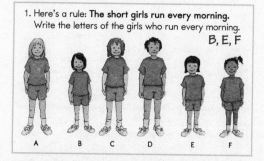

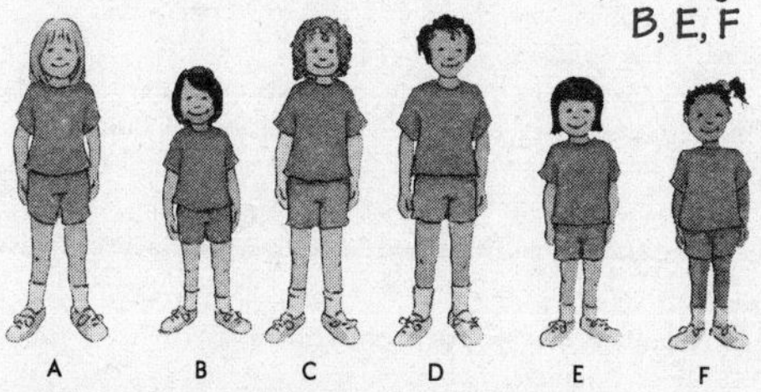
A
B
C
D
E
F

Here are titles for different stories:

a. Liz Goes to the Zoo
b. A Pretty New Hat
c. The Green Dog

2. One story tells about someone who went to look at animals. Write the letter of that title. a
3. One story tells about a funny-looking animal. Write the letter of that title. c
4. One story tells about something you put on your head. Write the letter of that title. b

TEXTBOOK

Review Items

5. How many centimeters long is a meter? 100
6. Which arrow shows the way the air will leave the jet engines? D
7. Which arrow shows the way the jet will move? T

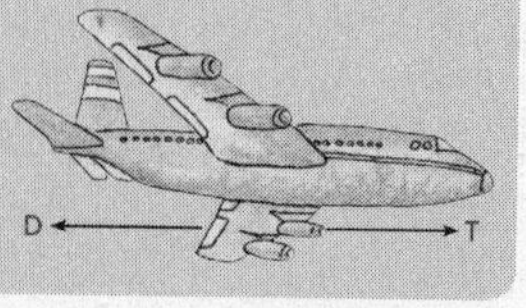
D
T

8. Write the letter of every line that is one inch long.
9. Write the letter of every line that is one centimeter long. C, D, E, G, I

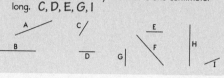

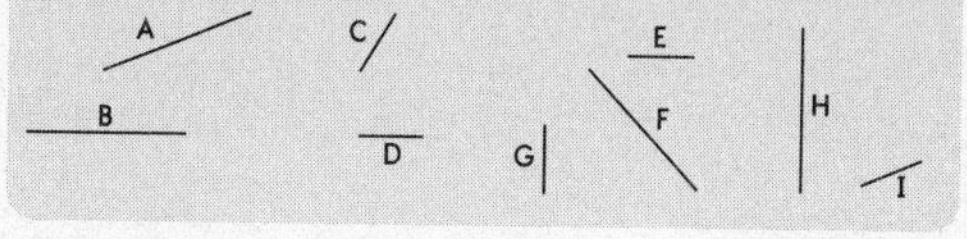
A
B
C
D
E
F
G
H
I

8. A, B, F, H

TEXTBOOK

10. Write the letter of each mole. D, G
11. Write the letter of each frog. A, H
12. Write the letter of each toad. B, E

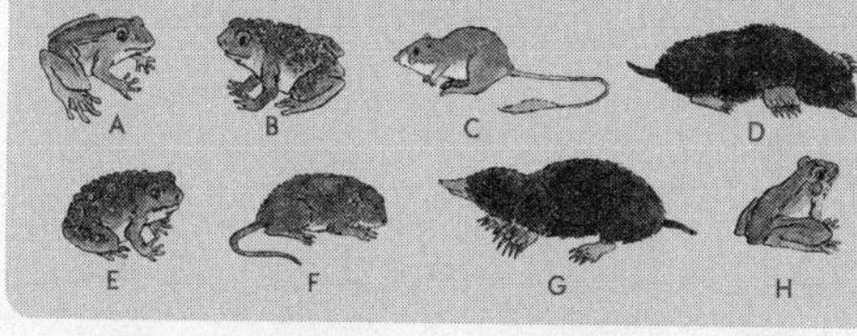
A
B
C
D
E
F
G
H

13. Name one way camel hooves are different from pig hooves. Idea: They're wider or they're flatter.
14. Which letter shows where the ground gets warm first? B
15. Which letter shows where the ground gets warm last? A

WORKBOOK

25

Name ______________________

A

Write 3 ways that tell how object A is different from object B. (Ideas:

1. Object A is big, but object B is small/not big.
2. Object A is circle/round, but object B is square/not round
3. Object A is gray, but object B is black)

Object A
Object B

B **Story Items**

4. What 2 things would Nancy do to get her own way?
   • ask • smile • laugh
   • cry • jump
5. Nancy didn't want to become bigger because she wouldn't be able to [redacted].
   • wear her shoes • act like a baby • play with Sally
6. Nancy knew that she was getting bigger because [redacted].
   • Sally looked smaller • she found a CD • her shoes were getting tight
7. What did Nancy find on her bed? a CD
8. The voice told the words to say if you want to stay small. Write those words. Broil, boil, dump that oil.

WORKBOOK

9. Who could do tricks that Nancy couldn't do? Sally

10. How did that make Nancy feel? (Idea: mad)

11. Did Nancy really think that the words would make her small?
no

Review Items

> Things that are this far apart on the map are 2 miles apart. ←——→
> Things that are this far apart are 4 miles apart. ←————→

12. Write **2** in the circle if the line stands for 2 miles.

13. Write **4** in the circle if the line stands for 4 miles.

14. How far is it from the school to the field? 2 miles

15. How far is it from the lake to the park? 4 miles

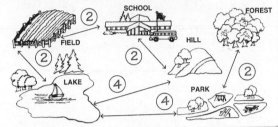

Here are names that tell how fast things move.

a. (inches) per second   c. (miles) per week
b. (meters) per minute   d. (centimeters) per hour

16. **Circle** the part of each name that tells about length.

17. **Underline** the part of each name that tells about time.

========= GO TO PART D IN YOUR TEXTBOOK. =========

46   Lesson 25

© SRA/McGraw-Hill. All rights reserved.

TEXTBOOK

you can't do. I can make myself small by saying some words that you don't know."

"No, you can't make yourself small," Sally said.

"Yes, I can," Nancy said. "But I don't feel like doing it now." Nancy didn't really think that she could make herself small, but she wouldn't tell that to Sally.

"You don't know any words that could make you small," Sally said.

Nancy was very mad. "Just listen to this," she said. Then she continued in a loud voice, "Broil, boil, dump that oil."

MORE NEXT TIME

D Number your paper from 1 through 10.

1. Which is longer, a centimeter or a meter? meter
2. How many centimeters long is a meter? 100

3. The names in one box tell about length. Write the letter of that box. A
4. The names in one box tell about time. Write the letter of that box. B

A	inch mile meter centimeter
B	month year hour second week minute

Lesson 25   155

TEXTBOOK

5. Which arrow shows the way the air leaves the balloon? B

6. Which arrow shows the way the balloon will move? A

7. Air rushes out of Goad this way ✎. Draw an arrow to show which way Goad will move. ↗

8. What part of the world is shown on the map?

9. The map shows how far apart some places are. One line shows 13 hundred miles. The other line shows 25 hundred miles. How far is it from **R** to **T**?

10. How far is it from **K** to **M**? 13 hundred miles

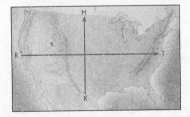

8. United States
9. 25 hundred miles

156   Lesson 25

WORKBOOK

26

Name _____

A

1. How many legs does an insect have? 6
2. How many legs does an ant have? 6
3. How many legs does a fly have? 6
4. How many legs does a flea have? 6
5. If an ant weighed as much as a beagle, the ant could carry an object as heavy as ▮▮▮. • 3 beagles   • 100 beagles   • 10 beagles
6. How many ants would it take to weigh as much as a peanut? 100

B Story Items

7. Did Nancy say the words on the CD? yes

8. Write the words Nancy said.
Broil, boil, dump that oil.

9. So what happened to Nancy? Idea: Nancy got small.

10. Why did Nancy think that the jump rope got bigger?
• The rope got bigger.   • The rope got smaller.
• Nancy got smaller.

11. How big did the ant seem to Nancy? the size of a horse

12. Nancy's voice sounded like a little squeak because she was so
small

13. Who gave the CD to Nancy? a little green man

14. Why did he give her the CD?
• She asked him to do it.   • She wanted to get bigger.
• So she would become smaller.

© SRA/McGraw-Hill. All rights reserved.

Lesson 26   47

30

WORKBOOK

Skill Item

15. Write 2 ways that tell how object A is different from object B.
Remember, you must name both objects. (Any 2 ideas:

① Object A is tall, but object B is short.

② Object A is striped, but object B is not striped/is plain, etc.)

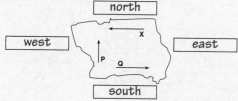

Object A   Object B

Review Items

16. Write **north**, **south**, **east**, and **west** in the right boxes.

```
              north
  west                    east
            P     Q
              south
```

17. An arrow goes from the Q. Which direction is that arrow going?
east

18. An arrow goes from the P. Which direction is that arrow going?
north

19. An arrow goes from the X. Which direction is that arrow going?
west

GO TO PART D IN YOUR TEXTBOOK.

48   *Lesson 26*   © SRA/McGraw-Hill. All rights reserved.

TEXTBOOK

The little man said, "You didn't want anybody to call you a big girl. And you got your wish. Nobody would call a tiny thing like you a big girl."

"I guess you're right," Nancy said. "But I really didn't want to be this little. I'm so little now that . . ."

"Now, now," the green man said. "You should be very, very happy. Even if you grow two times the size you are now, you'll be smaller than a blue fly. Even if you grow twenty times the size you are now, you'll be smaller than a mouse. So you should be very glad."

"Well, I don't . . ."

"I'll walk to your house with you and then I must go," the green man said. "Don't stay outside too long. There are cats and rats and loads of toads that love to eat things your size."

MORE NEXT TIME

D **Number your paper from 1 through 13.**

Skill Items

> Here's a rule: **All the green men are small.**

1. Lee is a green man. So what does the rule tell you about Lee? **He is small.**

2. Jack is not a green man. So what does the rule tell you about Jack? **nothing**

3. Fred is not a green man. So what does the rule tell you about Fred? **nothing**

160   *Lesson 26*

TEXTBOOK

Review Items

4. Write the letters of the 4 names that tell about time.
   - a. meter
   - b. hour
   - c. second
   - d. centimeter
   - e. minute
   - f. week
   - g. inch   **b, c, e, f**

5. Which animal can jump farther, a toad or a frog?

6. Which animal has smooth skin, a toad or a frog?

7. Do any frogs have teeth? **yes**

8. Write the letters of the 4 names that tell about length.
   - a. week
   - b. hour
   - c. second
   - d. mile
   - e. day
   - f. minute   **d, g, i, j**
   - g. centimeter
   - h. year
   - i. meter
   - j. inch

9. When wouldn't a fox bother a rabbit?
   • during spring   • during a fire   • at night

Lesson 26   161

TEXTBOOK

10. United States

10. What part of the world is shown on the map?
The map shows how far apart some places are. One line shows 13 hundred miles. The other line shows 25 hundred miles.

11. How far is it from A to B? **25 hundred miles**

12. How far is it from C to D? **13 hundred miles**

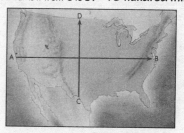

13. A mile is a little more than [____] feet.
   • 5 hundred   • 1 thousand   • <u>5 thousand</u>

162   *Lesson 26*

Name _____

Story Items

1. Could Nancy turn on the TV set? <u>no</u>

2. Where was the bed that Nancy napped in?
   • <u>in her dollhouse</u> • in her backyard • in her dog house

3. Whose voices did Nancy hear when she woke up from her nap?
   <u>Idea: her mother's and a police officer's voice</u>

4. Nancy's mother was crying because she could not find ▓▓.
   • money • the dollhouse • <u>Nancy</u>

5. Sally told what happened to Nancy. Did Nancy's mother believe the story? <u>no</u>

6. Nancy shouted at her mother. Her mother couldn't hear Nancy because Nancy's voice was too <u>squeaky/high/small</u>

   Here's a rule: **If you get smaller, your voice gets higher.**

7. **Circle** the picture that shows when Nancy's voice would be highest.

8. **Cross out** the picture that shows when Nancy's voice would be lowest.

9. Look at object A and object E. Write one way that tells how both objects are the same. _____

9. Ideas: They are both small; they are both standing; they are both girls; etc.

Skill Item

10. Write 2 ways that tell how object A is different from object B. Remember, you must name both. (Any 2 ideas:
    ❶ <u>A is a toad, but B is a frog/not a toad;</u>
    ❷ <u>A has bumpy skin, but B has smooth skin/does</u>
    not have bumpy skin.)

Object A

Object B

Review Items

11. Draw an arrow at **B** and an arrow at **C** to show which way the string will move when the toad moves the blue fly.

12. The arrow in each picture shows which way the wind is blowing. Start at the dot and **draw the smoke** in each picture.

Wind

Wind

Wind

GO TO PART C IN YOUR TEXTBOOK.

---

1. motioned

C Number your paper from 1 through 11.

Skill Items

He motioned to the flight attendant ahead of him.

1. One word tells about somebody using his hands to tell a person what to do. What's that word?

2. Which two words refer to a person who takes care of passengers on a plane? <u>flight attendant</u>

3. Which word means **in front**? <u>ahead</u>

Review Items

4. What do all living things need? <u>water</u>

5. What do all living things make? <u>babies</u>

6. Do all living things grow? <u>yes</u>

7. Which arrow shows the way the air will leave the jet engines? <u>T</u>

8. Which arrow shows the way the jet will move? <u>D</u>

9. A mile is a little more than ▓▓ feet.
   • 1 thousand • 5 hundred • <u>5 thousand</u>

10. If an ant weighed as much as a desk, the ant could carry an object as heavy as ▓▓. <u>10 desks</u>

11. How many ants would it take to weigh as much as a peanut? <u>100</u>

Name _____

A

1. If a grain of sugar were very big, it would look like a box made of <u>glass</u>

2. What kind of corners does a grain of sugar have? <u>sharp (corners)</u>

3. A grain of sugar is no bigger than a grain of <u>sand</u>

B **Story Items**

4. What did Nancy say to get small? <u>Broil, boil, dump that oil.</u>

5. The walk to the bedroom doorway was much longer for Nancy than for her mother because Nancy <u>Idea: was so small</u>

6. In this story, Nancy found something to eat. What did she find? <u>cookie crumb</u>

7. To Nancy it was the size of <u>a bucket</u>

8. Why did she sniff it before she started eating it?
   • to see if it was salty • to see if it was big
   • <u>to see if it was stale</u>

9. How much of it did she eat?
   • <u>half</u> • all • none

10. Why didn't she eat the whole thing? <u>Idea: She was full/wasn't hungry anymore.</u>

11. After Nancy finished eating, she wanted something. What did she want? _water_

12. Did she know how she was going to get it? _no_

13. **Circle** the picture that could be Nancy standing next to the big crumb she found.

14. **Underline** what Nancy has learned about being so small.
- Her voice got squeaky.   • The cookie crumb got bigger.
  • Her bed got bigger.

Skill Items

15. Write 2 ways that tell how object A is different from object B.

① (Any 2 ideas: A is tall, but B is not tall.

② A has dots/spots, but B is plain/does not have dots. A has a small base, but B has a wide base.)

Object A   **Object B**

GO TO PART D IN YOUR TEXTBOOK.

---

1. Hunters were |stationed| at |opposite| ends of the field.
2. He |motioned| to the |flight| attendant |ahead| of him.

"I need a glass of water," she said to herself. She didn't really need a glass of water. She needed much less than a drop of water. But how do you get water when you're smaller than a fly? How do you get water if you can't reach something as high as a sink? "Water," Nancy said to herself. "I must find water."

MORE NEXT TIME

D Number your paper from 1 through 17.

Skill Items

Use the words in the box to write complete sentences.

| thrown | changed | stationed | motioned |
| opposite | wonder | flight | after | ahead |

1. Hunters were ▓▓▓ at ▓▓▓ ends of the field.
2. He ▓▓▓ to the ▓▓▓ attendant ▓▓▓ of him.

Review Items

3. In which season is the danger of forest fires greatest?
4. Camels can go for ▓▓▓ days without drinking water.
5. How many pounds of water can a 1 thousand-pound camel drink at one time? _250_
6. Which is longer, an inch or a centimeter? _inch_
7. How many legs does an insect have? _6_
8. How many legs does a flea have? _6_

3. fall; 4. 10

---

9. If a fly is an insect, what else do you know about a fly? _It has 6 legs._
10. Which is longer, a centimeter or a meter? _meter_
11. How many centimeters long is a meter? _100_
12. A toad catches flies with its ▓▓▓.
- tongue   • feet   • legs

13. Why do flies stick to a toad's tongue?
- because the tongue is sticky
- because the tongue is dirty
- because the tongue is dry

14. If an ant weighed as much as a dog, the ant could carry an object as heavy as ▓▓▓. _10 dogs_

15. When do trees begin to grow?
- in the winter   • in the spring

16. Trees begin to grow when their roots get ▓▓▓. _warm_

17. Camel hooves keep camels from sinking in sand. How are camel hooves different from pig hooves?
- They are harder and longer.
- They are sharper and smaller.
- They are wider and flatter.

29

Name _____

A

1. What does the top of water have?   • a puddle   • hair   • skin

2. Look at the picture.
The tube is filled with water.
Draw the skin that covers the top of the water.

B

3. You can see drops of water on grass early in the morning. What are those drops called? _dew_

4. Does dew form in the middle of the day? _no_

5. Dew forms when the air gets ▓▓▓.
- warmer   • cooler   • windy

C   **Story Items**

6. If tiny animals fall from high places, they don't _get hurt_

7. When Nancy was thirsty, she didn't scream and yell and stamp her feet. Why not?
- She was tired.   • She was thirsty.
  • Nobody would hear her.

8. There wasn't any dew on the grass because it was not ▓▓▓.
- morning   • hot   • evening

9. Where did Nancy go to look for water?
- to the bedroom   • to the bathroom   • to the kitchen

10. Nancy slipped on the strip of wood because it was ▓▓▓.
   - hot
   - <u>moist with oil</u>
   - sticky
11. The cabinet was a <u>hundred</u> times taller than Nancy.
12. Did Nancy get hurt when she fell? <u>no</u>
13. Why not? <u>Idea: She was tiny and tiny things don't</u>
   <u>get hurt when they fall from high places.</u>

These animals fell from a cliff. **Underline** the words that tell what happened to each animal.

14. **ant**	15. **mouse**	16. **dog**	17. **squirrel**	18. **horse**
<u>not hurt</u>	<u>not hurt</u>	not hurt	not hurt	not hurt
hurt	hurt	<u>hurt</u>	<u>hurt</u>	hurt
killed	killed	<u>killed</u>	killed	<u>killed</u>

(Accept either)

Skill Items

19. Write 2 ways that tell how object A is different from object B.
(Any 2 ideas:
① <u>A is sitting, but B is standing.</u>
② <u>A has short/straight/spotted hair, but B does</u>
   <u>not. A is a pointer, but B is a poodle, etc.)</u>

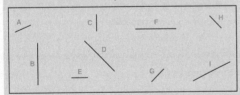

Object A    Object B

GO TO PART E IN YOUR TEXTBOOK.

The fall scared her. She landed on her back. For a moment she didn't move. Then she got up slowly, testing her arms and legs to make sure that they weren't hurt. She had fallen from something that was a hundred times taller than she was, but she wasn't hurt. She wasn't hurt at all, not one broken bone. Not one scratch. Not even an ouch.

"I don't know what's happening," Nancy said to herself. "But I'm not afraid to try climbing that cabinet again."

This time she got to the top.

MORE NEXT TIME

E Number your paper from 1 through 14.

Skill Items

Here's a rule: **Horses eat grass.**
1. A cow is not a horse. So what does the rule tell you about a cow? <u>nothing</u>
2. Jake is not a horse. So what does the rule tell you about Jake? <u>nothing</u>
3. Meg is a horse. So what does the rule tell you about Meg? <u>Meg eats grass.</u>

Review Items
4. Roots keep a tree from ▓▓▓. <u>falling over</u>
5. Roots carry ▓▓▓ to all parts of the tree. <u>water</u>
6. Camels can go for ▓▓▓ days without drinking water. <u>10</u>
7. How many pounds of water can a 1 thousand-pound camel drink at one time? <u>250</u>

Some of the lines in the box are one inch long and some are one centimeter long.
8. Write the letter of every line that is one centimeter long. <u>A, C, E, G, H</u>
9. Write the letter of every line that is one inch long.

[box with lines labeled A, B, C, D, E, F, G, H, I]

9. B, D, F, I

---

10. What part of the world is shown on the map?
The map shows how far apart some places are. One line shows 13 hundred miles. The other line shows 25 hundred miles.
11. How far is it from **F** to **G**? <u>25 hundred miles</u>
12. How far is it from **H** to **K**? <u>13 hundred miles</u>

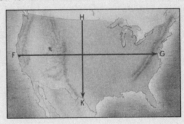

13. If a grain of sugar were very big, it would look like a box made of ▓▓▓. <u>glass</u>
14. What kind of corners does a grain of sugar have?

10. United States
14. sharp

TEXTBOOK

TEST 3 **30**

Number your paper from 1 through 25.

1. When wouldn't a fox bother a rabbit?
   - during spring
   - at night
   - <u>during a fire</u>

Here are names that tell how fast things move.
2. meters per minute
3. inches per second
4. centimeters per month
5. miles per hour **hour**

Write the part of each name that tells about time.

6. Which arrow shows the way the air will leave the jet engines?
7. Which arrow shows the way the jet will move? **D**

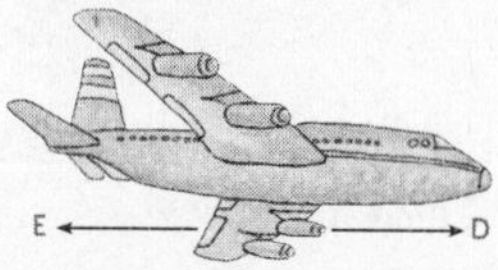

2. minute
3. second
4. month
6. E

TEXTBOOK

Let's say this line ←→ on the map is 3 miles long.
And this line ←——→ is 6 miles long.

8. Write the letter of a line on the map that is 3 miles long. **Accept A, B, C, E or F**
9. Write the letter of a line on the map that is 6 miles long. **Accept D or G**
10. How far is it from the hill to the lake? **6 miles**
11. How far is it from the forest to the school? **3 miles**

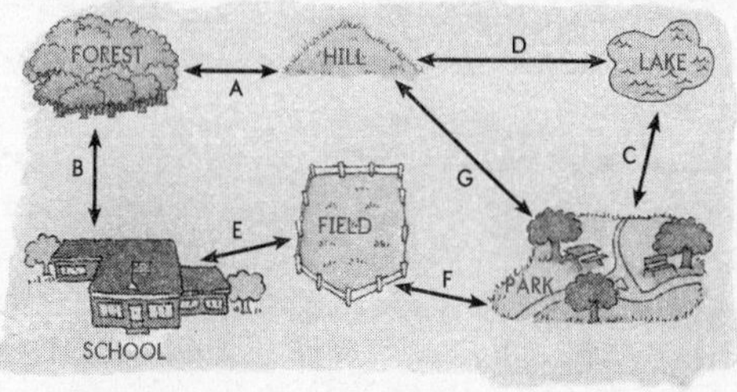

12. A mile is a little more than ▒▒ feet. **5 thousand**

TEXTBOOK

13. What part of the world is shown on the map?

One line on the map is 13 hundred miles long. The other line is 25 hundred miles long.

14. How far is it from **A** to **B**? **25 hundred miles**
15. How far is it from **P** to **T**? **13 hundred miles**

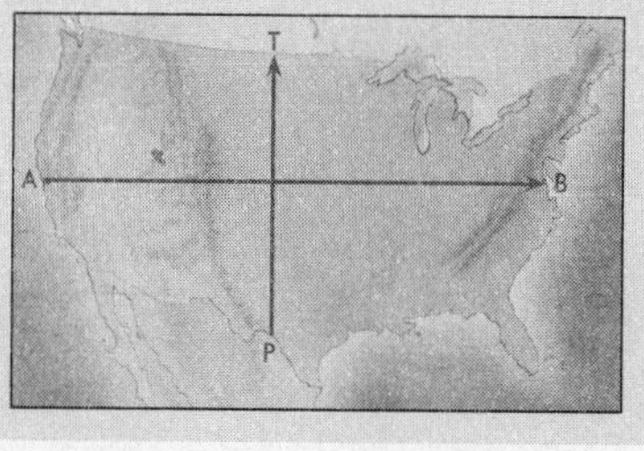

16. If an ant weighed as much as a bird, the ant could carry an object as heavy as ▒▒. **10 birds**
17. You can see drops of water on grass early in the morning. What are those drops called?
18. **Finish the rule.** If tiny animals fall from high places, they don't ▒▒. **get hurt**

13. United States
17. dew (drops)

TEXTBOOK

Skill Items

Here's a rule: **Dogs pant after they run fast.**

19. Fido is a dog. So what does the rule tell you about Fido? **Fido pants after he runs fast.**
20. Spot is not a dog. So what does the rule tell you about Spot? **nothing**

For each item, write the underlined word or words from the sentences in the box.

Hunters were <u>stationed</u> at <u>opposite</u> ends of the field.
He <u>motioned</u> to the <u>flight attendant</u> <u>ahead</u> of him.

21. What underlining tells about a person who takes care of passengers on a plane? **flight attendant**
22. What underlining tells they were not at the same end of the field? **opposite**
23. What underlining means **in front?** **ahead**
24. What underlining tells about something you could do with your hands? **motioned**
25. What underlining tells that the hunters had to stay where they were placed? **stationed**

END OF TEST 3

WORKBOOK

Name _____

A

Some hairs in the picture are being pushed down. Some are being pulled up. Look at the skin around each hair.

1. Make an arrow like this ↑ on every hair that is moving up.
2. Make an arrow like this ↓ on every hair that is moving down.

B Review Items

Things that are this far apart ⟵————⟶ on the map are 2 miles apart.

Things that are this far apart ⟵——————————⟶ are 4 miles apart.

3. Write **2** in the circle if the line stands for 2 miles.
4. Write **4** in the circle if the line stands for 4 miles.
5. How far is it from the school to the field? **2 miles**
6. How far is it from the lake to the park? **4 miles**

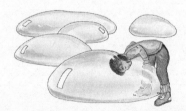

Lesson 31 55

WORKBOOK

7. What does the top of water have? • hair • <u>skin</u> • nails

8. A mile is a little more than ▇▇ feet.
   • 1 thousand   • <u>5 thousand</u>   • 5 hundred

9. If an ant weighed as much as a dog, the ant could carry an object as heavy as **10 dogs**

10. The tube is filled with water. Draw the skin that covers the top of the water.

11. You can see drops of water on grass early in the morning. What are those drops called? **dew**

12. If tiny animals fall from high places, they don't **get hurt**

13. Does dew form in the middle of the day? **no**

14. Dew forms when the air gets ▇▇.
   • warmer   • windy   • <u>cooler</u>

GO TO PART D IN YOUR TEXTBOOK.

TEXTBOOK

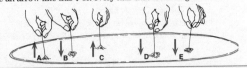

She drank quickly, trying not to get water in her nose. Then she pulled her head back. The skin of the water tugged at her neck. The water pulled at her neck the way a tight sweater pulls on your neck when you try to take it off. Nancy pulled hard, and **pop.** Her head came out of the drop.

"That was scary," she said out loud.
MORE NEXT TIME

D Number your paper from 1 through 22.

Story Items

1. Some drops of water were ▇▇ than Nancy.
   • bigger   • older   • hotter
2. When Nancy first touched the water drop, did her hand get wet? **no**

TEXTBOOK

3. What did Nancy have to do to get her hand inside the water drop?
   • look at the drop   • hit the drop
      • touch the drop
4. Did Nancy get her head inside the water drop? **yes**
5. What happened when Nancy tried to pull her head back out of the water drop?
   • It got smaller.   • It got stuck.   • It got wet.

6. Write the letters of the water striders. **A, C, F, G**

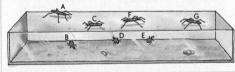

List the three things that Nancy has learned about being very small.

7. Small animals have a voice that is ▇▇.
8. Small animals don't get hurt when they ▇▇.
9. Water has a ▇▇. (tough) skin

7. Idea: small, squeaky, high
8. fall from high places

10. Is a water strider an insect? **yes**
11. How many legs does a water strider have? **6**
12. How many legs does an ant have? **6**
13. How many legs does a spider have? **8**
14. How many legs does a flea have? **6**
15. How many legs does a cat have? **4**

Skill Items

16. Write one way that tells how both objects are the same.
17. Write 2 ways that tell how object A is different from object B.

Object A

Object B

16. **Ideas: They are both dogs; they both have tails; they are both standing, etc.**
17. **Ideas (any 2): A is facing right, but B is facing left; A is three colors, but B is one; A has short hair/a long tail/ several colors, but B has long hair/a short tail/one color, etc.**

Lesson 31   **189**

Write the word from the box that means the same thing as the underlined part of each sentence.

heard	hoisted	long	sale
lawn	silly	boomed	stale

18. The cake was <u>old and not very good to eat</u>. **stale**
19. The <u>grass</u> was wet after the rain. **lawn**
20. They <u>lifted</u> the TV onto the truck. **hoisted**

Review Items

21. The names in one box tell about time. Write the letter of that box. **B**
22. The names in one box tell about length. Write the letter of that box. **A**

A	centimeter	inch	meter	mile	
B	week	year	second	month	minute	hour

190   *Lesson 31*

32

Name _____

A

1. When we weigh very small things, the unit we use is **gram(s)**

Some things in the picture weigh **1 gram**. Some weigh **2 grams**. Some weigh **5 grams**. Fill in the blanks to tell how much each object weighs.

2. **2 grams**
3. **2 grams**
 4. **1 gram**
5. **5 grams**
6. **5 grams**

B **Story Items**

7. The food that a very small animal eats each day weighs **more than the animal**.

8. Is a mouse a small animal? **yes**

9. Does the food a mouse eats each day weigh more than the mouse? **yes**

10. Are you a small animal? **no**

11. Does the food that you eat each day weigh as much as you do? **no**

12. How many times did Nancy wake up during the night? **2 times**

Lesson 32   **57**

13. Why did she wake up? **Idea: She was hungry (and thirsty).**

14. What did Nancy eat the first time she woke up? **cookie crumb**

15. Why didn't Nancy eat a cookie crumb the second time she woke up? **They were all gone.**

16. The food that 3 of the animals eat each day weighs more than those animals. **Circle** those animals.

17. Small animals don't get hurt when they **fall from high places**

18. Small animals have a voice that is **Ideas: high/squeaky/small**

19. Water has a **(tough) skin (if you're small)**

Review Item

Here's what you see through the circles made by your hands.

Draw what you would see through strong binoculars.

GO TO PART D IN YOUR TEXTBOOK.

58   *Lesson 32*

D Number your paper from 1 through 14.

Skill Items

1. Write one way that tells how both objects are the same.
2. Write 2 ways that tell how object A is different from object B.

Object A

Object B

The traffic was moving 27 miles per hour.

3. How fast was the traffic moving? **27 miles per hour**
4. If the traffic was moving 27 miles per hour, **how far** would a car go in one hour? **27 miles**
5. What word in the sentence refers to all the cars and trucks that were moving on the street? **traffic**
6. What word means **each**? **per**

1. Ideas: They're both boxes/square/yellow/ have dots, etc.
2. Ideas (any 2): Object A is small/has three dots/has black dots, but object B is large/has five dots/has red dots, etc.

194   Lesson 32

Review Items

7. Which arrow shows the way the air leaves the balloon? **B**
8. Which arrow shows the way the balloon will move? **A**

9. Write the letters of the 4 names that tell about length.

a. minute   d. centimeter   g. mile   i. year
b. hour   e. second   h. meter   j. inch
c. day   f. week   **d, g, h, j**

Look at the skin around each hair.
• Make an arrow like this ↑ if the hair is moving up.
• Make an arrow like this ↓ if the hair is moving down.

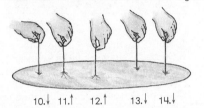

10. ↓   11. ↑   12. ↑   13. ↓   14. ↓

Lesson 32   195

33

Name _____

Story Items

1. Why couldn't Nancy see very well when she walked to the kitchen?
   • She was tired.   • <u>It was dark.</u>   • She was hungry.

2. Why didn't Nancy act like a baby when she was very hungry?
   • She was mad.   • Her voice was too small.
   • <u>Crying wouldn't do any good.</u>

3. Was Nancy frightened when she climbed the kitchen counter?
   no

4. If she fell, she wouldn't get **hurt**

5. What did Nancy smell on the kitchen counter? **toast**

6. How many pieces of toast were on the plate? **3**

7. That pile looked as tall as a **ten-story building** to Nancy.

8. Did Nancy have to climb the pile of toast to get something to eat?
   no

9. What did she find to eat on the counter? **crumbs**

10. How many toast crumbs did Nancy eat? **2**

11. Each crumb was as big as **a football**

12. Nancy hated toast when she was full-sized. Why doesn't she hate toast now? **Idea: because she was so hungry**

13. How much does Nancy weigh?
    • almost a gram   • <u>much less than a gram</u>   • a gram

14. Nancy ate a lot of food in one day. How much did that food weigh?
    a gram

Lesson 33   59

15. Water has a **skin**

16. Small animals don't get hurt when they **fall from high places**

17. The food that a small animal eats each day weighs **more than the animal**

18. Small animals have a voice that is **Ideas: high/squeaky/small**

Skill Items

19. Write one way that tells how both objects are the same.
    Ideas: They are both mugs/have handles, etc.

20. Write 2 ways that tell how object A is different from object B. **Ideas (any 2):**
    ① **A is striped, but B is plain/not striped;**
    ② **A is small/short, but B is tall/big;**
    A is full, but B is not, etc.

Object A

Object B

Review Items

Here are names that tell how fast things move.

a. (centimeters) per <u>month</u>   c. (meters) per <u>year</u>
b. (miles) per <u>week</u>   d. (inches) per <u>second</u>

21. **Circle** the part of each name that tells about length.

22. **Underline** the part of each name that tells about time.

GO TO PART D IN YOUR TEXTBOOK.

60   Lesson 33

Now that she was small and hungry all the time, she didn't hate toast. In fact, that crumb of toast tasted so good that she ate another piece the size of a football.

Nancy weighed much less than a gram. In one day, she had eaten food that weighed a gram.

MORE NEXT TIME

D Number your paper from 1 through 14.
1. Does a housefly weigh **more than a gram** or less than a gram?
2. Does a glass of water weigh more than a gram or **less than a gram**?
3. How many ants would it take to weigh one gram?

4. How many grams are on the left side of the scale?
5. So how much weight is on the side of the scale with the water striders? *1 gram*

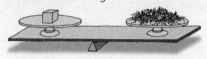

6. Which weighs more, one gram or one water strider?

3. about 100
4. 1 gram

Lesson 33 **201**

Skill Items
Use the words in the box to write complete sentences.

stationed	traffic	after	ahead	opposite
per	motioned	wonder	attendant	

7. He ▮▮▮ to the flight ▮▮▮ ▮▮▮ of him.
8. The ▮▮▮ was moving forty miles ▮▮▮ hour.

Review Items
9. Write the letters of the 4 names that tell about time.
   a. week   b. inch   c. centimeter   d. second
   e. minute   f. meter   g. hour
10. If a grain of sugar were very big, it would look like a box made of ▮▮▮. *glass*
11. What kind of corners does a grain of sugar have?
12. When we weigh very small things, the unit we use is ▮▮▮. *gram(s)*

7. He |motioned| to the flight |attendant| |ahead| of him.
8. The |traffic| was moving forty miles |per| hour.
9. a, d, e, g
11. sharp

202   *Lesson 33*

---

13. The food that 3 of the animals eat each day weighs as much as those animals. Write the letters of those animals. *C, D, E*
14. The food that 4 of the animals eat each day does not weigh as much as those animals. Write the letters of those animals. *A, B, F, G*

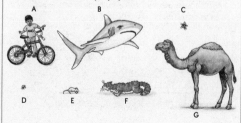

Lesson 33   **203**

34

Name _____
Story Items

1. Was Nancy afraid to jump down from the counter top? *no*
2. Did she get hurt when she jumped? *no*
3. Tell why. *Idea: because small things don't get hurt when they fall from high places*
4. Who woke Nancy? *green man*
5. Was Nancy happy about being so little? *no*
6. Did Nancy change her mind about growing up? *yes*
7. Nancy learned that she doesn't have to act like a baby because *she can take care of herself*
8. Small animals don't get hurt when they *fall from high places*
9. Small animals have a voice that is *Ideas: high/small/squeaky*
10. Water has a *skin*
11. The food that a small animal eats each day weighs *more than the animal*

Skill Items

Here's a rule: **Every little girl wants to grow up.**

12. Jan is a little girl. So what does the rule tell you about Jan? *Jan wants to grow up.*
13. Ron is not a little girl. So what does the rule tell you about Ron? *nothing*

Lesson 34   **61**

WORKBOOK

14. Peg is a little girl. So what does the rule tell you about Peg?

Peg wants to grow up.

Review Item

15. At each dot, draw an arrow to show which way the string will move when the girl pulls it.

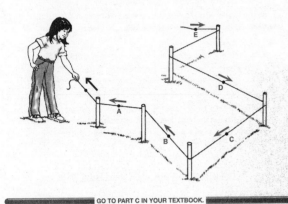

GO TO PART C IN YOUR TEXTBOOK.

TEXTBOOK

C Number your paper from 1 through 20.

Skill Items

Write the word from the box that means the same thing as the underlined part of each sentence.

| hoist | fish | tadpoles | squeak |
| remove | climb | moist | wrong |

1. The pond is full of <u>baby frogs</u>. _tadpoles_
2. The grass is <u>a little wet</u> today. _moist_
3. She will <u>take</u> the books from the desk. _remove_

Review Items

Some things happen as tadpoles grow.
4. Write the letter of what happens first. _d_
5. Write the letter of what happens last. _b_
   a. They grow front legs.   c. They turn blue.
   b. Their tail disappears.   d. They grow back legs.

TEXTBOOK

6. The picture shows Goad filled up with air. Arrow A shows air leaving Goad this way ⟶.
   Write the letter of the arrow that shows the way Goad will move. _G_

7. A mile is a little more than ▉ feet.
   • 2 thousand   • |5 thousand| • 1 thousand
8. If an ant weighed as much as a cat, the ant could carry an object as heavy as ▉. _ten cats_

These animals fell from a cliff. Write the words that tell what happened to each animal.
   • not hurt   • hurt   • killed

flea

9.   10.   11.   12.   13.

9. killed; 10. not hurt; 11. not hurt;
12. (accept either) hurt, killed; 13. hurt

TEXTBOOK

14. Does a housefly weigh **more than a gram** or |less than a gram|?
15. Does a dog weigh |more than a gram| or **less than a gram**?

16. How many grams are on the left side of the scale? _1 gram_
17. So how much weight is on the side of the scale with the houseflies? _1 gram_

---

18. An arrow goes from the **F.** Which direction is that arrow going? _north_

19. An arrow goes from the **G.** Which direction is that arrow going? _west_

20. An arrow goes from the **J.** Which direction is that arrow going? _south_

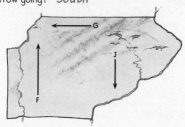

210   Lesson 34

35

Name _____

A

1. If you get smaller, your voice _gets higher_ _____.

2. Fran got smaller. So what do you know about Fran's voice? _It got higher._ _____

3. **Circle** the ruler that will make the highest sound.

4. **Cross out** the ruler that will make the lowest sound.

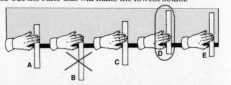

B Story Items   Ideas: because she was so glad to see her mother/have her mother hold her

5. Why did Nancy cry when she saw her mother? _____

_____

Nancy told about two things to prove that she had been very small.

6. There were crumbs of _toast_ _____ on the counter.

7. There were drops of _water_ _____ in the _bathroom_ _____

8. Does Nancy want to be called a baby now? _no_ _____

9. Does Nancy want to grow up now? _yes_ _____

10. When things go wrong, Nancy tells herself, "I can take _care of myself_ _____."

Lesson 35   **63**

---

11. One of these pictures shows Nancy when she was very small. Which picture is that? _C_ _____

Review Items

Here's a picture of a food trap. The arrow at **A** shows the way the fly will move when the toad grabs it.

12. **Draw an arrow** to show which way the string will move at **B.**

13. **Draw an arrow** to show which way the pole will move at **C.**

GO TO PART D IN YOUR TEXTBOOK.

D Number your paper from 1 through 24.

Skill Items

He is supposed to make a decision in a couple of days.
1. What part means **should**? _supposed to_
2. What word means **two**? _couple_
3. What part means **make up his mind**? _make a decision_

4. Write one way that tells how both objects are the same.

5. Write 2 ways that tell how object A is different from object B.

Object A   Object B

4. 1 Idea: They are both toads/sitting/ facing right.
5. 2 Ideas: A is big/is catching a fly/has tongue out, but B is small/not catching a fly/does not have tongue out

216   Lesson 35

41

Review Items

Some of the lines in the box are one inch long and some are one centimeter long.
6. Write the letter of every line that is one inch long.
7. Write the letter of every line that is one centimeter long. B, C, E, G, I

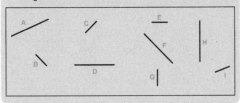

8. Which arrow shows the way the air will leave the jet engines? C
9. Which arrow shows the way the jet will move? B

6. A, D, F, H

---

10. Write the letter of each water strider. B, E, F

11. Is a water strider an insect? yes
12. How many legs does a water strider have? 6
13. How many legs does a fly have? 6
14. How many legs does a dog have? 4
15. How many legs does a spider have? 8
16. How many legs does an ant have? 6
17. When we weigh very small things, the unit we use is ▓▓▓. gram(s)

Some things in the picture weigh **1 gram.** Some weigh **2 grams.** Some weigh **5 grams.** Write how much each object weighs.

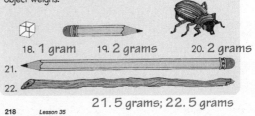

18. 1 gram   19. 2 grams   20. 2 grams
21.
22.
21. 5 grams; 22. 5 grams

---

23. The food that 3 of the animals eat each day weighs more than those animals. Write the letters of those animals. C, B, G
24. The food that 4 of the animals eat each day does not weigh as much as those animals. Write the letters of those animals. A, D, E, F

36

Name _____

Story Items

1. When something tries to move in one direction, something else tries to move *in the opposite direction* _____.

2. Which arrow shows the direction the air will leave the balloon? A

3. Which arrow shows the direction the balloon will move? B

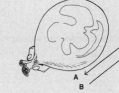

4. Which arrow shows the direction the canoe is moving? D

5. Which arrow shows the direction the paddle is moving in the water? C

The picture shows Goad filled up with air.

6. Which arrow shows the direction the air will leave Goad? E

7. Which arrow shows the direction Goad will move? E

8. The arrow shows which direction the boy will jump. **Make an arrow** on the block of ice to show which direction it will move.

9. The arrow shows which direction the girl will jump. **Make an arrow** on the back of the boat to show which way the boat will move.

Skill Items

Fill in each blank with a word from the box.

decision	traffic	weather	perfect	per
frightened	supposed	forward	couple	

10. The _traffic_ was moving forty miles _per_ hour.

11. He is _supposed_ to make a _decision_ in a _couple_ of days.

GO TO PART D IN YOUR TEXTBOOK.

D Number your paper from 1 through 25.

Each statement tells about **how far** something goes or **how fast** something goes. Write **how far** or **how fast** for each item.
1. They walked 6 miles. _how far_
2. They walked 6 miles per hour. _how fast_
3. The bus was moving 20 miles per hour. _how fast_
4. The bus was 20 miles from the city. _how far_

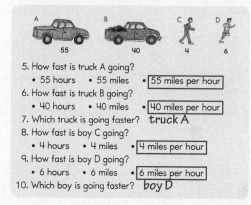

5. How fast is truck A going?
   • 55 hours   • 55 miles   • _55 miles per hour_
6. How fast is truck B going?
   • 40 hours   • 40 miles   • _40 miles per hour_
7. Which truck is going faster? _truck A_
8. How fast is boy C going?
   • 4 hours   • 4 miles   • _4 miles per hour_
9. How fast is boy D going?
   • 6 hours   • 6 miles   • _6 miles per hour_
10. Which boy is going faster? _boy D_

---

11. When we talk about miles per hour, we tell how ▮▮▮ something is moving. _fast_

Skill Items

Here are titles for different stories:
   a. The Pink Flea   b. Pete Gets a Reward
      c. The Ant That Escaped
12. One story tells about an insect that was a strange color. Write the letter of that title. _a_
13. One story tells about an insect that got away from something. Write the letter of that title. _c_
14. One story tells about someone who got something for doing a good job. Write the letter of that title. _b_

Review Items

15. If you get smaller, your voice gets ▮▮▮. _higher/ smaller_
16. Jean got smaller. So what do you know about Jean's voice? _Jean's voice got higher._

---

17. Write the letter of the ruler that will make the lowest sound. _B_
18. Write the letter of the ruler that will make the highest sound. _D_

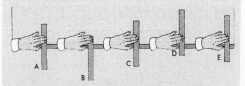

19. The food that a very small animal eats each day weighs ▮▮▮.
   • less than the animal   • 5 pounds
   • _more than the animal_
20. Does dew form in the middle of the day? _no_
21. Dew forms when the air gets ▮▮▮.
   • _cooler_   • windy   • warmer
22. What do all living things need? _water_
23. What do all living things make? _babies_
24. Do all living things grow? _yes_
25. If tiny animals fall from high places, they don't ▮▮▮. _get hurt_

37

Name _____

Story Items

1. When something tries to move in one direction, something else tries to move **in the opposite direction** _____

2. Which arrow shows the direction the air will leave the jet engines?
P _____

3. Which arrow shows the direction the jet will move?
Q _____

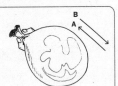

4. Which arrow shows the direction the canoe is moving? **Y** _____

5. Which arrow shows the direction the paddle is moving in the water? **X**

6. If the paddle of a canoe is moving east through the water, in which direction is the boat moving? **west** _____

7. Which arrow shows the direction the air will leave the balloon? **A** _____

8. Which arrow shows the direction the balloon will move? **B** _____

Lesson 37   **67**

The picture shows Goad filled up with air.

9. Which arrow shows the direction the air will leave Goad? **R** _____

10. Which arrow shows the direction Goad will move? **S** _____

11. When a boy jumps from the mud this way ⬉, the mud tries to move which way? ⬊ _____

Skill Items

12. Write one way that tells how both objects are the same.
Ideas: They are both trees/living things, etc.

13. Write 2 ways that tell how object A is different from object B.

① **(Ideas (any 2): A has a thick trunk, but B does**
② **not; A has long branches/is short, but B has short branches/is tall, etc.)**

Object A   Object B

■ GO TO PART D IN YOUR TEXTBOOK. ■

68   *Lesson 37*

D Number your paper from 1 through 21.
Review Items
1. A mile is more than ▨▨ feet.
   • 2 thousand   • 1 thousand   • 5 thousand

2. What part of the world is shown on the map?
3. The map shows how far apart some places are. One line shows 13 hundred miles. The other line shows 25 hundred miles. How far is it from **B** to **T**?
4. How far is it from **G** to **H**?   **13 hundred miles**

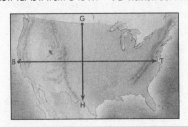

2. **United States**
3. **25 hundred miles**

232   *Lesson 37*

---

5. Which letter shows where the ground gets warm first? **D**
6. Which letter shows where the ground gets warm last? **A**

7. Which has a tall straight trunk, a forest tree or an apple tree?
8. Which has larger branches, a forest tree or an apple tree?
9. Which is longer, a centimeter or an inch?

Lesson 37   **233**

44

10. Write the letter of each toad in the picture. **B, E**
11. Write the letter of each frog in the picture. **A, H**
12. Write the letter of each mole in the picture. **D, G**

13. Which animal has smooth skin, a frog or a toad?
14. Which animal can jump farther, a frog or a toad?
15. Do any frogs have teeth? **yes**
16. If an ant weighed as much as a desk, the ant could carry an object as heavy as ▓▓▓. **10 desks**
17. You can see drops of water on grass early in the morning. What are those drops called? **dew**
18. Which weighs more, one gram or one water strider?
19. About how many ants would it take to weigh one gram? **100**
20. Roots keep a tree from ▓▓▓. **falling over**
21. Roots carry ▓▓▓ to all parts of the tree. **water**

234   *Lesson 37*

Name _____

A

1. What part of a car tells how fast the car is moving?

   • the tires   • <u>the speedometer</u>   • the clock

Each speedometer in the picture shows how fast the car is moving.

2. How fast is car A going? **45 miles per hour**

3. How fast is car B going? **30 miles per hour**

4. Which car is going faster? **A**

5. A speedometer tells about ▓▓▓.

   • miles   • hours   • <u>miles per hour</u>

B **Story Items**

6. What city was Herman born in?

   • <u>New York City</u>   • Toadsville   • Portland

7. What airport was close to where Herman was born?

   • O'Hare   • <u>Kennedy</u>   • O'no

8. How far was the airport from where Herman was born?

   5 miles

Lesson 38   **69**

---

9. Why didn't Herman fly off the cab?

   • Flies don't fly in the morning.
   • Flies don't take off near airports.
   • <u>Flies don't take off in big winds.</u>

10. How many legs does Herman have? **6**

11. The two women were part of the crew of a **jumbo jet**

12. Herman went into the woman's purse ▓▓▓.

   • to stay warm   • to chew gum   • <u>to eat candy</u>

13. **Underline** 2 things that Herman liked about the cab.

   • <u>It was warm.</u>   • It was new.
   • It was fast.   • It was green.   • <u>It was yellow.</u>

14. When was the wind blowing fastest on Herman?

   • when the cab was standing still
   • <u>when the cab was going 35 miles per hour</u>
   • when the cab was going 15 miles per hour

Look at the pictures.

15. **Underline** the thing that Herman rode on to the airport.

16. **Make an X** on the thing the two women were going to work on.

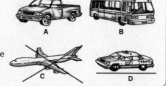

GO TO PART D IN YOUR TEXTBOOK.

70   *Lesson 38*

D Number your paper from 1 through 18.

Skill Items

Here's the rule: **Toads have warts.**
1. Zorm is a toad. So what does the rule tell you about Zorm? **Zorm has warts.**
2. Gleeb is not a toad. So what does the rule tell you about Gleeb? **nothing**

Write the word from the box that means the same thing as the underlined part of each sentence.

apart	warts	behind	motioned
ahead	propped	hair	broiled	boasted

3. She <u>bragged</u> about winning the race. **boasted**
4. The cab was <u>in front</u> of the bus. **ahead**
5. The animal was covered with <u>little bumps</u>. **warts**

240   *Lesson 38*

Things that are this far apart on the map ←——→ are 1 mile apart.

Things that are this far apart ←————————→ are 2 miles apart.

6. How far is it from the pool to the park?   **2 miles**
7. How far is it from the park to the forest?   **1 mile**

AIRPORT
FOREST
MALL
HILL
POOL
PARK

Lesson 38   **241**

---

8. What part of the world is shown on the map?   **United States**
9. The map shows how far apart some places are. How far is it from **M** to **P**?
   • 13 hundred miles   • 35 hundred miles
   • 25 hundred miles
10. How far is it from **X** to **Y**?
   • 13 hundred miles   • 35 hundred miles
   • 25 hundred miles

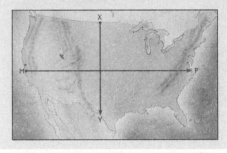

X
M   P
Y

11. A mile is more than ▨▨▨ feet.
   • 5 thousand   • 3 thousand   • 1 thousand

242   Lesson 38

Each statement tells about how far something goes or how fast something goes. Write **how far** or **how fast** for each item.

12. She walked 3 miles.   **how far**
13. The bus was going 50 miles per hour.   **how fast**
14. She walked 3 miles per hour.   **how fast**
15. He chased the dog 6 miles.   **how far**

16. How **fast** is truck **R** going?   **25 miles per hour**
17. How **fast** is truck **S** going?   **30 miles per hour**
18. Which truck is going faster?   **S**

R   S
25   30

Lesson 38   **243**

39

Name _____

A

Look at the cut-away picture of an airplane.

1. There are 3 flight attendants on the plane. **Make a box** around each flight attendant.

2. **Cross out** the pilot.

B   Story Items

3. How far is it from New York City to San Francisco?
   25 hundred miles

4. Make an **X** where New York City is.

5. Make a **Y** where San Francisco is.

6. Why did Herman fly into the woman's purse?
   • to get warm   • to get candy   • to find a dark place

Lesson 39   **71**

---

7. Why did it get dark inside the purse?
    - • <u>The woman closed the purse.</u>   • The sun went down.
        - • The woman went into a dark place.
8. Herman tried to take a nap on something. What was it?
        - • a wall   • a window   • <u>a seat</u>
9. Why did that place feel great to Herman?
        - • It was big.   • <u>It was warm and sunny.</u>   • It was cool.
10. **Underline** the plane that Herman was in.

A   B   C

Here's the crew of a jumbo jet.
11. **Circle** the crew member who brought Herman on board.
12. **Make an X** to show where Herman was.

A   B   C   D

GO TO PART D IN YOUR TEXTBOOK.

---

good to Herman. They were the clean smells of clean seats and clean floors and clean windows.

Herman took off to find some better smells or some better light. He found a nice, warm red. It was fuzzy and very warm. Herman took a nap. He was on the back of a seat, right next ✷ to the window. The sun was shining through the window. That felt great.

MORE NEXT TIME

D Number your paper from 1 through 22.

Skill Items

Several paths continued for a great distance.
1. What part means a **long way**?   a great distance
2. What word refers to more than two but less than a lot?   several
3. What word means **kept on going**?   continued

Review Items

4. What color are the flowers that apple trees make?   white
5. What grows in each place where there was a flower?   apple

---

6. Which has a tall straight trunk, a forest tree or an apple tree?
7. How many years could it take for a forest to grow back after a forest fire?
    - • 10 years   • 200 years   • 100 years

Some things happen as tadpoles grow.
8. Write the letter of what happens first.   c
9. Write the letter of what happens last.   a
    a. Their tail disappears.
    b. They grow front legs.
    c. They grow back legs.

10. Write the letter of each statement that is make-believe.   a, c
    a. A toad flew away.
    b. A bird flew away.
    c. A dog flew away.
    d. A fly flew away.
11. When we talk about miles per hour, we tell how ▨ something is moving.   fast
12. A speedometer tells about ▨.
    - • hours   • miles per hour   • miles

Some of the lines in the box are one inch long and some are one centimeter long.
13. Write the letter of every line that is one centimeter long.   C, D, E, G, I
14. Write the letter of every line that is one inch long.

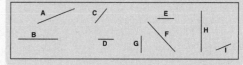

15. Which is longer, a centimeter or a meter?   meter
16. How many centimeters long is a meter?   100
17. Write the letters of the 4 names that tell about length.
    a. inch   d. day   g. hour   i. mile
    b. year   e. second   h. week   j. minute
    c. centimeter   f. meter

14. A, B, F, H
17. a, c, f, i

47

United States

18. What part of the world is shown on the map?
The map shows how far apart some places are. One line shows 13 hundred miles. The other line shows 25 hundred miles.
19. How far is it from **A** to **B**? 13 hundred miles
20. How far is it from **C** to **D**? 25 hundred miles

21. Arrow **X** shows the direction the boy will jump. Which arrow shows the direction the block of ice will move? P

22. Arrow B shows the direction the girl will jump. Which arrow shows the direction the boat will move? E

TEST 4   **40**

Number your paper from 1 through 26.

Some hairs in the picture are being pushed down. Some are being pulled up. Look at the skin around each hair.
1. Write the letter of each hair that is being pushed down. A, D
2. Write the letter of each hair that is being pulled up.

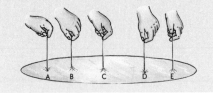

3. When we weigh very small things, the unit we use is ▨. gram(s)

2. B, C, E

4. The food that 3 of the animals eat each day weighs more than those animals. Write the letters of those animals. D, E F
5. The food that 4 of the animals eat each day does not weigh as much as those animals. Write the letters of those animals. A, B, C, G

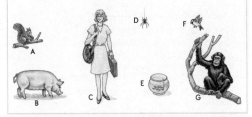

6. If you get smaller, your voice gets ▨. higher
7. Tom got smaller. So what do you know about Tom's voice? Idea: It got higher.

8. Write the letter of the ruler that will make the highest sound. C

9. Write the letter of the ruler that will make the lowest sound. B

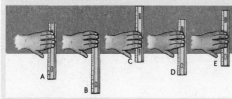

Each statement tells about how far something goes or how fast something goes. Write **how far** or **how fast** for each item.

10. He ran 5 miles per hour. how fast
11. He ran 5 miles. how far
12. The plane was 500 miles from New York City. how far
13. The plane was flying 500 miles per hour. how fast

14. When we talk about miles per hour, we tell how ▬ something is moving. fast
15. When something tries to move in one direction, something else tries to move ▬. in the opposite direction

---

16. How fast is car **A** going? 25 miles per hour
17. How fast is car **B** going? 30 miles per hour
18. Which car is going faster? B

19. How far is it from New York City to San Francisco?

Skill Items   19. 25 hundred miles
Look at object A and object B.
20. Write one way that tells how both objects are the same.
21. Write 2 ways that tell how object A is different from object B.

Object A   Object B

20. Ideas: They are both cups/containers/vases, they both have shadows, etc.
21. Ideas (any 2): A is tall, but B is not/is short; A has dots, but B does not/is plain, etc.

For each item, write the underlined word or words from the sentences in the box.

> The traffic was moving forty miles per hour.
> He is supposed to make a decision in a couple of days.

22. What underlining means **two**? couple
23. What underlining means **each**? per
24. What underlining means **make up his mind**?
25. What underlining refers to all the cars and trucks that were moving on the street? traffic
26. What underlining means **should**? supposed to

24. make a decision

■ END OF TEST 4 ■

41

Name _____

A

1. **Underline** the names of 4 insects:

   • mouse   • bee   • crab   • spider   • ant
   • fish   • snake   • fly   • turtle   • beetle

2. How many parts does the body of an insect have? 3
3. How many parts does the body of an ant have? 3
4. Is a spider an insect? no
5. All insects have 6 legs.
6. How many legs does a spider have? 8
7. How many parts does a spider's body have? 2

B   Story Items

8. Mark New York City with the letters **NY**.
9. Mark San Francisco with the letters **SF**.
10. Draw an arrow from New York City to San Francisco.

11. How far would you travel to go from New York City to San Francisco?
   25 hundred miles

12. What did a passenger almost drop on Herman?
    • a purse • a shoe • <u>a coat</u>

13. When Herman flew away, he bumped into a living. What part of a living did he bump into?
    • a hand • <u>a face</u> • a coat

14. Herman got away by using a <u>W</u>-shaped move.

15. Who was telling the passengers what to do in case of danger?
    • the pilot • <u>a flight attendant</u> • a doctor

16. The flight attendants made sure that passengers were wearing ▓▓▓.
    • seats • coats • <u>seat belts</u>

17. How many passengers were on the jumbo jet? <u>300</u>

Review Items

The arrow in each picture shows which way the wind is blowing. Start at the dot and draw the smoke in each picture.

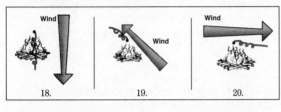

18.   19.   20.

▓▓▓ GO TO PART E IN YOUR TEXTBOOK. ▓▓▓

E Number your paper from 1 through 18.

Skill Items

Here's a rule: **Fish live in water.**

1. Alex is not a fish. So what does the rule tell you about Alex? *nothing*

2. A trout is a fish. So what does the rule tell you about a trout? *A trout lives in water.*

3. A lizard is not a fish. So what does the rule tell you about a lizard? *nothing*

Use the words in the box to write complete sentences.

continued	cleared	supposed	service	distance
	decision	dead	couple	quite	several

4. He is ▓▓▓ to make a ▓▓▓ in a ▓▓▓ of days.

5. ▓▓▓ paths ▓▓▓ for a great ▓▓▓.

Review Items

6. A mile is more than ▓▓▓ feet.
   • 1 thousand • ⟨5 thousand⟩ • 2 thousand

7. What part of a car tells how fast the car is moving?

4. He is ⟨supposed⟩ to make a ⟨decision⟩ in a ⟨couple⟩ of days.

5. ⟨Several⟩ paths ⟨continued⟩ for a great ⟨distance⟩.

7. speedometer

---

8. *500 miles per hour;* 9. *35 miles per hour*
10. *20 miles per hour*

Here's how fast different things can go:
• 20 miles per hour
• 35 miles per hour
• 200 miles per hour
• 500 miles per hour

8. Which speed tells how fast a jet can fly?

9. Which speed tells how fast a fast dog can run?

10. Which speed tells how fast a fast man can run?

11. What part of the world is shown on the map?

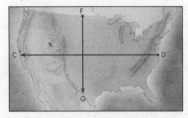

12. The map shows how far apart some places are. How far is it from **F** to **G**? *13 hundred miles*

11. *United States*

The speedometers are in two different cars.

A   B

13. How fast is car A going? *30 miles per hour*

14. How fast is car B going? *45 miles per hour*

15. Which car is going faster? *B*

16. Which weighs more, ⟨one gram⟩ or one water strider?

17. How many ants would it take to weigh one gram?

18. Arrow B shows the direction the girl will jump. Which arrow shows the direction the boat will move? *C*

17. *about 100*

50

WORKBOOK

Name _____

A

1. When we talk about how hot or cold something is, we tell about the __temperature__ of the thing.

2. When an object gets hotter, the temperature goes __up__.

3. When the earth gets cold, which way does the temperature go?

   __down__

4. An oven gets hotter. So what do you know about the temperature of the oven?

   • It goes up.   • It goes down.

The arrows show that the temperature is going up on thermometer A and going down on thermometer B.

5. In which picture is the water getting colder?   • A   • <u>B</u>

6. In which picture is the water getting hotter?   • <u>A</u>   • B

A   B

Lesson 42   **75**

WORKBOOK

B **Story Items**

7. The plane went up and up after it left New York City. How high did it go?

   • 5 miles   • <u>6 miles</u>   • 100 miles

8. How fast does a jumbo jet fly?

   • 5 miles per hour   • 6 miles per hour
   • <u>500 miles per hour</u>

9. When a plane goes 5 hundred miles per hour, do the passengers feel that they're moving **fast** or **not at all**?

   • fast   • <u>not at all</u>

10. How many flies were on the plane? __6__

---

11. Which arrow shows the way the air will leave Goad's mouth? __F__

12. Which arrow shows the way Goad will move? __G__

---

13. Which arrow shows the way the air shoots from the jet engine? __T__

14. Which arrow shows the way the jet moves? __D__

GO TO PART D IN YOUR TEXTBOOK.

76   *Lesson 42*

TEXTBOOK

"You may remove your seat belts and move around the plane now." The passengers start to talk to each other now. They feel safe. The plane doesn't seem to be moving at all. Walking around inside the plane is just like walking around inside a building. But the passengers inside the plane are moving along at the speed of five hundred miles per hour.

Herman was moving at five hundred miles per hour. But he wasn't thinking much about it. He didn't feel like a super fly. In fact, he wasn't the only fly in that jumbo jet. Like most jumbo jets that fly in the summer, it had flies in it. There were six flies and one beetle.

MORE NEXT TIME

D Number your paper from 1 through 27.

Story Items

1. Pretend you are in an airplane that is flying over a city. What would look different about the city?

   • Things would be darker.
   • | Things would be smaller. |
   • Things would be bigger.

TEXTBOOK

Skill Items

Here are the titles of some stories:
   a. Glenn Found Gold
   b. Four Skunks Under the House
   c. The Day Uncle Bill Came to Visit

2. One story tells about a bad, bad smell. Write the letter of that title. __b__

3. One story tells about a man who went to somebody's home. Write the letter of that title. __c__

4. One story tells about a man who became very rich. Write the letter of that title. __a__

Write the word from the box that means the same thing as the underlined part of each sentence.

| spider | apart | couple | per | weather |
| pilot | insect | passenger | service | |

5. Tom picked fifty apples <u>each hour</u>. __per__
6. The <u>bug with six legs</u> walked up my arm. __insect__
7. The <u>person who flew the plane</u> told about the trip.

   __pilot__

8. 200 miles per hour 9. 500 miles per hour
10. 20 miles per hour

Review Items

Here's how fast different things can go:
- 20 miles per hour
- 35 miles per hour
- 200 miles per hour
- 500 miles per hour

8. Which speed tells how fast a racing car can go?
9. Which speed tells how fast a jet can fly?
10. Which speed tells how fast a fast man can run?

11. Which animal has smooth skin, a frog or a toad?
12. Which animal can jump farther, a toad or a frog?
13. A speedometer tells about ▓▓▓.
   - hours   • miles   • miles per hour
14. Write the names of the 4 insects.
   - spider   • bird   • beetle   • bee   • snake
   - toad   • fly   • worm   • ant
15. How many parts does the body of an insect have? 3
16. How many legs does an insect have? 6
17. How many legs does a spider have? 8
18. How many parts does a spider's body have? 2
19. What's the boiling temperature of water?
   - 112 degrees   • 121 miles   • 212 degrees
20. When something tries to move in one direction, something else tries to move ▓▓▓.
   in the opposite direction

21. Arrow **X** shows the direction the boy will jump. Which arrow shows the direction the block of ice will move? N

22. When we weigh very small things, the unit we use is ▓▓▓. gram(s)

Some things in the picture weigh **1 gram.** Some weigh **2 grams.** Some weigh **5 grams.** Write how much each object weighs.

23. ▬▬▬▬▬
24. ◻
25. ▬▬▬
26. ▬▬▬▬▬
27. 🪲

23. 5 grams   24. 1 gram
25. 2 grams   26. 5 grams
27. 2 grams

43

Name _____

1. **Underline** the city on the east coast that Herman flew from.
   - Chicago   • New York City   • San Francisco

2. **Underline** the city on the west coast that Herman flew to.
   - Chicago   • New York City   • San Francisco

3. How far is the trip from New York City to San Francisco?
   25 hundred miles

4. The kitchen on an airplane is called ▓▓▓.
   - a kitchen   • a galley   • an alley

5. Herman went from New York City to San Francisco. **Underline** 3 cities he flew over.
   - Chicago   • Denver   • New England
   - Lake Michigan   • Alaska   • Salt Lake City

6. **Circle** the pictures that show what Herman had for his meal service.

   A   B   C   D   E   F

7. Herman took a nap on something. What was that thing?
   - a wooden panel   • a plastic panel
   - a metal panel

8. Why did Herman like that place?
   - It was quiet.   • It was warm.   • It was smooth.

9. Write **east** next to the city on the east coast.
10. Write **west** next to the city on the west coast.
11. **Draw an arrow** that shows the trip the jet plane took.
12. Make a **D** where Denver is.
13. Make a **C** where Chicago is.

west   San Francisco D   Salt Lake City C   New York City east

14. How many flies were on the plane when it left New York City?
   6

15. How many flies got off the plane in San Francisco? 3

GO TO PART D IN YOUR TEXTBOOK.

D Number your paper from 1 through 24.

Story Items

Look at the picture. It tells how many degrees each object is.
1. Which object is the hottest? B
2. What is the temperature of that object?
3. Which object is coldest? A
4. What is the temperature of that object?

A   B   C

20 degrees   60 degrees   35 degrees

5. When an object gets hotter, the temperature goes ▩. up
6. When the temperature goes up, what gets bigger?
   • the number of degrees
   • the number of miles per hour
   • the time

2. 60 degrees
4. 20 degrees

Skill Items

Here's a rule: **Every insect has six legs.**
7. Jub is an insect. So what does the rule tell you about Jub? Jub has six legs.
8. Frig is not an insect. So what does the rule tell you about Frig? nothing

Boiling water will thaw ice in a few moments.
9. What word means **melt**? thaw
10. What 2 words mean **not very many seconds**?
11. What word tells you that the water was 212 degrees?

Review Items

Each statement tells about how far something goes or how fast something goes. Write **how far** or **how fast** for each item.
12. The car that won the race drove 200 miles per hour.
13. The woman ran 3 miles to get home. how far
14. The dog was running 35 miles per hour. how fast
15. They drove 200 miles without stopping. how far

10. few moments
11. boiling
12. how fast

---

16. Write the names of the 4 insects.
   • fish   • beetle   • fly   • spider   • bird
   • frog   • bee   • snake   • worm   • ant
17. How many legs does an insect have? 6
18. How many parts does the body of an insect have? 3
19. How many parts does a spider's body have? 2
20. How many legs does a spider have? 8
21. When we talk about how hot or cold something is, we tell about the ▩ of the thing.
   • length   • weight   • temperature
22. When an object gets hotter, the temperature goes ▩. up

23. The arrow on the thermometer shows that the temperature is going down. Is the water getting **hotter** or **colder**?
24. The arrow on the thermometer shows that the temperature is going up. Is the water getting **hotter** or **colder**?

Name _____

A

1. Write **north, south, east,** and **west** in the shaded boxes.

2. Write the letter of the animal that is facing into the wind.
   C _____

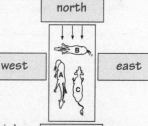

north

west   east

south

3. Which direction is that animal facing?
   north

4. So what's the name of the wind? north _____ wind

B Story Items

5. How many flies were on the plane when it left New York City?
   6 _____

6. How many flies got off the plane in San Francisco? 3 _____

7. How many flies died on the plane? 2 _____

8. What killed them?
   • Herman   • fly spray   • cold air

9. When fly spray filled the air, Herman was near ▨.
   - • <u>an open door</u>   • a red seat   • a window

10. The air that blew on Herman was ▨.
   - • filled with fly spray   • <u>fresh air</u>   • hot air

11. Some workers stacked dinners in the galley. Why didn't those dinners smell very good to Herman?
   - • They were rotten.   • They were small.
   - • <u>They were frozen.</u>

Look at the map below. The **Y** shows where the wind starts.

12. Write **north**, **south**, **east**, and **west** in the shaded boxes.

13. Make a **Z** where San Francisco is.

14. If you were in San Francisco, which direction would you face if you wanted the wind to blow in your face? <u>west</u>

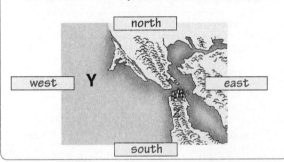

north
west   Y   east
south

━━━━━ GO TO PART D IN YOUR TEXTBOOK. ━━━━━

80   Lesson 44

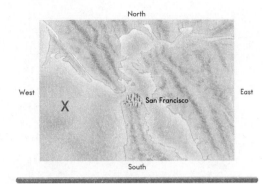

North

West   East

        X   San Francisco

South

D Number your paper from 1 through 25.

Story Items

1. How many hours did it take to fly from New York City to San Francisco? 6 (hours)

2. Will it take **more time** or **less time** to fly from San Francisco to New York City?

---

3. Would a plane fly **faster** or **slower** when it goes in the same direction as the wind?

4. When the plane flies from San Francisco to New York City, is it flying in the **same direction** or the **opposite direction** as the wind?

Skill Items

5. Write one way that tells how both objects are the same.

6. Write **2** ways that tell how object A is **different** from object B.

Object A   Object B

5. Ideas: They are both animals; they both have a tail; they both have four legs; etc.
6. Ideas (any 2): A has a hump, but B doesn't; A is a camel, but B is a pig; A is facing left/west, but B is facing right/east; etc.

286   Lesson 44

---

9. Several paths continued for a great distance.
10. Boiling water will thaw ice in a few moments.

The faster the cab moves, the faster the wind blows on Herman.

7. Write the letter of the cab where the wind will blow fastest on Herman. D

8. Write the letter of the cab where the wind will blow slowest on Herman. B

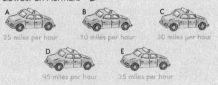

A   B   C
25 miles per hour   10 miles per hour   30 miles per hour

D   E
45 miles per hour   35 miles per hour

Use the words in the box to write complete sentences.

| figure | thaw | distance | seven | moments |
| several | frozen | boiling | continued | circled |

9. ▨ paths ▨ for a great ▨.
10. ▨ water will ▨ ice in a few ▨.

Review Items

11. When a room gets colder, which way does the temperature go? down

12. A car gets hotter. So what do you know about the temperature of the car? Idea: It goes up.

The arrows show that the temperature is going down on thermometer A and going up on thermometer **B**.

13. In which picture is the water getter colder, A or **B**?
14. In which picture is the water getter hotter, A or **B**?

15. Write the **name** of the city that's on the **west** coast.
16. Write the **name** of the city that's on the **east** coast.
17. Which letter shows where Chicago is? D
18. Which letter shows where Denver is? C

15. San Francisco; 16. New York (City)

288   Lesson 44

19. When we talk about how hot or cold something is, we tell about the ▨▨▨ of the thing.
    • weight   • temperature   • length
20. When the temperature goes up, the number of ▨▨▨ gets bigger.
    • miles   • degrees   • hours
21. What's the boiling temperature of water?
    • 212 miles   • 212 degrees   • 112 degrees
22. How fast does a jumbo jet fly?
    • 5 miles per hour   • 50 miles per hour
    • 500 miles per hour
23. The kitchen on an airplane is called ▨▨▨.
    • an alley   • a galley   • a kitchen
24. Does a housefly weigh **more than a gram** or less than a gram?
25. Does a table weigh more than a gram or **less than a gram?**

Lesson 44   289

45

Name _____

A

1. **Draw a circle** around the plane in each picture that will go the fastest.

2. **Draw an arrow** on the cloud in each picture to show which direction it is moving.

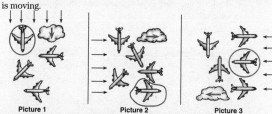

Picture 1   Picture 2   Picture 3

B Story Items

3. How long did the trip to San Francisco take? 6 hours
4. How long did the trip back to New York City take? 5 hours
5. The trip back to New York City took less time because the plane went in ▨▨▨.
    • the same direction as the wind
    • the opposite direction as the wind
6. What month was it when Herman landed in San Francisco?
    • May   • June   • July
7. What was the temperature when Herman landed in San Francisco?
    63 _____ degrees
8. Was it **hotter** or **colder** in San Francisco when the plane left?
    colder _____

Lesson 45   81

9. Write **north, south, east,** and **west** in the shaded boxes.
10. **Draw an arrow** on the cloud to show which way the cloud will move.
11. **Fill in the blanks.** That wind is blowing from the west . So that wind is called a west wind.

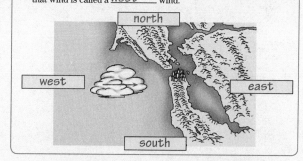

north
west   east
south

12. What made the trip to New York City a rough trip?
    • the pilot   • the copilot   • the clouds
13. Why did the captain tell the passengers to keep their seat belts fastened?
    • because of meal service   • because of rough air
    • because of low temperature
14. Did the passengers enjoy the trip?   • yes   • no
15. **Underline 2** words that tell how most passengers felt.
    • happy   • sick   • sleepy
    • frightened   • hungry

GO TO PART D IN YOUR TEXTBOOK.

82   Lesson 45

The crew on the plane didn't mind the rough air very much. They knew that they would be out of the rough air as soon as they got above the clouds. They weren't the only ones who were not afraid. Herman had found a candy wrapper. And it was good, good, GOOD. The plane was much warmer now. And the food in the ovens was starting to thaw out. The smells of food filled the plane. While the passengers were thinking, "I'm going to be sick," Herman was thinking, "This place is good, good, GOOD."

The trip going to San Francisco had taken six hours. The trip back to New York took only five hours.

Can you figure out why?

MORE NEXT TIME

D Number your paper from 1 through 23.

Skill Items

Here are titles for different stories:
- a. The Man Who Stayed for Dinner
- b. Ten Ways to Trap Moles
- c. Mary Buys a Car

1. One story tells about a person who got something new. Write the letter of that title. *c*

2. One story tells about a person who wanted to eat. Write the letter of that title. *a*

3. One story tells about things you can do to catch some animals. Write the letter of that title. *b*

Lesson 45   293

Review Items

4. When a plane flies from New York City to San Francisco, is it flying in the **same direction** or the opposite direction as the wind?

5. Write the name of the city that's on the west coast.
6. Write the name of the city that's on the east coast.
7. Which letter shows where Chicago is? *D*
8. Which letter shows where Salt Lake City is? *B*

5. San Francisco
6. New York (City)

294   Lesson 45

---

9. How many parts does the body of an insect have? *3*
10. How many legs does an insect have? *6*
11. How many legs does a spider have? *8*
12. How many parts does a spider's body have? *2*

Here's how fast different things can go:
- 20 miles per hour
- 35 miles per hour
- 200 miles per hour
- 500 miles per hour

13. Which speed tells how fast a fast man can run?
14. Which speed tells how fast a jet can fly?
15. Which speed tells how fast a fast dog can run?

16. Arrow B shows the direction the girl will jump. Which arrow shows the direction the boat will move? *R*

R ⟶
S ⟵

13. 20 miles per hour
14. 500 miles per hour
15. 35 miles per hour

Lesson 45   295

---

17. What does the top of water have?
    • hair   • nails   • skin
18. If tiny animals fall from high places, they don't ▊▊▊.
19. The food that very small animals eat each day may weigh ▊▊▊.
    • 20 pounds   • 5 pounds   • more than the animal

20. If you get smaller, your voice gets ▊▊▊. *higher*
21. Jean got smaller. So what do you know about Jean's voice? *Idea: It got higher.*

22. Does dew form in the middle of the day? *no*
23. Dew forms when the air gets ▊▊▊.
    • cooler   • windy   • warmer

18. get hurt

296   Lesson 45

WORKBOOK

Name _____

46

A

1. Write **north, south, east,** and **west** in the right boxes.

2. Make an **H** where New York City is.

3. Make an **F** where San Francisco is.

4. Make a **J** where Japan is.

5. Make a **P** where the Pacific Ocean is.

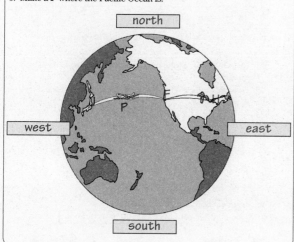

north

west

east

south

WORKBOOK

B Story Items

6. Did the fly spray kill Herman? **no**

7. Where was Herman when fly spray filled the air?
   - on a paper panel   • **inside an oven**   • on a red seat

8. After the plane left New York City, where did it stop first?
   - Japan   • Chicago   • <u>San Francisco</u>

9. Then the plane left for ▓▓▓▓.
   - **Japan**   • Chicago   • San Francisco

10. In what direction did the plane fly? **west**

11. How far is it from New York City to San Francisco?
    25 hundred _____ miles

12. How far is it from San Francisco to Japan?
    5 thousand _____ miles

13. What ocean do you cross to get from San Francisco to Japan?
    - Atlantic   • <u>Pacific</u>   • Peaceful

14. What did Herman get stuck in? **(spider) web**

15. **Cross out** Herman's enemy.

A   B   C

GO TO PART D IN YOUR TEXTBOOK.

TEXTBOOK

The trip to San Francisco took six hours. After the plane left San Francisco, the passengers napped and talked and ate. While they did that, Herman met an enemy. Herman was buzzing around near one of the coat closets in the jumbo jet. It was dark inside the coat closets, but some smells caught Herman's attention, so he buzzed inside one of the closets. He buzzed up into one of the corners. And then he kept trying to fly, but his legs were stuck to something. He buzzed his wings harder and harder. But he couldn't pull himself free. Once more, he buzzed. Time to rest.

Herman, like other flies, had big strange eyes that could see in all directions at the same time. Suddenly, Herman's eyes saw something moving toward him very fast. It was a large hairy thing with eight legs and a mean-looking mouth. Herman was stuck in a spider web, and the spider was ready to eat dinner.

MORE NEXT TIME

D Number your paper from 1 through 23.

Skill Items

Here's a rule: **Fish live in water.**

1. A trout is a fish. So what does the rule tell you about a trout? **A trout lives in water.**

2. A frog is not a fish. So what does the rule tell you about a frog? **nothing**

TEXTBOOK

3. speedometer

Review Items

3. What part of a car tells how fast the car is moving?

The speedometers are in 2 different cars.

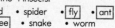

4. How fast is car A going? **55 miles per hour**
5. How fast is car B going? **45 miles per hour**
6. Which car is going faster? **A**

7. Write the names of the 4 insects.
   - beetle • bird • spider • fly • ant
   - frog • bee • snake • worm

8. When a glass of water gets colder, which way does the temperature go? **down**

9. A pot gets hotter. So what do you know about the temperature of the pot? **It is going up.**

10. When a plane flies from New York City to San Francisco, is it flying in the **same direction** or the **opposite direction** as the wind?

57

TEXTBOOK

Write the letter of the plane in each picture that will go the fastest.

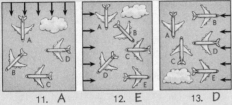

11. A   12. E   13. D

14. Which arrow shows the way the cloud will move? M

San Francisco

M ⟶
P ⟵

15. That wind is blowing from the ▇▇▇. west
16. So that wind is called a ▇▇▇ wind. west

TEXTBOOK

17. If a grain of sugar were very big, it would look like a box made of ▇▇▇. glass
18. What kind of corners does a grain of sugar have? sharp
19. You can see drops of water on grass early in the morning. What are those drops called? dew

20. Write the letter of each water strider. A, C, E, G

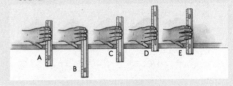

21. Write the letter of the ruler that will make the lowest sound. B
22. Write the letter of the ruler that will make the highest sound. D

23. How fast does a jumbo jet fly?
• 50 miles per hour   • 500 miles per hour
• 5 miles per hour

WORKBOOK

47

Name _____

Ⓐ

1. Which eye works like one drop, a human's eye or a fly's eye?
• <u>human eye</u>   • fly eye

2. Which eye works like many drops?
• human eye   • <u>fly eye</u>

3. Which eye can see more things at the same time?
• human eye   • <u>fly eye</u>

Ⓑ **Story Items**

4. When a spider wraps an insect in a web, the insect looks like a ▇▇▇.
• fly   • <u>mummy</u>   • spider

5. **Circle** the spider.
6. **Cross out** Herman.
7. **Make a box** around the dead insect.

WORKBOOK

Review Items

8. Write **north, south, east,** and **west** in the right boxes.
9. Which letter shows where New York City is? C
10. Which letter shows where San Francisco is? D
11. Which letter shows where Japan is? B
12. Which letter shows where the Pacific Ocean is? A
13. Is the United States shown on this map? yes

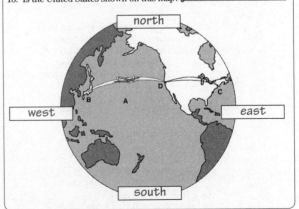

north

west   east

south

▇▇▇ GO TO PART D IN YOUR TEXTBOOK. ▇▇▇

The passengers in the jumbo jet were talking to each other or ✳ leaning back in their seats thinking about what they would do when they reached Japan. Once in a while, passengers would look below at the ocean. They would think, "Ocean, ocean, ocean. All you can see is ocean."

While the passengers sat and talked and thought, Herman was fighting for his life.

Herman was lucky. The spider tried to turn Herman around and wrap him up. But when the spider turned Herman, the spider freed Herman's legs from the web. Herman gave a great buzz with his wings. Suddenly, he was in the air, with some sticky stuff still on his legs.

"Get out of that dark," Herman thought. He flew from the closet to the bright part of the jet. A moment later, Herman landed on a warm red and rubbed his front legs together. As Herman sat on the seat back, he did not remember what had just happened. For Herman, things were warm and red. And he was tired. Time to nap.

MORE NEXT TIME

D Number your paper from 1 through 25.

Story Items

1. Herman took a nap on something that was warm and red. What was it?
   - an oven • a closet • **a seat**

---

2. In today's story the plane left San Francisco to go to ▮▮▮. **Japan**
3. In which direction did the plane fly? **west**
4. How far is it from San Francisco to that country?
   - **5 thousand miles** • 5 hundred miles
   - 2 thousand miles
5. What ocean did the plane cross? **Pacific (Ocean)**

6. Why did Herman have a hard time escaping from the spider web?
   - His wings were stuck. • He couldn't see.
   - **His legs were stuck.**
7. How do most spiders kill insects?
   - **by biting them** • by crushing them
   - by wrapping them
8. Did the spider kill Herman? **no**

Skill Items

Write the word or words from the box that mean the same thing as the underlined part of each sentence.

continued	ahead	cook	figured out
pilot	decision	record	far apart	copilot

9. The houses were <u>not close to each other</u>. **far apart**
10. The <u>person in charge</u> of the plane told us where we were. **pilot**
11. She <u>learned</u> how to put the table together. **figured out**

They were eager to hear the announcement.

12. What word means **message**? **announcement**
13. What word tells how they felt about hearing the announcement? **eager**

Review Items

14. How fast is truck **A** going? **50 miles per hour**
15. How fast is truck **B** going? **30 miles per hour**
16. Which truck is going faster? **A**

---

17. How fast is boy C going? **5 miles per hour**
18. How fast is boy D going? **8 miles per hour**
19. Which boy is going faster? **D**

20. Which arrow shows the way the air will leave the jet engines? **S**
21. Which arrow shows the way the jet will move? **R**

22. When the temperature goes up, the number of ▓▓ gets bigger.
    • miles   • degrees   • hours   • miles per hour

23. Write the letter of the animal that is facing into the wind. A
24. Which direction is that animal facing? south
25. So what's the **name** of that wind? south wind

Lesson 47   313

Name _____

A

1. The United States is a ▓▓.
    • state   • <u>country</u>   • city

2. Japan is a ▓▓.
    • state   • <u>country</u>   • city

3. The United States is made up of fifty ▓▓.
    • countries   • cities   • <u>states</u>

4. The biggest state in the United States is ▓▓.
    • Texas   • <u>Alaska</u>   • California

5. The second biggest state in the United States is ▓▓.
    • <u>Texas</u>   • Alaska   • California

6. The third biggest state in the United States is ▓▓.
    • Texas   • Alaska   • <u>California</u>

7. **Underline** the state in the United States that is bigger than Japan.
    • Ohio   • <u>Alaska</u>   • New York

8. **Underline** the 9 places that are in the United States.
    • <u>Chicago</u>   • <u>Lake Michigan</u>   • <u>California</u>
    • <u>San Francisco</u>   • <u>Denver</u>   • Japan
    • <u>Texas</u>   • <u>Ohio</u>   • <u>New York City</u>
    • <u>Alaska</u>

9. What's the name of the state you live in? (Student's state) _____

Lesson 48   87

B Story Items

10. What country is shown in the picture? Japan _____

11. What did Herman do after he escaped from the spider?
    • <u>took a nap</u>   • ate candy   • flew into a closet

12. The plane landed in the country of Japan _____

13. Why were the passengers excited about landing there?
    • They were hungry.
    • <u>They had been on the plane for many hours.</u>
    • They were tired.

14. A passenger told the others that the tiny lines they saw showed where ▓▓.
    • the ocean was
    • the mountains were
    • <u>the airport was</u>

▓▓▓ GO TO PART E IN YOUR TEXTBOOK. ▓▓▓

88   Lesson 48

---

1. Boiling water will thaw ice in a few moments.
2. They were eager to hear the announcement.

E Number your paper from 1 through 23.

Skill Items

Use the words in the box to write complete sentences.

strength	eager	enemy	boiling	announcement
	thaw	free	moments	cross

1. ▓▓ water will ▓▓ ice in a few ▓▓.
2. They were ▓▓ to hear the ▓▓.

3. Look at object A and object B. Write one way that tells how both objects are the same.
4. Write **2** ways that tell how object A is **different** from object B.

Object A   Object B

Review Items

5. A mile is around ▓▓ feet.
    • 5 hundred   • 5 thousand   • 1 thousand

6. A speedometer tells about ▓▓.
    • hours   • miles per hour   • miles

320   Lesson 48

3. Ideas: They are both spiders/have 8 legs/have 2 body parts; etc.
4. Ideas (any 2): A is brown, but B is black; A is hairy, but B isn't; A has a web, but B doesn't.

---

7. How many legs does an insect have? 6
8. How many legs does a fly have? 6
9. How many legs does a bee have? 6
10. How many legs does a spider have? 8
11. How many parts does a spider's body have? 2
12. How many parts does a fly's body have? 3

13. Some of the objects in the picture are insects, and some are spiders. Write the letter of each spider.
14. Write the letter of each insect. A, B, D, F, G

15. Object D is not a spider. Tell why. Ideas: It doesn't have 8 legs; it doesn't have 2 body parts.

13. C, E, H

Lesson 48 **321**

Here's how fast different things can go:
- 20 miles per hour
- 35 miles per hour
- 200 miles per hour
- 500 miles per hour

16. Which speed tells how fast a fast man can run?
17. Which speed tells how fast a fast dog can run?
18. Which speed tells how fast a jet can fly?

19. Which eye works like one drop, a human's eye or a fly's eye?
20. Which eye works like many drops, a human's eye or a fly's eye?
21. Which eye can see more things at the same time, a human's eye or a fly's eye?

16. 20 miles per hour
17. 35 miles per hour
18. 500 miles per hour

322 *Lesson 48*

Things that are this far apart ←——→ on the map are 2 miles apart.
Things that are this far apart ←————→ on the map are 4 miles apart.
22. How far is it from the pool to the store? 4 miles
23. How far is it from the park to the bus stop? 2 miles

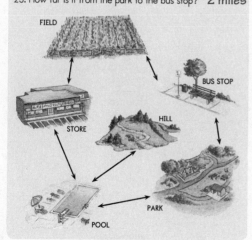

Lesson 48 **323**

49

Name _____
Story Items

1. Let's say that you are outside when the temperature is 50 degrees. What is the temperature inside your body?
   - 50 degrees   - 90 degrees   - <u>98 degrees</u>

2. Let's say you are outside when it is 90 degrees. What is the temperature inside your body?
   - 50 degrees   - 90 degrees   - <u>98 degrees</u>

3. Let's say a fly is outside when the temperature is 50 degrees. What is the temperature inside the fly's body?
   - <u>50 degrees</u>   - 90 degrees   - 98 degrees

4. Let's say a fly is outside when the temperature is 90 degrees. What is the temperature inside the fly's body?
   - 50 degrees   - <u>90 degrees</u>   - 98 degrees

5. Herman wanted to get out of the jet because ▇▇▇.
   - he was old   - <u>he was cold</u>   - he was hungry

6. Would it be easier to catch a fly on a hot day or on a cold day?
   - hot day   - <u>cold day</u>

7. Tell why.
   - <u>because the fly is moving slowly</u>
   - because the fly is hungry
   - because the fly is moving quickly

Lesson 49 **89**

Underline **warm-blooded** or **cold-blooded** for each animal.

8. Herman	warm-blooded	<u>cold-blooded</u>
9. fly	warm-blooded	<u>cold-blooded</u>
10. ant	warm-blooded	<u>cold-blooded</u>
11. dog	<u>warm-blooded</u>	cold-blooded
12. cat	<u>warm-blooded</u>	cold-blooded
13. flea	warm-blooded	<u>cold-blooded</u>
14. spider	warm-blooded	<u>cold-blooded</u>
15. horse	<u>warm-blooded</u>	cold-blooded

Review Items

16. Write **north**, **south**, **east**, and **west** in the right boxes.
17. Make an **F** where San Francisco is.
18. Make a **C** where Chicago is.
19. Make an **X** where New York City is.

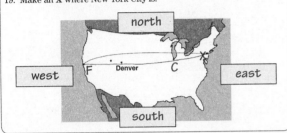

GO TO PART C IN YOUR TEXTBOOK.

Try catching a fly when the weather is very cool. The fly is slow and easy to catch. The fly is slow because everything inside the fly's body is cool and is working very slowly. Remember: A fly's body slows down when it gets cold.

Herman didn't know this ✿ rule. He did know that he didn't like cool places and he didn't like dark places unless they were warm. He was in Japan. He wanted to leave the jet because it was getting too cool for him. The air temperature was down to 45 degrees. He was slowing down. And his eyes could see that something was coming toward him.

MORE TO COME

C Number your paper from 1 through 18.

Skill Items

Here's a rule: **The colder the temperature, the slower the insects move.**
1. Write the letter of the insect that will move the slowest. **C**
2. Write the letter of the insect that will move the fastest. **D**

A	B	C	D	E
60 degrees	45 degrees	30 degrees	95 degrees	50 degrees

Review Items

3. When we talk about miles per hour, we tell how ▮▮▮ something is moving. **fast**

4. Which object is the hottest? **C**
5. What is the temperature of that object? **60 degrees**

A	B	C
45 degrees	30 degrees	60 degrees

6. When the temperature goes up, the number of ▮▮▮ gets bigger.
   • miles per hour   • hours   • miles   • <u>degrees</u>
7. How many legs does an insect have? **6**
8. How many legs does an ant have? **6**
9. How many legs does a spider have? **8**
10. How many parts does a spider's body have? **2**
11. How many parts does a fly's body have? **3**

---

12. Which letter shows where San Francisco is? **C**
13. Which letter shows where New York City is? **B**
14. Which letter shows where the Pacific Ocean is? **A**
15. Which letter shows where Japan is? **D**
16. Is the United States shown on this map? **yes**

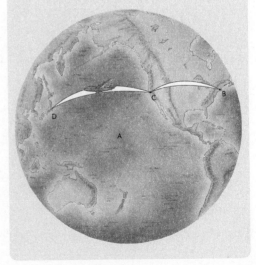

Some of the objects in the picture are insects, and some are spiders.

17. Write the letters of the spiders. B, H
18. Write the letters of the insects. A, D, F, G

Number your paper from 1 through 33.

Here's how fast different things can go:
- 20 miles per hour
- 200 miles per hour
- 35 miles per hour
- 500 miles per hour

1. Which speed tells how fast a fast man can run?
2. Which speed tells how fast a jet can fly?
3. Which speed tells how fast a fast dog can run?

4. When an object gets hotter, the temperature goes ____. up

The arrows show that the temperature is going up on thermometer A and going down on thermometer B.
5. In which picture is the water getting colder, A or B?
6. In which picture is the water getting hotter, A or B?

1. 20 miles per hour
2. 500 miles per hour
3. 35 miles per hour

---

7. Which letter shows where San Francisco is? X
8. If you were in San Francisco, which direction would you face if you wanted the wind to blow in your face? west

9. When a plane flies from New York City to San Francisco, is it flying in the **same direction** or the opposite direction as the wind?

---

10. Which letter shows where New York City is? R
11. Which letter shows where San Francisco is? P
12. Which letter shows where Japan is? N
13. Which letter shows where the Pacific Ocean is? M

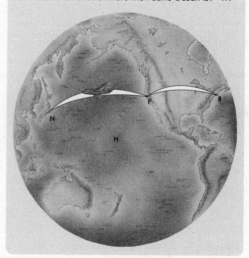

Write **W** for warm-blooded animals and **C** for cold-blooded animals.
14. beetle C
15. camel W
16. spider C
17. dog W
18. fly C

19. What's the boiling temperature of water?
   • 212 miles   • 112 degrees   • ☐212 degrees☐

20. Write the letter of the animal that is facing into the wind. Y
21. Which direction is that animal facing? south
22. So what's the **name** of that wind? south wind

23. How many states are in the United States? 50
24. The biggest state in the United States is ▓▓▓. Alaska

334   Lesson 50

---

25. Texas   26. 5 thousand miles

25. The second-biggest state in the United States is ▓▓▓.
26. How far is it from San Francisco to Japan?

Skill Items

For each item, write the underlined word or words from the sentences in the box.

> Several paths continued for a great distance.
> Boiling water will thaw ice in a few moments.
> They were eager to hear the announcement.

27. What underlining means **melt**? thaw
28. What underlining means **message**?
29. What underlining means **kept on going**?
30. What underlining refers to more than two but less than a lot? several
31. What underlining tells how they felt about hearing the announcement? eager

Here's a rule: **Every spider has eight legs.**
32. Keb is a spider. So what does the rule tell you about Keb? Keb has 8 legs.
33. Bop is not a spider. So what does the rule tell you about Bop? nothing

━━━━ END OF TEST 5 ━━━━
28. announcement   29. continued
                          Lesson 50   335

51

Name

A

1. Jean is 2 miles high. Fran is 5 miles high. Who is colder? Fran

2. Tell why.
   • because she is colder
   • because she is higher
   • because she is lower

B Story Items

3. How far is the trip from Japan to Italy?
   • 6 hundred miles   • 6 thousand miles
   • 60 thousand miles
4. How long should that trip take?
   • 6 hours   • 12 hours   • 13 hours
5. **Underline** 2 countries the plane flew over on the trip.
   • Turkey   • United States   • Canada
   • England   • China
6. **Underline** the state in the United States that is bigger than Italy.
   • Ohio   • Alaska   • New York
7. Italy is shaped something like a ▓▓▓.
   • horn   • shoe   • boot

Lesson 51   1

---

8. When could Herman move fastest?
   • when it is 60 degrees   • when it is 50 degrees
   • when it is 80 degrees   • when it is 45 degrees

9. Write **north, south, east,** and **west** in the right boxes.
10. Make a **J** where Japan is.
11. Make a **C** where China is.
12. Make a **T** where Turkey is.
13. Make an **I** where Italy is.
14. Is the United States shown on this map? no

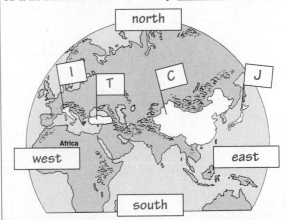

━━━━ GO TO PART D IN YOUR TEXTBOOK. ━━━━

2   Lesson 51

The country of Italy is very small compared to the United States. Italy is about the same size as Japan. So Italy is smaller than the state of Alaska. Italy is small, but 60 million people live there.

Italy is shaped something like a boot.

The jumbo jet circled several times and then landed. The passengers cheered and waved as they got off the plane. Nobody cheered for Herman. But Herman had just traveled farther than any other insect that ever lived.

MORE NEXT TIME

D Number your paper from 1 through 26.

1. Write the letter of the plane that is in the coldest air. **A**
2. Write the letter of the plane that is in the warmest air. **D**

	5 miles high
A	4 miles high
B	3 miles high
C	2 miles high
D	1 mile high

Story Items

3. Why was Herman moving so slowly at the beginning of the story? Write the letter that answers the question.
   a. He was tired.   b. <u>He was cold.</u>
   c. He was hot.
4. What made Herman start moving faster? Write the letter that answers the question.
   a. <u>The plane got warmer.</u>
   b. The plane got colder.   c. Herman woke up.

5. After the plane took off, how high did it go? **6 miles**
6. Write the letter of the temperature inside the plane. **a**
   a. 70 degrees   b. 80 degrees below zero
   c. 90 degrees
7. Write the letter of the temperature outside a plane that is 6 miles high. **b**
   a. 70 degrees   b. 80 degrees below zero
   c. 90 degrees
8. Write the letter of the country the plane left. **b**
   a. United States   b. Japan   c. Italy
9. Write the letter of the country where the plane was going. **c**
   a. United States   b. Japan   c. Italy

---

10. Write the letters of the 9 places that are in the United States.
    <u>a.</u> Lake Michigan   h. Ohio
    <u>b.</u> Alaska   i. Italy
    c. Japan   j. China
    <u>d.</u> Chicago   <u>k.</u> Denver
    <u>e.</u> California   <u>l.</u> New York City
    <u>f.</u> San Francisco   m. Turkey
    <u>g.</u> Texas

Skill Items

The lifeboat disappeared in the whirlpool.
11. What word names an emergency boat that's on a large ship? **lifeboat**
12. What word tells what happened to the lifeboat when you couldn't see it any more? **disappeared**
13. What word refers to water that goes around and around as it goes down? **whirlpool**

Review Items
14. The United States is a ▨.
    • <u>country</u>   • city   • state
15. Japan is a ▨. **country**
16. How many states are in the United States? **50**

---

17. The biggest state in the United States is ▨.
    • Texas   • <u>Alaska</u>   • Ohio   • California
18. The second biggest state in the United States is ▨.
19. Write the name of the state in the United States that is bigger than Japan.
    • New York   • <u>Alaska</u>   • Ohio
20. Let's say you are outside when the temperature is 35 degrees. What is the temperature inside your body?
21. Let's say you are outside when the temperature is 70 degrees. What is the temperature inside your body?
22. Let's say a fly is outside when the temperature is 70 degrees. What is the temperature inside the fly's body?

Write **warm-blooded** or **cold-blooded** for each animal.
23. beetle **cold-blooded**
24. cow **warm-blooded**
25. cat **warm-blooded**
26. spider **cold-blooded**

18. Texas
20. 98 degrees
21. 98 degrees
22. 70 degrees

65

WORKBOOK

Name _____

Story Items

1. **Circle** 2 of the things below that would smell very good to Herman.
2. **Underline** one thing that would smell bad to Herman. **(Any 2)**

   • (meat)   • soap   • (candy)   • (garbage)   • gum

3. A plane that flies from Italy to New York City goes in which direction? _west_

4. What airport did Herman fly to in this story?
   • San Francisco   • <u>Kennedy</u>   • Italy

5. In what city is that airport?
   • Chicago   • San Francisco   • <u>New York City</u>

6. Where are the fuel tanks on a big jet?
   • in the rear   • <u>in the wings</u>   • in the galley

7. It was hard for Herman to move around in the fall because ▓▓▓.
   • it was raining   • the temperature went up
   • <u>the temperature went down</u>

8. What killed Herman?
   • <u>freezing</u>   • boiling   • sleeping

Lesson 52   3

WORKBOOK

9. Which letter shows where Italy is? B _____
10. Which letter shows where New York City is? C _____
11. Which letter shows where Turkey is? A _____

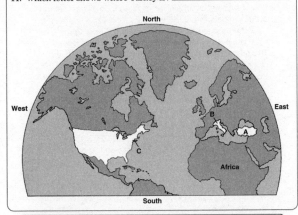

Review Items

12. Sue is 10 miles high. Lynn is 6 miles high. Who is colder? Sue _____

13. Tell why. Idea: She is higher.

GO TO PART C IN YOUR TEXTBOOK.

4   Lesson 52

TEXTBOOK

But Herman had a lot of children and grandchildren. In fact, the next spring, when the days got warm, Herman's 8 thousand children and grandchildren were born. They were maggots, and they looked just like Herman had looked when he was a maggot. And many of these maggots grew up to be flies, just like Herman.

The next time you look at a fly, take a good look. Maybe that fly is one of Herman's children or grandchildren.

THE END

C Number your paper from 1 through 26.

Skill Items

Write the word from the box that means the same thing as the underlined part of each sentence.

| froze | figured out | weren't | boiled |
| continued | distance | thawed | moments |

1. The snow <u>melted</u> when the sun came out. thawed
2. The girls <u>were not</u> at home. weren't
3. He <u>kept on</u> reading as he ate. continued

Lesson 52   13

TEXTBOOK

4. Ideas: They are both animals/are cold-blooded/have 4 legs; etc.

4. Look at object A and object B. Write one way that both objects are the same.
5. Write **2** ways that tell how object A is **different** from object B.   5. Ideas (any 2:) A is a toad, but B is a frog; A is big, but B isn't; A has warts, but B doesn't; etc.

Object A   Object B

Use the words in the box to write complete sentences.

| finally | whirlpool | eager | colder | lifeboat |
| announcement | traveled | disappeared | early |

6. They were ▓▓▓ to hear the ▓▓▓.
7. The lifeboat ▓▓▓ in the ▓▓▓.

Review Items

8. When we talk about miles per hour, we tell how ▓▓▓ something is moving. fast

6. They were eager to hear the announcement.
7. The lifeboat disappeared in the whirlpool.

14   Lesson 52

66

9. Which arrow shows the way the air will leave the jet engines? **B**
10. Which arrow shows the way the jet will move? **A**

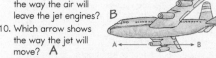

Write **warm-blooded** or **cold-blooded** for each animal.
11. flea   12. dog   13. horse   14. spider

15. Write the letter of the plane that is in the **warmest** air. **A**
16. Write the letter of the plane that is in the **coldest** air. **C**

C	5 miles high
	4 miles high
B	3 miles high
	2 miles high
D	1 mile high
A	

17. Name a state in the United States that is bigger than Italy. **Alaska (accept Texas or California)**
18. Italy is shaped something like a ▓▓▓. **boot**

**11. cold-blooded   12. warm-blooded
13. warm-blooded   14. cold-blooded**

20. **98 degrees**   21. **98 degrees**

19. Let's say a fly is outside when the temperature is 85 degrees. What is the temperature inside the fly's body? **85 degrees**
20. Let's say you are outside when the temperature is 85 degrees. What is the temperature inside your body?
21. Let's say you are outside when the temperature is 50 degrees. What is the temperature inside your body?

22. What part of the world is shown on the map? **United States**
23. How far is it from A to B? **25 hundred miles**
24. How far is it from C to D? **13 hundred miles**

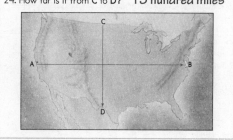

25. Would it be easier to catch a fly on a **hot day** or a cold day ?
26. Would a fly move faster on a hot day or a cold day?

━━━━ END OF LESSON 52 INDEPENDENT WORK ━━━━

53

Name _____

A

The picture shows 4 objects caught in a whirlpool.

1. Write **1** on the object that will go down the hole in the whirlpool first.
2. Write **2** on the object that will go down next.
3. Number the rest of the objects.

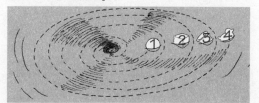

B

4. Put a **B** on 2 bulkheads.
5. Put an **X** on 2 decks.
6. Put a **W** at the bow.
7. Put an **S** at the stern.

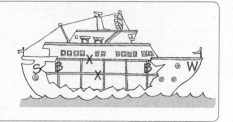

C

The picture below shows jars of water on a very cold day.

32 degrees	32 degrees	32 degrees	32 degrees	32 degrees	32 degrees
A	B	C	D	E	F

8. What is the temperature of the water in each jar?
   32 degrees

9. Write **OW** on each jar that is filled with ocean water.

10. Jar F is filled with ocean water. How do you know?
    Idea: It is not frozen.

11. What does ocean water taste like? **salt(y)**

12. What will happen if you drink a lot of ocean water?
    Idea: You will get thirsty.

━━━━ GO TO PART F IN YOUR TEXTBOOK. ━━━━

F Number your paper from 1 through 28.

1. Look at the picture. Jar A is filled with ocean water. Jar B is filled with fresh water. Which jar is heavier? **A**

2. Which jar will freeze at 32 degrees? **B**

3. Will the other jar freeze when it is **more than 32 degrees** or **less than 32 degrees?**

ocean water   fresh water

Skill Items

Look at object A and object B. Compare the objects.

4. Tell a way the objects are the same.

5. Tell a way the objects are different.

Object A   Object B

4. Ideas: They're both squares; they both have (13) spots; etc.

5. Ideas: A is little, but B is not; A has red spots, but B has blue spots; A is crowded, but B is not; etc.

24   Lesson 53

Here's a rule: **Dogs have hair.**

6. Sam is not a dog. So what does the rule tell you about Sam? **nothing**

7. Rex is a dog. So what does the rule tell you about Rex? **Rex has hair.**

8. A jay is not a dog. So what does the rule tell you about a jay? **nothing**

9. A poodle is a dog. So what does the rule tell you about a poodle? **A poodle has hair.**

Review Items   **25 hundred miles**

10. How far is it from New York City to San Francisco?

11. What ocean do you cross to get from San Francisco to Japan? **Pacific (Ocean)**

12. How far is it from San Francisco to Japan?
   • 15 hundred miles   • <u>5 thousand miles</u>
   • 3 thousand miles

13. How many legs does an insect have? **6**

14. How many legs does a fly have? **6**

15. How many legs does a bee have? **6**

16. How many legs does a spider have? **8**

17. How many parts does a spider's body have? **2**

18. How many parts does a fly's body have? **3**

Lesson 53   25

---

19. Which letter shows where Italy is? **B**

20. Which letter shows where China is? **A**

21. Which letter shows where Turkey is? **D**

22. Which letter shows where Japan is? **C**

23. Is the United States shown on this map? **no**

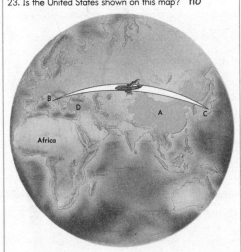

26   Lesson 53

---

24. A plane that flies from Italy to New York City goes in which direction? **west**

25. Where are the fuel tanks on a big jet? **in the wings**

26. It was hard for Herman to move around in the fall because ████. **Idea: It was cold.**

27. What killed Herman? **Idea: freezing**

28. Write the letters of the 5 places that are in the United States.
   a. Denver   e. Alaska
   b. California   f. Lake Michigan
   c. Japan   g. Italy
   d. New York City   h. China

Lesson 53   27

WORKBOOK

Name _____

Story Items

1. Linda and Kathy were on a ship that was going from the United States to ▮▮▮▮.
   - Canada   • England   • <u>Japan</u>

2. The girls were on their way to visit their <u>father</u>

3. Did Linda and Kathy go in one of the lifeboats when the ship sank?
   <u>no</u>

4. What did the girls plan to use for a lifeboat?
   - a raft   • <u>a crate</u>   • a boat

5. Which girl could swim well?
   - <u>Linda</u>   • Kathy

6. Which girl was older? <u>Linda</u>

7. How much older? <u>3 years</u>

8. When the ship sank, it was in the middle of the <u>Pacific</u> Ocean.

9. A stranger lifted ▮▮▮▮ into a lifeboat.
   - <u>Linda</u>   • Kathy

10. Why didn't she stay in the lifeboat?
    - <u>She went to find her sister.</u>   • She was scared.
    - She couldn't swim.

Lesson 54   7

WORKBOOK

Review Items

11. Write **north, south, east,** and **west** in the right boxes.
12. Which letter shows where Japan is? <u>W</u>
13. Which letter shows where Italy is? <u>Z</u>
14. Which letter shows where Turkey is? <u>Y</u>
15. Which letter shows where China is? <u>X</u>
16. Is the United States shown on this map? <u>no</u>

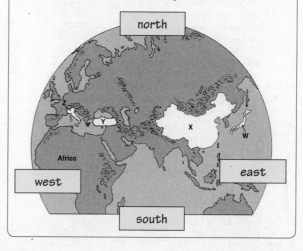

GO TO PART C IN YOUR TEXTBOOK.

8   Lesson 54

TEXTBOOK

C Number your paper from 1 through 24.

Skill Items   1. Ideas: They're both animals/sitting down. A is a pig, but B is a camel, etc.

1. Compare object A and object B. Remember, first tell how they're the same. Then tell how they're different.

object A   object B

32   Lesson 54

TEXTBOOK

> The smoke swirled in enormous billows.

2. What word means that the smoke spun around and around? **swirled**

3. What word means **very, very large?** **enormous**

4. What word means that the clouds were swelling up? **billows**

Review Items

The picture shows objects caught in a whirlpool.

5. Write the letter of the object that will go down the whirlpool first. **A**

6. Write the letter of the object that will go down the whirlpool next. **B**

7. Write the letter of the object that will go down the whirlpool last. **D**

Lesson 54   33

8. B   9. C

8. Write the letter of the plane that is in the warmest air.
9. Write the letter of the plane that is in the coldest air.

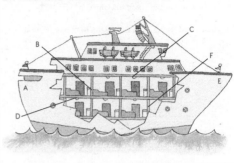

10. Name a state in the United States that is bigger than Italy. **Accept: Alaska, Texas or California.**
11. Italy is shaped something like a ▨▨▨. *boot*
12. The biggest state in the United States is ▨▨▨. *Alaska*
13. The second biggest state in the United States is ▨▨▨.
14. Write the name of the state in the United States that is bigger than Japan.
   • Ohio   • <u>Alaska</u>   • New York

15. Which eye works like one drop, a <u>human's eye</u> or a fly's eye?
16. Which eye works like many drops, a human's eye or a <u>fly's eye</u>?
17. Which eye can see more things at the same time, a human's eye or a <u>fly's eye</u>?

13. Texas

18. Write 2 letters that show bulkheads. B, F
19. Write 2 letters that show decks. C, D
20. Which letter shows where the bow is? E
21. Which letter shows where the stern is? A

22. What is the temperature of the water in each jar?
23. Write the letter of each jar that is filled with ocean water. B, D, E
24. Jar B is filled with ocean water. How do you know?

32 degrees 32 degrees 32 degrees 32 degrees 32 degrees 32 degrees
   A   B   C   D   E   F

22. 32 degrees
24. Idea: It is not frozen.

Name _____

Story Items

1. Why did Linda have a hard time swimming to the crate?
   • She could not swim well.   • <u>Currents held her back.</u>
                    • She was weak.
2. What did Linda and Kathy use for a lifeboat?
   • a raft   • a craft   • <u>a crate</u>
3. What did the girls use for paddles? • oars   • <u>hands</u>   • boards
4. What made Linda's feet sore?
   • the crate   • <u>the salt water</u>   • the sun
5. If you drank lots of ocean water, you would get ▨▨▨.
   • sillier   • tired   • <u>thirstier</u>

Here's a picture of Kathy and Linda on their crate.
6. Which arrow shows the way Linda's hand will move? B
7. Which arrow shows the way the crate will move? A

8. Something made sounds that told Linda they were near the shore. What made those sounds?
   • <u>waves on the beach</u>   • birds in the trees   • fish in the waves
9. As the girls walked along the beach, they could hardly see where they were going. Tell why. <u>Idea: It was dark.</u>

Review Items

10. Write **north, south, east,** and **west** in the right boxes.
11. Which letter shows where China is? H
12. Which letter shows where Japan is? K
13. Is the United States shown on this map? no

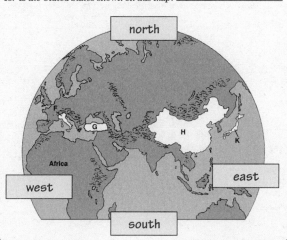

GO TO PART D IN YOUR TEXTBOOK.

"I'm thirsty," Kathy said. She sounded as if she was ready to cry.

"So am I," Linda said. "But it won't do us any good to cry."

MORE NEXT TIME

D Number your paper from 1 through 23.

1. There are 3 islands on the map. Write the letter of each island. B, C, E
2. A is not an island. Tell why.

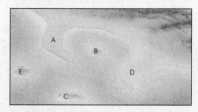

2. Idea: A is not surrounded by water.

Skill Items

Use the words in the box to write complete sentences.

| swirled | announced | enormous | smelly |
| lifeboat | billows | crowd | whirlpool |

3. The ▬▬▬ disappeared in the ▬▬▬.
4. The smoke ▬▬▬ in ▬▬▬ ▬▬▬.

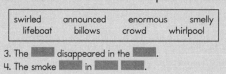

5. Compare object A and object B. Remember, first tell how they're the same. Then tell how they're different.

Object A   Object B

3. The lifeboat disappeared in the whirlpool.
4. The smoke swirled in enormous billows.
5. Idea: They are both dogs. A is sitting, but B is standing, etc.

Review Items

The closer an object is to the center of a whirlpool, the faster it moves.

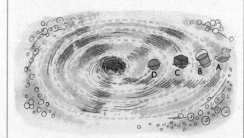

6. Write the letter of the object that is going the fastest.
7. Write the letter of the object that is going the slowest.
8. The path is shown for objects A and D. Which object will go around more times, A or D? A
9. Which path will go around the most times, the path for B, C, or D? B

6. D
7. A

10. When we talk about how hot or cold something is, we tell about the ▨ of the thing.
    • weight   • length   • <u>temperature</u>
11. When the temperature goes up, the number of ▨ gets bigger.
    • miles   • <u>degrees</u>
    • hours   • miles per hour

12. Write the name of the city that's on the east coast.
13. Write the name of the city that's on the west coast.
14. Which letter shows where Denver is? C
15. Which letter shows where Chicago is? D

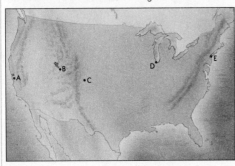

12. New York (City)
13. San Francisco

44   Lesson 55

16. Which letter shows where Italy is? B
17. Which letter shows where New York City is? C
18. Which letter shows where Turkey is? A

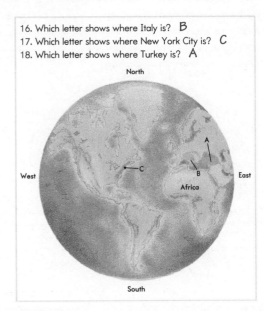

Lesson 55   45

19. A plane that flies from Italy to New York City goes in which direction? **west**

Jar X is filled with fresh water. Jar Y is filled with ocean water.
20. Which jar is heavier? Y
21. Which jar will freeze at 32 degrees? X
22. Will the other jar freeze when it is **less than 32 degrees** or **more than 32 degrees?**

X   Y

23. Linda and Kathy were on a ship that was going from the United States to ▨. Japan

46   Lesson 55

56

Name _____

Ⓐ

1. Palm trees cannot live in places that get ▨.
    • wet   • <u>cold</u>   • moist
2. What are the branches of palm trees called?
    • fans   • fonds   • <u>fronds</u>
3. When the author told about palm trees, was the purpose to **persuade, inform,** or **entertain?** <u>inform</u>

Ⓑ Story Items

4. Underline 2 words that tell about the stream water.
    • <u>cold</u>   • warm   • salty   • smelly   • dark   • <u>fresh</u>
5. A strange sound woke Linda in the morning. What was making that strange sound?
    • sailors   • <u>birds</u>   • waves
6. Whose footprints did Linda and Kathy find on the beach?
    <u>Idea: their own</u>
7. Linda said, "We have been walking in a circle. That means we're ▨."
    • in a forest   • near Japan   • <u>on an island</u>
8. Did Linda and Kathy see anyone else when they were walking? <u>no</u>
9. When the author told about Linda and Kathy, was the purpose to **persuade, inform,** or **entertain?** <u>entertain</u>

Lesson 56   11

The map shows the island that Linda and Kathy were on.

10. Write **north, south, east,** and **west** in the right boxes.

11. **Draw a line** from the crate to show where Linda and Kathy walked.

12. **Make an X** to show where Linda was when she saw footprints.

13. **Make a Y** to show where they landed on the island.

14. **Make an S** to show where the stream is.

15. **Circle** the grove where they found bananas.

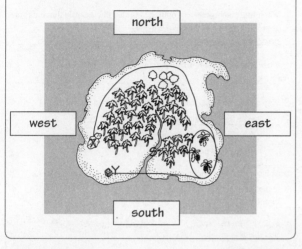

north

west

east

south

GO TO PART D IN YOUR TEXTBOOK.

have been walking in a circle. That means we're on an island. We walked all the way around the island."

Kathy started to cry.

Linda said, "Don't cry. Everything will be all right."

Linda didn't cry, but she felt like crying, too. She and her sister were all alone on an island. There was nothing on that island but trees and sand and a stream. How would they let anybody know where they were? How would they ever get off the island?

MORE NEXT TIME

D Number your paper from 1 through 26.

1. Name 2 things that grow on different palm trees.   coconuts, dates

2. What part does the A show?   frond(s)

3. What part does the B show?   coconut(s)

4. What part does the C show?   trunk

5. What part does the D show?   roots

Skill Items

Here's a rule: **Birds have feathers.**

6. A crow is a bird. So what does the rule tell you about a crow?   It has feathers.

7. A bass is not a bird. So what does the rule tell you about a bass?   nothing

8. A jay is a bird. So what does the rule tell you about a jay?   It has feathers.

Review Items

9. What does ocean water taste like?   salty

10. If you drank lots of ocean water, you would get [____].

Jar M is filled with fresh water. Jar P is filled with ocean water.

11. Which jar is heavier?   P

12. Which jar will freeze at 32 degrees?   M

13. Will the other jar freeze when it is **more than 32 degrees** or **less than 32 degrees?**

10. Idea: thirsty

The ship in the picture is sinking. It is making currents as it sinks.

14. Write the letter of the object that will go down the whirlpool first.   P

15. Write the letter of the object that will go down the whirlpool next.   Q

16. Write the letter of the object that will go down the whirlpool last.   S

17. When a plane flies from New York City to San Francisco, is it flying in the same direction or the **opposite direction** as the wind?

18. A mile is a little more than [____] feet.   5 thousand

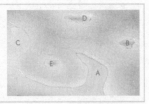

19. Write the letter of each island on the map. **B, D, E**

20. C is not an island. Tell why. **Idea: It is not surrounded by water.**

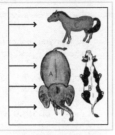

21. Write the letter of the animal that is facing into the wind. **C**

22. Which direction is that animal facing? **west**

23. So what's the name of that wind? **west wind**

24. Let's say you are outside when the temperature is 40 degrees. What is the temperature inside your body?

25. Let's say a fly is outside when the temperature is 85 degrees. What is the temperature inside the fly's body?

26. Let's say you are outside when the temperature is 85 degrees. What is the temperature inside your body?

24. **98 degrees**   25. **85 degrees**

54   Lesson 56   26. **98 degrees**

Name _____

Story Items

1. What was wrong with the first coconuts that the girls found?
   - They were too high in the trees.
   - They were not ripe.
   - <u>They were rotten.</u>

2. When Kathy shook the coconut, it sounded like a bottle that had water in it. What made the sound like water?
   <u>coconut milk</u>

3. What did Linda and Kathy use to open the coconut?
   <u>rock</u>

4. Why did the girls want to make the monkeys mad?
   - <u>so they would throw coconuts</u>
   - so they would go away
   - so they would make noise

The picture shows a coconut.

5. Make an **X** on the part that the girls ate.

6. Make a **Y** on the part that the girls drank.

Lesson 57   **13**

Review Items

The map shows the island that Linda and Kathy were on.

7. Write **north, south, east,** and **west** in the right boxes.

8. **Draw a line** from the crate to show where Linda and Kathy walked.

9. **Make an A** to show where Linda was when she saw footprints.

10. **Make a B** to show where they landed on the island.

11. **Make a C** to show where the stream is.

12. **Circle** the grove where they found bananas.

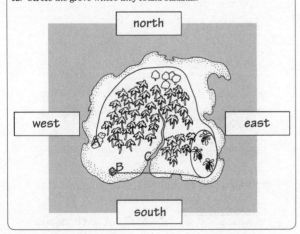

north

west   east

south

▬▬▬ GO TO PART D IN YOUR TEXTBOOK. ▬▬▬

14   *Lesson 57*

---

and screeched at Linda. "Choo, choo, cha, cha, chee, chee, chee," they screeched.

Linda made a face and waved her arms at them. The monkeys got madder and madder. Linda went over to one of the trees and tried to shake it.

One of the monkeys picked a coconut and threw it down at Linda. Linda tried to shake the tree again. Another monkey threw a coconut at her. Other monkeys started to throw coconuts. Coconuts were coming down like raindrops.

Linda ran away from the trees. By now the ground was covered with fresh coconuts.

Kathy laughed. "We will have enough coconuts to last us for days and days," she said.
                    MORE NEXT TIME

D Number your paper from 1 through 27.

1. How many shells does a coconut have? **2**

2. Is it easy to break open a coconut? **no**

3. What is the juice inside a coconut called?
   coconut milk

Lesson 57   **59**

The picture below shows a coconut that is cut in half.

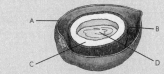

- inner shell
- fronds
- trunk
- coconut milk
- coconut meat
- coconuts
- outer shell
- dates
- roots

4. What part does the A show? **outer shell**
5. What part does the B show? **inner shell**
6. What part does the C show? **coconut meat**
7. What part does the D show? **coconut milk**

Skill Items   Idea: A and B are both rabbits. A is black and white, but B is all white, etc.

8. Compare object A and object B. Remember, first tell how they're the same. Then tell how they're different.

Object A   Object B

60   Lesson 57

The occasional foul smell was normal.
9. What word means **once in a while**? **occasional**
10. What word means **bad**? **foul**
11. What word means **usual**? **normal**

Review Items

The picture below shows a coconut tree.

- inner shell
- fronds
- trunk
- coconut milk
- coconut meat
- coconuts
- outer shell
- dates
- roots

12. What part does the A show? **frond(s)**
13. What part does the B show? **coconut(s)**
14. What part does the C show? **trunk**
15. What part does the D show? **roots**

Lesson 57   61

---

16. Write **A, B, C** or **D** to name the arrow that shows the way the cloud will move. **B**
17. That wind is blowing from the ▨. **west**
18. So that wind is called a ▨ wind. **west**

San Francisco

19. Which eye works like one drop, <u>a human's eye</u> or a fly's eye?
20. Which eye works like many drops, a human's eye or a <u>fly's eye</u>?
21. Which eye can see more things at the same time, a human's eye or a <u>fly's eye</u>?

62   Lesson 57

Some of the objects in the picture are insects, and some are spiders.

A   B   C   D
E   F   G   H

22. Write the letters of the spiders. **C, F**
23. Write the letters of the insects. **B, E, G, H**

24. Write the letters of the 9 places that are in the United States.

a. Denver   h. Italy
b. Turkey   i. Lake Michigan
c. Chicago   j. California
d. New York City   k. San Francisco
e. Texas   l. Japan
f. China   m. Ohio
g. Alaska

25. When something tries to move in one direction, something else tries to move ▨. **in the opposite direction**

Lesson 57   63

75

26. Which arrow shows the direction the canoe is moving?
27. Which arrow shows the direction the paddle is moving in the water? **T**

26. **Z**

58

Name _____

A

1. All machines make it easier for someone to **do work** _____.

2. You would have the most power if you pushed against handle C. Which handle would give you the least amount of power?

E _____

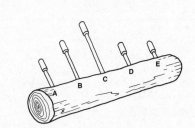

B Story Items

3. What were the only things Linda and Kathy ate for two days?

- carrots
- coconuts
- corn
- fronds
- cabbage
- bananas

---

4. Why did Linda and Kathy want to catch some fish?
- They were tired.
- They wanted to eat something new.
- They could not open the coconuts.

5. What did they use for fish hooks? **nails (from the crate)** _____

6. What did they use for a fishing line? **vines** _____

7. Were there many fish in the water? **yes** _____

8. Did Linda and Kathy catch many fish with their hooks and lines? **no** _____

9. The girls made hooks and lines to catch fish. Then they made something else to catch fish. What else did they make? **net** _____

10. What did they make it out of? **vines** _____

11. What happened when the girls tried to pull the net out of the water?
- The fish jumped out of the water.
- The fish pulled the girls into the water.
- The crate fell in the water.

GO TO PART D IN YOUR TEXTBOOK.

D Number your paper from 1 through 27.
Skill Items

Use the words in the box to write complete sentences.

foul	swirled	echoed	normal	enough
billows	juice	enormous	inner	occasional

1. The smoke ▮▮▮ in ▮▮▮.
2. The ▮▮▮ ▮▮▮ smell was ▮▮▮.

1. **swirled, enormous, billows**

Write words from the box that mean the same thing as the underlined parts of the sentences.

- the reason
- coconuts
- fronds
- echo
- crate
- finally
- the outcome
- frost

3. She was happy with how things turned out.
4. Many of the palm trees' branches broke off in the storm.
5. He filled the wooden box with dishes. **crate**

Review Items
Write **W** for **warm-blooded** animals and **C** for **cold-blooded** animals.

6. dog **W**   8. pig **W**   10. bee **C**
7. cow **W**   9. spider **C**

2. **occasional, foul, normal**
3. **the outcome**
4. **fronds**

TEXTBOOK

The picture shows objects caught in a giant whirlpool.
11. Write the letter of the object that will go down the hole in the whirlpool first. **Z**
12. Write the letter of the object that will go down the hole in the whirlpool next. **Y**
13. Write the letter of the object that will go down the hole in the whirlpool last. **W**

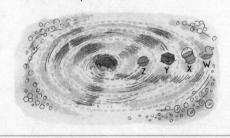

14. Palm trees cannot live in places that get ▮▮▮. **cold**
15. What are the branches of palm trees called? **fronds**
16. Name 2 things that grow on different palm trees.
coconuts, dates

72   Lesson 58

TEXTBOOK

17. What part does the H show? **outer shell**
18. What part does the G show? **inner shell**
19. What part does the E show? **coconut milk**
20. What part does the F show? **coconut meat**

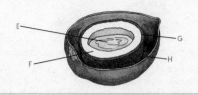

21. Lee is 8 miles high. Sam is 6 miles high. Who is colder? **Lee**
22. Tell why. **Idea: because Lee is higher**

23. The United States is not a state. It is a ▮▮▮. **country**
24. Japan is a ▮▮▮. **country**
25. How many states are in the United States? **50**
26. When we weigh very small things, the unit we use is ▮▮▮. **gram(s)**
27. You can see drops of water on grass early in the morning. What are those drops called? **dew**

Lesson 58   73

WORKBOOK

59

Name _____
Story Items

1. Linda and Kathy built something to help them ▮▮▮.
   • pull the nails from the crate
   • <u>pull the net from the ocean</u>
   • pull Kathy's teeth

2. What did the girls find floating in the water?
   • a ship   • <u>a first-aid kit</u>   • boards
3. The white box probably came from ▮▮▮.
   • <u>their ship</u>   • their crate   • Italy
4. What was the most important thing inside the box?
   • candy   • food   • <u>matches</u>
5. Why didn't the girls test them right away?
   • <u>They would need them later.</u>
   • They didn't know how.
   • They were tired.

6. The girls made a ▮▮▮.
   • building   • <u>machine</u>   • motor
7. What did the girls use for a handle?
   • <u>a board</u>   • a log   • a vine

© SRA/McGraw-Hill. All rights reserved.   Lesson 59   17

WORKBOOK

8. The girls hammered the handle to the end of ▮▮▮.
   • a shoe   • <u>a log</u>   • a crate
9. The girls got nails from ▮▮▮.
   • a shoe   • a log   • <u>a crate</u>
10. They tied one end of the vine to the log and the other end of the vine to the ▮▮▮.
   • beach   • crate   • <u>net</u>
11. When the fish were in the net, the girls ▮▮▮.
   • <u>turned the handle</u>   • ran into the water
   • climbed a tree

12. The arrow by the handle shows which way it turns. Start at the dot on the log. Make an arrow on the log to show which way it turns.
13. Make an arrow by the vine to show which way it moves.

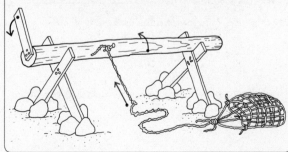

GO TO PART C IN YOUR TEXTBOOK.

18   Lesson 59   © SRA/McGraw-Hill. All rights reserved.

77

Idea: They're both insects. A is brown, but B is yellow and black; etc.

C Number your paper from 1 through 27.

Skill Item

1. Compare object A and object B. Remember, first tell how they're the same. Then tell how they're different.

Object A   Object B

Review Items   2. *98 degrees*   3. *98 degrees*

2. Let's say you are outside when the temperature is 40 degrees. What is the temperature inside your body?

3. Let's say you are outside when the temperature is 85 degrees. What is the temperature inside your body?

4. Let's say a fly is outside when the temperature is 85 degrees. What is the temperature inside the fly's body? *85 degrees*

5. The stream water that Linda and Kathy found was different from the ocean water. **Tell 2 ways it was different.** *cold, fresh (not salty)*

6. How many shells does a coconut have? *2*

7. What is the juice inside a coconut called? *coconut milk*

8. All machines make it easier for someone to ▢. *do work*

9. Name a state in the United States that is bigger than Italy. *Accept: Alaska, Texas or California.*

---

10. Italy is shaped something like a ▢. *boot*

11. Write 2 letters that show bulkheads. *M, Q*
12. Write 2 letters that show decks. *R, S*
13. Which letter shows where the bow is? *P*
14. Which letter shows where the stern is? *N*

15. Which arrow shows the way Linda's hand will move? *E*
16. Which arrow shows the way the crate will move? *G*

E ⟵
G ⟶

---

18. Texas

17. The biggest state in the United States is ▢. *Alaska*
18. The second biggest state in the United States is ▢.
19. A mile is a little more than ▢ feet. *5 thousand*
20. Write the name of the state in the United States that is bigger than Japan. *Alaska*
    • Ohio   • Alaska   • New York

21. You would have the least power if you pushed against one of the handles. Which handle is that? *I*
22. Which handle would give you the most power? *F*

---

23. Write the letter of the plane that is in the warmest air. *E*
24. Write the letter of the plane that is in the coldest air. *D*

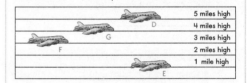

25. Does dew form in the middle of the day? *no*
26. Dew forms when the air gets ▢.
    • cooler   • windy   • warmer
27. What's the boiling temperature of water?
    • 212 miles   • 212 degrees   • 112 degrees

60 TEST 6

Number your paper from 1 through 32.

1. Write the letter of each island on the map. **C, D, E**

2. Jar A is filled with fresh water. Jar B is filled with ocean water. Which jar is heavier? **B**
3. Which jar will freeze at 32 degrees? **A**
4. Will the other jar freeze when it is **less than** 32 degrees or **more than** 32 degrees? **less than 32 degrees**

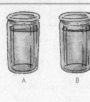

---

5. Write the letters of the 9 places that are in the United States.
   a. Denver
   b. Lake Michigan
   c. China
   d. Alaska
   e. New York City
   f. Chicago
   g. Texas
   h. San Francisco
   i. Ohio
   j. Japan
   k. Turkey
   l. California
   m. Italy

6. The ship in the picture is sinking. It is making currents as it sinks. Write the letter of the object that will go down the whirlpool first. **Y**
7. Write the letter of the object that will go down the whirlpool last. **Z**

---

8. A plane that flies from Italy to New York City goes in which direction? **west**

9. Which letter shows where Italy is? **A**
10. Which letter shows where China is? **C**
11. Which letter shows where Turkey is? **D**
12. Is the United States shown on this map? **no**

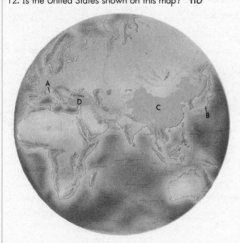

---

13. Which arrow shows the way Linda's hand will move? **B**
14. Which arrow shows the way the crate will move? **A**

15. Write the letter of the plane that is in the warmest air. **D**

	5 miles high
A	4 miles high
B	3 miles high
C	2 miles high
D	1 mile high

16. Palm trees cannot live in places that get ▇▇▇▇. **cold**
17. Name 2 things that grow on different palm trees. **coconuts, dates**

18. All machines make it easier to for someone to ▨. *do work*

19. You would have the most power if you pushed against one of the handles. Which handle is that? *E*

20. Which handle would give you the least amount of power? *B*

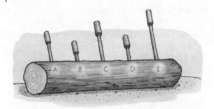

The arrow on the handle shows which way it turns.
21. Which arrow shows the way the log moves? *Z*
22. Which arrow shows the way the vine moves? *X*

23. What part does the **G** show? *roots*
24. What part does the **H** show? *trunk*
25. What part does the **K** show? *coconuts*
26. What part doe the **J** show? *fronds*

Skill Items

27. Compare object A and object B. Remember, first tell how they're the same. Then tell how they're different.
Idea: They're both dogs. A has three colors, but B is all white; etc.

Object A

Object B

For each item, write the underlined word from the sentences in the box.

> The <u>lifeboat</u> <u>disappeared</u> in the <u>whirlpool</u>.
> The smoke <u>swirled</u> in <u>enormous</u> <u>billows</u>.
> The <u>occasional</u> <u>foul</u> smell was <u>normal</u>.

28. What underlining names an emergency boat that is on a large ship? *lifeboat*
29. What underlining means **usual**? *normal*
30. What underlining names water that goes around and around as it goes down? *whirlpool*
31. What underlining means **very, very large**? *enormous*
32. What underlining means **once in a while**? *occasional*

■■■■■■■ **END OF TEST 6** ■■■■■■■

61

Name _____

A

1. What is it called when the sun goes down?
   • sunrise   • <u>sunset</u>

2. What is it called when the sun comes up?
   • <u>sunrise</u>   • sunset

B   Story Items

3. What did Kathy have to do to the outside of the fish?
   • remove fins   • <u>remove scales</u>   • remove shells

4. What did she use for a tool?
   • a fin   • a scale   • <u>a shell</u>

5. What was Linda's job when the girls cleaned the fish?
   • removing the scales   • <u>removing the insides</u>
   • removing the fins

6. What did she use for a tool?
   • <u>a belt buckle</u>   • a nail   • a rock

7. Linda made her tool sharp by ▨.
   • <u>rubbing it against a rock</u>   • putting it in the fire
   • making it red hot

8. Name 2 things the girls ate for dinner.
   ① *fish* _____
   ② *(green) plants* _____

9. Linda and Kathy drank fresh water with their dinner.

   Where did they get the fresh water? <u>stream</u>

10. **Underline** 4 things that the girls used to make their simple machine.

    - <u>vines</u>
    - <u>nails</u>
    - coconuts
    - <u>boards</u>
    - rope
    - <u>a tree trunk</u>
    - turtle shell
    - matches

Review Items

11. The arrow by the handle shows which way it turns. Make an arrow on the log to show which way it moves.

12. Make an arrow by the vine to show which way it moves.

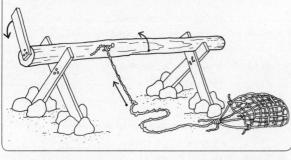

GO TO PART D IN YOUR TEXTBOOK.

20   Lesson 61

before one of those ships would find Kathy and her. Suddenly Linda felt cold and unhappy.

MORE NEXT TIME

D Number your paper from 1 through 26.

The picture shows the sun at different times of day.

1. Write the letter of the sun you see early in the morning. **E**
2. Write the letter of the sun you see at noon. **C**
3. Write the letter of the sun you see at sunset. **A**
4. Write the letter of the sun that shows when the girls made the fire. **C**
5. Write the letter of the sun that shows when the girls finished dinner. **A**

Skill Items

They constructed an enormous machine.

6. What word means **built**? **constructed**
7. What word means **very large**? **enormous**
8. What word names something that helps people do work? **machine**

Review Items

9. Linda and Kathy made a ▓▓▓ to help them pull the fish net from the water. **machine**
10. What did the girls use for a handle? **board**
11. The girls hammered the handle to the end of a ▓▓▓.
12. The girls got nails from ▓▓▓. **the crate**
13. They tied one end of the vine to the log and the other end of the vine to the ▓▓▓. **net**
14. When the fish were in the net, how did the girls get the net out of the water?

15. Would it be easier to catch a fly on a hot day or a <u>cold day</u>?
16. Would a fly move faster or <u>slower</u> on a cold day?

11. log (or tree trunk)
14. Idea: They turned the handle on the machine.

17. A plane that flies from Italy to New York City goes in which direction? **west**
18. Where are the gas tanks on a big jet? **on the wings**

19. What is the temperature of the water in each jar? **32**
20. Write the letter of each jar that is filled with ocean water. **C, F** **degrees**
21. Jar B is not filled with ocean water. How do you know? **Idea: It is frozen.**

22. A mile is around ▓▓▓ feet. **5 thousand**

Jar A is filled with fresh water. Jar B is filled with ocean water.

23. Which jar is heavier? **B**
24. Which jar will freeze at 32 degrees? **A**
25. Will the other jar freeze when it is **more than 32 degrees** or **less than 32 degrees**?

A   B

26. Write the letters of the 8 places that are in the United States.

a. Denver
b. Texas
c. Turkey
d. San Francisco
e. Ohio
f. Chicago
g. China
h. Italy
i. Lake Michigan
j. Japan
k. New York City
l. California

Lesson 61   **99**

62

Name _____

A

1. The temperature inside your body is about __98__ degrees.
2. Most fevers don't go over __101__ degrees.
3. When people have very high fevers, they may see and hear things that are not __real__

B Story Items

4. How long had Linda and Kathy been on the island when they saw the airplane?
   • <u>15 days</u>   • 3 weeks   • 12 days
5. Did the people in the plane see Linda and Kathy? __no__
6. What did the girls use to make a signal for planes?
   • paint   • <u>rocks</u>   • leaves
7. What word did they spell? __help__
8. The word was more than __20__ feet long.
9. What kind of signal did the girls have ready for ships?
   • rocks   • fog   • <u>smoke</u>
10. What would make the fire smoke?
   • sticks   • <u>green leaves</u>   • bananas

Lesson 62   **21**

---

11. How did Linda know that Kathy had a fever?
   • <u>Linda felt her forehead.</u>
   • Linda took her temperature.
   • Linda felt her feet.

12. Linda thought that Kathy's temperature was over __101__ degrees.

Review Items

13. The United States is a __country__
   • city   • state   • country

14. Japan is a __country__

15. How many states are in the United States? __50__

━━━━━━━ GO TO PART D IN YOUR TEXTBOOK. ━━━━━━━

---

4. Ideas: They are both cups; they both have handles; etc. A is tall, but B is short; A is full, but B is empty; A is striped, but B is not; etc.

D Number your paper from 1 through 24.

Skill Items

Write the word from the box that means the same thing as the underlined part of each sentence.

supported	attached	jungle	contest
image	startled	rushed	fever

1. The <u>picture</u> was faded. **image**
2. The gloves were <u>connected</u> to the jacket. **attached**
3. He was <u>suddenly surprised</u> by the loud noise. **startled**

4. Compare object A and object B. Remember, first tell how they are the same. Then tell how they're different.

Object A   Object B

Use the words in the box to write complete sentences.

attached	constructed	occasional	steady
machine	normal	hauled	foul	force

5. The ▨ ▨ smell was ▨.
6. They ▨ an enormous ▨.

5. **occasional, foul, normal**
6. **constructed, machine**

104   *Lesson 62*

82

Review Items

7. How far is it from New York City to San Francisco?
   • 5 hundred miles   • <u>25 hundred miles</u>
          • 5 thousand miles
8. How far is it from San Francisco to Japan?
   • 5 hundred miles   • 25 hundred miles
          • <u>5 thousand miles</u>
9. What ocean do you cross to get from San Francisco to Japan? *Pacific (Ocean)*

10. How many legs does an insect have? *6*
11. How many legs does a fly have? *6*
12. How many legs does a bee have? *6*
13. How many legs does a spider have? *8*
14. How many parts does a spider's body have? *2*
15. How many parts does a fly's body have? *3*

---

16. Write the letter of the sun you see at noon. *K*
17. Write the letter of the sun you see at sunset. *H*
18. Write the letter of the sun you see early in the morning. *M*
19. Write the letter of the sun that shows when Linda and Kathy finished dinner. *H*

Look at the skin around each hair. Make an arrow like this ↑ if the hair is moving up. Make an arrow like this ↓ if the hair is moving down.

20.↑ 21.↓ 22.↓ 23.↑ 24.↓

Name _____

A

1. Put a **T** on each tugboat.
2. Put a **D** on each dock.
3. Put an **S** on each ship.

B Story Items

4. How long had Linda and Kathy been on the island when they saw the airplane?
   • <u>15 days</u>   • 3 weeks   • 12 days
5. Did the people in the plane see Linda and Kathy? *no*

6. What did the girls use to make a signal for planes?
   • paint   • <u>rocks</u>   • leaves
7. What word did they spell? *help*
8. The word was over *20* _____ feet long.

9. What kind of signal did the girls have ready for ships?
   - rocks   - fog   - <u>smoke</u>
10. What made the fire smoke so much?
   - sticks   - <u>green leaves</u>   - bananas

11. What was the name of the ship that rescued the girls?
   - S. S. Mason   - <u>S. S. Milton</u>   - S. S. Sisters
12. Kathy's forehead was hot because she had a *fever*

13. How long were the girls on the island?
   - one week   - 2 weeks   - <u>almost 3 weeks</u>
14. How long were the girls on the S.S. Milton?
   - <u>one week</u>   - 2 weeks   - almost 3 weeks
15. Where did the S.S. Milton take them? *Japan*
16. Who took them to their new home? *Idea: their father*
17. Did Linda think it would be dull there? *no*

18. Linda showed Captain Reeves 4 things that she and Kathy had used to survive on the island. **Underline** those 4 things.
   - <u>machine</u>   - <u>belt buckle</u>   - table   - books
   - TV   - wagon   - house   - socks
   - bathtub   - <u>fish net</u>   - <u>vines</u>

Review Items

19. The temperature inside your body is about <u>98</u> degrees when your body is healthy.
20. Most fevers don't go over <u>101</u> degrees.

GO TO PART D IN YOUR TEXTBOOK.

D Number your paper from 1 through 18.
1. Airplanes land at airports. Ships land at ▓▓▓.
   - gates   - <u>harbors</u>   - airports
2. Airplanes are pulled by little trucks. Ships are pulled by little ▓▓▓. (tug) boats
3. Airplanes unload at gates. Ships unload at ▓▓▓.
   - gates   - <u>docks</u>   - harbors

Skill Items

Here's a rule: **Fish are cold-blooded.**
4. A whale is not a fish. So what does the rule tell you abut a whale? *nothing*
5. A shark is a fish. So what does the rule tell you about a shark? *A shark is cold-blooded.*
6. A snapper is a fish. So what does the rule tell you about a snapper? *A snapper is cold-blooded.*

Review Items

7. Which object is the hottest? *B*
8. What is the temperature of that object? *60 degrees*
9. Which object is the coldest? *A*
10. What is the temperature of that object? *20 degrees*

20 degrees   60 degrees   35 degrees

11. Write the letter of every line that is one inch long.
12. Write the letter of every line that is one centimeter long. *B, C, E, G, I*

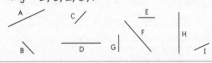

13. Palm trees cannot live in places that get ▓▓▓. *cold*
14. What are the branches of palm trees called? *fronds*
15. Name 2 things that grow on different palm trees.
16. All machines make it easier for someone to ▓▓▓.
   do work
11. *A, D, F H*
15. *coconuts, dates*

The arrow by the handle shows which way it turns.
17. Which arrow shows the way the log moves? *A*
18. Which arrow shows the way the vine moves? *D*

END OF LESSON 63 INDEPENDENT WORK

Name _____

A

1. Make a **K** on the map where Troy used to be.
2. Make a **P** where Greece is.
3. Make an **X** on Italy.

4. The place that was called Troy is now part of what country?
   • Italy   • Greece   • <u>Turkey</u>

A **Story Items**

5. What year is it now? <u>(current year)</u>
6. In what year were you born? <u>(student's birth year)</u>
7. In what year was the first airplane made? <u>1903</u>
8. What was the year 1 hundred years ago? <u>(correct response)</u>
9. What was the year 2 hundred years ago? <u>(correct response)</u>
10. In what year did the United States become a country? <u>1776</u>
11. What was the year 3 hundred years ago? <u>(correct response)</u>

Lesson 64   25

---

12. Write the years where they belong on the time line.

   • 1995   • 1994
   • 1997   • 1998
   • 1990

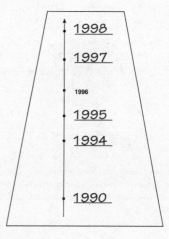

<u>1998</u>

<u>1997</u>

1996

<u>1995</u>

<u>1994</u>

<u>1990</u>

GO TO PART D IN YOUR TEXTBOOK.

26   Lesson 64

TEXTBOOK

D Number your paper from 1 through 24.

Skill Items

> She survived until she was rescued.
>
> 1. What word means **saved from danger**? rescued
> 2. What word means **managed to stay alive**? survived

Review Items

3. What does ocean water taste like? salty
4. If you drank lots of ocean water you would get ███.
   Idea: thirsty

5. Which arrow shows the way Linda's hand will move? E
6. Which arrow shows the way the crate will move? G

E ⟵
G ⟶

Lesson 64   125

TEXTBOOK

Jar A is filled with fresh water. Jar B is filled with ocean water.

7. Which jar is heavier? B
8. Which jar will freeze at 32 degrees? A
9. Will the other jar freeze **above 32 degrees** or **<u>below</u> 32 degrees**?

A   B

10. Write the letter of each place that is in the United States.
    a. New York City   f. Alaska   j. Chicago
    <u>b</u>. California   <u>g</u>. Texas   <u>k</u>. Japan
    c. Italy   h. Denver   l. China
    d. San Francisco   <u>i</u>. Lake Michigan   <u>m</u>. Ohio
    e. Turkey

11. Write the letter of each water strider. P, R, U, V

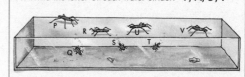

126   Lesson 64

12. What part does the A show? **fronds**
13. What part does the B show? **coconuts**
14. What part does the C show? **trunk**
15. What part does the D show? **roots**

16. How many shells does a coconut have? **2**
17. What is the juice inside a coconut called? *coconut milk*
18. All machines make it easier for someone to ▨.
    do work

Lesson 64   127

19. Write the letter that shows a tugboat. **E**
20. Write two letters that show ships. **D, G**
21. Write two letters that show docks. **F, H**

22. Airplanes land at airports. Ships land at ▨. **harbors**
23. Airplanes are pulled by little trucks. Ships are pulled
    by ▨. **tugboats**
24. Airplanes unload at gates. Ships unload at ▨.
    docks

128   Lesson 64

65

Name _____
Story Items

1. When did the story of Troy take place?
   - 300 years ago   • <u>3 thousand years ago</u>
         • 1 thousand years ago

2. Why didn't the people of Troy have cars?
   - They didn't like cars.   • <u>There were no cars yet.</u>
         • Cars cost too much.

3. The people of Troy got in and out of the city through the great
   <u>gate</u>

4. **Underline** the weapons that soldiers used when they had battles with
   Troy.
   - <u>swords</u>   • guns   • <u>spears</u>   • tanks
   - planes   • rockets   • <u>bows</u>   • <u>arrows</u>

5. When an army put ladders against the wall of Troy, what did the
   people of Troy do to the ladders?
   Idea: pushed them away

6. When an army dug holes under the wall, what did the people of Troy
   dump into the holes? **boiling water**

7. When an army tried to knock down the gate, what did the people of
   Troy dump on them? **boiling water**

8. An army could not starve the people of Troy because the people had
   Idea: lots of food and water

Lesson 65   27

9. Write the years where they belong on the timeline.

   • 1985   • 1982   • 1987   • 1981   • 1989

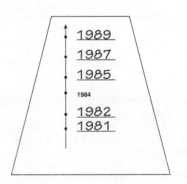

1989
1987
1985
1984
1982
1981

▭▭▭▭▭ GO TO PART C IN YOUR TEXTBOOK. ▭▭▭▭▭

28   Lesson 65

TEXTBOOK

1. They constructed an enourmous machine.
2. She survived until she was rescued.

   4. The army could not starve the people of Troy because the people of Troy had lots of food and water inside the wall.

   In the next story, you will read about a great war that took place in Troy. This war lasted a long, long time because the army could not get inside the wall.

MORE NEXT TIME

C Number your paper from 1 through 26.

Skill Items

Use the words in the box to write complete sentences.

imagined	rescued	disappeared	machine
constructed	image	survived	twice

1. They ▇▇ an enormous ▇▇.
2. She ▇▇ until she was ▇▇.

Review Items

3. Write the letter of each island on the map. **S, U, V**
4. T is not an island. Tell why. **Idea: It is not surrounded by water.**

134   *Lesson 65*

TEXTBOOK

5. Palm trees cannot live in places that get ▇▇. **cold**
6. What are the branches of palm trees called? **fronds**
7. Name two things that grow on different palm trees. **coconuts, dates**
8. What part does the A show? **outer shell**
9. What part does the B show? **inner shell**
10. What part does the C show? **coconut meat**
11. What part does the D show? **coconut milk**

12. The temperature inside your body is about ▇▇ degrees when you are healthy. **98**
13. Most fevers don't go over ▇▇ degrees. **101**
14. When people have very high fevers, how do they feel? **Ideas: sick, hot**
15. They may see and hear things that are not ▇▇. **real**

Lesson 65   135

TEXTBOOK

16. Which letter shows where San Francisco is? **B**
17. Which letter shows where Japan is? **C**
18. Which letter shows where the Pacific Ocean is? **A**

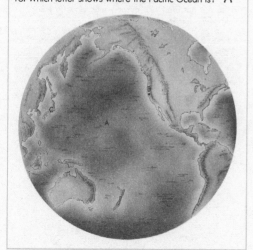

136   *Lesson 65*

TEXTBOOK

19. The place that is called Troy is now part of what country?
   • Greece   • Turkey   • Italy
20. What year is it now? **(current year)**
21. In what year were you born?
22. In what year was the first airplane made? **1903**
23. What was the year 1 hundred years ago?
24. What was the year 2 hundred years ago?
25. In what year did the United States become a country?
26. What was the year 3 hundred years ago?

21. **(correct response)**
23. **(correct response)**
24. **(correct response)**
25. **1776**
26. **(correct response)**

Lesson 65   137

WORKBOOK

Name _____

A

Fill in the blanks on the time line.

1. Write **NOW** next to the dot that shows the year now.
2. Write **3 thousand years ago** next to the right dot.
3. Write **2 thousand years ago** next to the right dot.
4. Write **1 hundred years ago** next to the right dot.
5. Write **1 thousand years ago** next to the right dot.

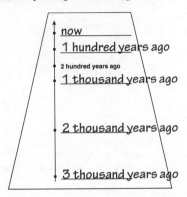

now
1 hundred years ago
2 hundred years ago
1 thousand years ago

2 thousand years ago

3 thousand years ago

Lesson 66   **29**

WORKBOOK

6. How long ago did the story of Troy take place?
   <u>3 thousand years ago</u>

7. About how long ago did Jesus Christ live?
   <u>2 thousand years ago</u>

B Story Items

8. Greece went to war with Troy because of a woman named
   <u>Helen</u>.

9. The woman from Greece was important because she was a
   <u>queen</u>.

10. The woman from Greece went away with a man from <u>Troy</u>.

11. How many ships sailed to Troy? <u>1 thousand</u>

12. When the Greek army put ladders against the wall of Troy, what did
    the people of Troy do? <u>Idea: pushed them over</u>

13. When the Greek army dug holes under the wall, what did the people
    of Troy do? <u>Idea: poured boiling water on them</u>

14. When the Greek army tried to knock down the gate, what did the
    people of Troy do? <u>Idea: poured boiling water on them</u>

15. Why couldn't the Greek army starve the people of Troy?
    <u>Idea: because they had lots of food and water</u>

16. How long did the war go on? <u>10 years</u>

17. If the Greek army got a few men inside the wall of Troy, these men
    could <u>open the gate</u>.

GO TO PART D IN YOUR TEXTBOOK.

30   *Lesson 66*

TEXTBOOK

D Number your paper from 1 through 21.
Review Items

1. Write 2 letters that show decks. C, D
2. Write 2 letters that show bulkheads. B, F
3. Which letter shows where the stern is? A
4. Which letter shows where the bow is? E

TEXTBOOK

5. 32 degrees

5. What is the temperature of the water in each jar?
6. Write the letter of each jar that is filled with ocean
   water. C, F
7. Jar A is not filled with ocean water. How do you
   know? **Idea: It is frozen.**

32 degrees   32 degrees   32 degrees   32 degrees   32 degrees   32 degrees
A   B   C   D   E   F

8. You would have the least amount of power if you
   pushed against one of the handles. Which handle is
   that? I
9. Which handle would give you the most power? F

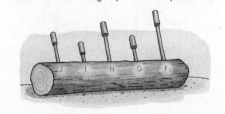

The arrow by the handle shows which way it turns.
10. Which arrow shows the way the log moves? **A**
11. Which arrow shows the way the vine moves? **D**

12. When did the story of Troy take place?
    • 1 thousand years ago   • 1 hundred years ago
    • 3 thousand years ago
13. Why didn't the people of Troy have cars?
    • Cars were too much trouble.   • There were no cars yet.
    • They didn't like cars.
14. The people of Troy got in and out of the city through the great ▨. **gate**
15. Write the letters of the 4 kinds of weapons that soldiers used when they had battles with Troy.
    a. rockets   b. planes   c. spears   d. guns
    e. swords   f. bows   g. arrows   h. tanks

146   Lesson 66

16. Write the letter of the sun you see at sunset. **A**
17. Write the letter of the sun you see at noon. **C**
18. Write the letter of the sun you see early in the morning. **E**

19. Airplanes land at airports. Ships land at ▨. **harbors**
20. Airplanes are pulled by little trucks. Ships are pulled by ▨. **tugboats**
21. Airplanes unload at gates. Ships unload at ▨. **docks**

Lesson 66   147

67

Name _____
Story Items

The army of Greece kept using the same four plans.
1. The army put ladders against **the wall**
2. The army dug holes **under the wall**
3. The army tried to knock down **the gate**
4. The army kept the people of Troy **Idea: inside the city**

5. How long did the war between Greece and Troy go on?
   10 years
6. What did the Greek army build to help them get inside Troy?
   big wooden horse
7. Where did the army put the horse after they finished building it?
   in front of the gate
8. What did the people of Troy think the wooden horse was?
   • a cow   • a trick   • a gift
9. After the people of Troy fell asleep, what came out of the horse?
   3 soldiers (men)
10. What did they do after they came out of the horse?
    opened the gate

11. Was the great wooden horse a gift, or was it a trick?
    a trick
12. Who won the war, Troy or Greece? **Greece**

Lesson 67   **31**

Review Items

Fill in the blanks on the time line.
13. Write **now** next to the dot that shows the year now.
14. Write **1 thousand years ago** next to the right dot.
15. Write **3 thousand years ago** next to the right dot.
16. Write **2 hundred years ago** next to the right dot.
17. Write **2 thousand years ago** next to the right dot.

now

1 hundred years ago

2 hundred years ago

1 thousand years ago

2 thousand years ago

3 thousand years ago

GO TO PART C IN YOUR TEXTBOOK.

32   Lesson 67

Troy could get their swords and spears, the war was over. The army of Greece had won.

The story of the wooden horse may be make-believe. But we know that there was a great war between Greece and Troy. And the story of Troy tells us something that is important. If you can't solve a problem one way, try something else.

The army of Greece kept trying to get inside the wall by using their old tricks. Then they tried something else. It worked.

THE END

C Number your paper from 1 through 19.

Skill Items

The soldiers protected their equipment.
1. What word names men and women in the army?
2. What word means **large machines and tools?**
3. What word tells how they made sure nothing could hurt their equipment? **protected**

1. soldiers
2. equipment

152   Lesson 67

Review Items
4. Name a state in the United States that is bigger than Italy. **Alaska**
5. Italy is shaped something like a ▬. **boot**

6. What place does the **W** show? **Italy**
7. What place does the **X** show? **Turkey**
8. What place does the **Y** show? **China**
9. What place does the **Z** show? **Japan**

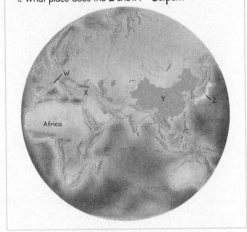

Africa

Lesson 67   153

---

10. Greece went to war with Troy because of a woman named ▬. **Helen**
11. The woman from Greece was important because she was a ▬. **queen**
12. The woman from Greece went away with a man from ▬. **Troy**
13. How many ships sailed to Troy? **1 thousand**
14. How long did the war go on? **10 years**

15. If the Greek army could get a few men inside the wall of Troy, those men could ▬.
16. When the Greek army put ladders against the wall of Troy, what did the people of Troy do?
17. When the Greek army dug holes under the wall, what did the people of Troy do?
18. When the Greek army tried to knock down the gate, what did the people of Troy do?
19. Why couldn't the Greek army starve the people of Troy?

15. Idea: open the gate
16. Idea: pushed them away
17. Idea: poured boiling water on them
18. Idea: poured boiling water on them
19. Idea: They had lots of food and water.

154   Lesson 67

Name _____

A Story Items
1. How old was Bertha? **15 years old**
2. What kind of school did Bertha go to? **high school**
3. Bertha had a super sense of **smell**.
4. Who had a better sense of smell, Bertha or a hound dog? **Bertha**
5. Bertha and her friends played Pin the Tail on the Donkey. Did any of Bertha's friends pin the tail in the right place? **no**
6. Did Bertha pin the tail in the right place? **yes**
7. Bertha knew what her friends at the party were doing without looking at them. How did she know? **Idea: She smelled them.**
8. **Underline** 2 things that were in the cans that the school tester used to test Bertha's sense of smell.
   • pepper • <u>roses</u> • oranges • lilies • <u>lemon</u>
9. Bertha was sorry that she had let people know about her sense of smell because she didn't want to be ▬.
   • the same as others • <u>different from others</u> • others

B Skill Items

10. Compare Bertha and a hound dog. Remember, first tell how they're the same. Then tell how they're different.
    <u>Idea: They both have a good sense of smell.</u>
    <u>Bertha is a person, but a hound dog is a</u>
    <u>dog, etc.</u>

Lesson 68   33

WORKBOOK

Review Items

Write **W** for warm-blooded animals and **C** for cold-blooded animals.

11. beetle _C_
12. cow _W_
13. horse _W_
14. spider _C_
15. bee _C_

The ship in the picture is sinking. It is making currents as it sinks.

16. Write the letter of the object that will go down the whirlpool first. _A_
17. Write the letter of the object that will go down the whirlpool next. _B_
18. Write the letter of the object that will go down the whirlpool last. _D_

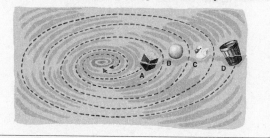

19. The temperature inside your body is about _98_ degrees when you are healthy.
20. Most fevers don't go over _101_ degrees.

GO TO PART C IN YOUR TEXTBOOK.

TEXTBOOK

1. survived, rescued
2. soldiers, protected, equipment

C Number your paper from 1 through 15.

Skill Items

Use the words in the box to write complete sentences.

failed	beauty	protected	peeked	equipment
rescued	imagine	secret	survived	soldiers.

1. She ▮▮▮ until she was ▮▮▮.
2. The ▮▮▮ ▮▮▮ their ▮▮▮.

Review Items

3. Tom is 4 miles high. Jack is 20 miles high. Who is colder? **Jack**
4. Tell why. **Idea: Jack is higher up.**
5. A plane that flies from Italy to New York City goes in which direction? **west**

6. When did the story of Troy take place?
   • 1 thousand years ago   • ⟨3 thousand years ago⟩
        • 1 hundred years ago
7. During the war with Troy, what did the Greek army build to help them get inside Troy?
8. What was inside this object? **3 soldiers**
9. What did they do after they came out of the object?
10. Who won the war, Troy or ⟨Greece⟩?

7. a big wooden horse
9. They opened the gate of Troy.

TEXTBOOK

The picture shows objects caught in a whirlpool. The path is shown for object A.
11. Will the path for object B go around ⟨more times⟩ or **fewer times?**
12. Which path will go around the fewest times, the path for ⟨A,⟩ B, or C?

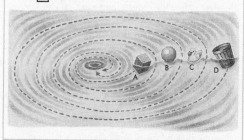

13. Airplanes land at airports. Ships land at ▮▮▮. **harbors**
14. Airplanes are pulled by little trucks. Ships are pulled by ▮▮▮. **tugboats**
15. Airplanes unload at gates. Ships unload at ▮▮▮. **docks**

WORKBOOK

69

Name _____

A Story Items

1. Bertha became restless after school got out for the summer. Tell why.
   • <u>She didn't have anything to do.</u>   • She didn't have a car.
        • She had a fight with her neighbors.
2. What is Maria Sanchez's job?
        • investor   • <u>investigator</u>   • illustrator
3. Had Maria finished her report? _no_
4. Where was the oil company supposed to get its water?
        • <u>from deep wells</u>   • from the creek
5. Where did Maria think the oil company was getting its water?
        • from deep wells   • <u>from the creek</u>
6. Could Maria prove that what she thought was true? _no_
7. How could Bertha help Maria? **Idea: With her sense of smell she could tell if the water was well water or creek water.**

B Skill Items

8. Compare Bertha and a normal 15-year-old girl. Remember, first tell how they're the same. Then tell how they're different.
   Idea: They're both girls. Bertha has a great sense of smell, but a normal 15-year-old girl does not; they're both in high school. Bertha is tall, but a normal 15-year-old girl is not tall.

Review Items

Fill in the blanks on the time line.

9. Write **now** next to the dot that shows the year now.
10. Write **3 thousand years ago** next to the right dot.
11. Write **1 hundred years ago** next to the right dot.
12. Write **2 thousand years ago** next to the right dot.
13. Write **2 hundred years ago** next to the right dot.

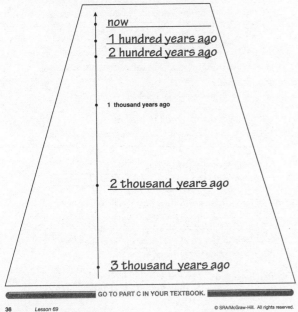

now _____
1 hundred years ago
2 hundred years ago

1 thousand years ago

2 thousand years ago

3 thousand years ago

GO TO PART C IN YOUR TEXTBOOK.

36   Lesson 69   © SRA/McGraw-Hill. All rights reserved.

said. "The dotted line shows an old pipe that goes from the creek to the oil plant. The people who run the oil company tell me that they don't use this pipe to take water from the creek. They say they haven't used the pipe in ten years." Maria shook her head. "I don't believe them, but I can't prove that they are taking water from the creek."

Bertha said, "I think I can help you."
MORE NEXT TIME

C Number your paper from 1 through 24.

Review Items

Some of the lines below are one inch long and some are one centimeter long.
1. Write the letter of every line that is one centimeter long. B, C, E, G, I
2. Write the letter of every line that is one inch long.

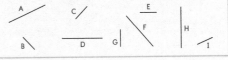

2. A, D, F, H

166   Lesson 69

3. A mile is a little more than [ ] feet.
   • 1 thousand   • 5 hundred   • 5 thousand
4. Does dew form in the middle of the day? **no**
5. Dew forms when the air gets [ ].
   • cooler   • windy   • warmer
6. When we weigh very small things, the unit we use is [ ]. **gram(s)**

Each statement tells about how far something goes or how fast something goes. Write **how far** or **how fast** for each item.
7. She walked 4 miles. **how far**
8. She walked 4 miles per hour. **how fast**
9. The plane was flying 300 miles per hour. **how fast**
10. The plane was 300 miles from Denver. **how far**

11. How fast is truck **A** going? **25 miles per hour**
12. How fast is truck **B** going? **30 miles per hour**
13. Which truck is going faster? **B**

A   B
25   30

14. How many parts does the body of an insect have? **3**
15. How many legs does an insect have? **6**

Lesson 69   167

19. New York
20. San Francisco

16. How many legs does a spider have? **8**
17. How many parts does a spider's body have? **2**
18. What's the boiling temperature of water? **212 degrees**

19. Write the name of the city that's on the east coast.
20. Write the name of the city that's on the west coast.
21. Which letter shows where Denver is? **C**
22. Which letter shows where Chicago is? **D**

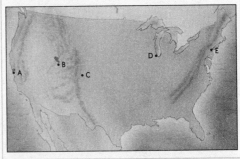

23. Why didn't the people of Troy have cars?
   • They didn't like cars.   • There were no cars yet.
   • Cars were too much trouble.
24. The people of Troy got in and out of the city through the great [ ]. **gate**

168   Lesson 69

Number your paper from 1 through 36.

1. Write the letter of the sun you see early in the morning. E
2. Write the letter of the sun you see at sunset. A
3. Write the letter of the sun you see at noon. C

4. The temperature inside your body is about ▨▨▨ degrees when you are healthy. 98
5. Most fevers don't go over ▨▨▨ degrees. 101
6. Airplanes land at airports. Ships land at ▨▨▨. harbors
7. Airplanes are pulled by little trucks. Ships are pulled by ▨▨▨. tugboats
8. Airplanes unload at gates. Ships unload at ▨▨▨. docks

TEXTBOOK

13. (student's birth year)   15. 1776

9. Which letter shows where Troy used to be? B
10. Which letter shows where Greece is? A
11. Which letter shows where Italy is? C

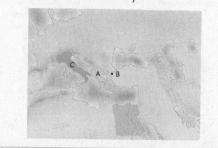

12. In what year was the first airplane made? 1903
13. In what year were you born?
14. What year is it now? (current year)
15. In what year did the United States become a country?
16. What was the year 2 hundred years ago?
17. What was the year 1 hundred years ago?
18. What was the year 3 hundred years ago?
19. When did the story of Troy take place?
   • 1 thousand years ago   • 1 hundred years ago
   • 3 thousand years ago

16. (correct response)
17. (correct response)
18. (correct response)

TEXTBOOK

20. Greece went to war with Troy because of a woman named ▨▨▨. Helen
21. The woman from Greece was important because she was a ▨▨▨. queen
22. The woman from Greece went away with a man from ▨▨▨. Troy
23. How many ships sailed to Troy? 1 thousand
24. How long did the war go on? 10 years
25. If the Greek army could get a few men inside the wall of Troy, those men could ▨▨▨. open the gate
26. During the war with Troy, what did the Greek army build to help them get inside Troy?
27. What was inside this object? 3 soldiers
28. What did they do after they came out of the object?
29. Who won the war, Troy or Greece? Greece

26. big wooden horse
28. opened the gate

TEXTBOOK

Skill Items

30. Compare Linda and Kathy. Remember, first tell how they're the same. Then tell how they're different.

For each item, write the underlined word from the sentences in the box.

> They constructed an enormous machine.
> She survived until she was rescued.
> The soldiers protected their equipment.

31. What word means **saved from danger?** rescued
32. What word means **very large?** enormous
33. What word means **large machines and tools?**
34. What word names something that helps people do work? machine
35. What word means **managed to stay alive?** survived
36. What word means **built?** constructed

━━━━━━━━━━ END OF TEST 7 ━━━━━━━━━━

30. Ideas: They are both sisters/girls. Linda is 13, but Kathy is 10./Linda is a good swimmer, but Kathy isn't.
33. equipment

Name _____

A

1. Name two kinds of wells. oil (wells), water (wells)

Write these names on the picture to show where each liquid is: **crude oil, fresh water, salt water.**

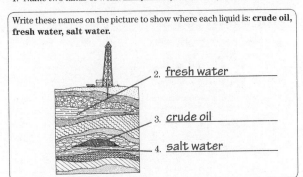

2. fresh water

3. crude oil

4. salt water

5. Fill in the boxes with the names for the **crude oil, pipeline,** and **refinery.**

6. Draw an arrow at A to show which way the crude oil is moving.

7. Draw an arrow at B to show which way the crude oil is moving.

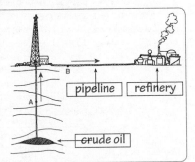

pipeline   refinery

crude oil

B   Story Items

8. Gasoline comes from a liquid called (crude) oil _____.

9. When Bertha first told Maria about her talent, did Maria believe her? no

10. How many glasses of water did Maria use to test Bertha's talent? 3

11. **Underline** the items that tell where the water came from.
- fish bowl   • bath tub   • <u>jug in refrigerator</u>   • sink
- <u>water heater</u>   • frog pond   • <u>watering can</u>

12. Did Bertha pass Maria's test? yes

13. After the test, did Maria believe what Bertha said about her talent? yes

14. Bertha will help Maria by telling where ▯▯.
- the oil wells are   • <u>the water came from</u>   • the snow was

Review Items

15. The arrow by the handle shows which way it turns. Which arrow shows the way the log moves? Z

16. Which arrow shows the way the vine moves? X

GO TO PART D IN YOUR TEXTBOOK.

D   Number your paper from 1 through 19.

Skill Items

Lawyers with talent normally succeed.
1. What word means the opposite of **fail**? succeed
2. What word names people who help us when we have questions about the law? lawyers
3. What word means **usually**? normally
4. What word refers to the special skills a person has? talent

Review Items

5. You can see drops of water on grass early in the morning. What are those called? dew

6. Which letter shows the coconut milk? H
7. Which letter shows the inner shell? G
8. Which letter shows the coconut meat? F
9. Which letter shows the outer shell? E

---

10. do work

10. All machines make it easier for someone to ▯▯.

11. You would have the most power if you pushed against one of the handles. Which handle is that? V

12. Which handle would give you the least amount of power? S

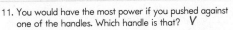
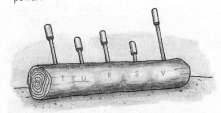

13. When people have very high fevers, how do they feel? Ideas: sick, hot

14. They may see and hear things that are not ▯▯. real

TEXTBOOK

15. Write the letter that shows a tugboat. E
16. Write two letters that show ships. D, G
17. Write two letters that show docks. F, H

18. The place that is called Troy is now part of what country?
    • Greece   • Italy   •□Turkey

19. Write the letters of the 4 kinds of weapons that soldiers used when they had battles with Troy.
    a.│bows   c.│arrows   e.│spears   g. planes
    b.│swords   d. rockets   f. guns   h. tanks

180   Lesson 71

WORKBOOK

Name _____

72

Story Items

1. What was the name of the oil refinery? Reef Oil Refinery
2. Name two ways that the oil refinery was like a prison. (Any 2 ideas:
   ① fence, guard at gate, guard with gun,
   ② far away from city)

3. Was the guard at the gate angry? yes
4. Did he act as if he was angry? no
5. How did Bertha know that he was angry? Idea: by his smell

6. Name the building that Maria and Bertha drove to.
   building C
7. How many floors did that building have? 5
8. What was on the second floor of the building? restaurant
9. What was on the third floor of the building? offices, lawyers
10. Bertha smelled something on the third floor that told her who had offices there. What did she smell?
    • lawyers and fish   • books   • doctors   • typists and roast beef
11. What was on the fourth floor of the building? typists
12. How many people did Bertha think worked on the top floor of the building? Idea: not more than 10
13. Was the author's purpose in this story to **persuade, inform,** or **entertain**? entertain

© SRA/McGraw-Hill. All rights reserved.

Lesson 72   **39**

WORKBOOK

Review Items

14. **Underline** each place that is in the United States.
    • Alaska   • New York City   • California
    • China   • Japan   • Ohio
    • Chicago   • Lake Michigan   • San Francisco
    • Turkey   • Italy   • Texas
    • Denver

15. When the Greek army put ladders against the wall of Troy, what did the people of Troy do? Idea: pushed them away
16. When the Greek army dug holes under the wall, what did the people of Troy do? Idea: poured boiling water into the holes
17. When the Greek army tried to knock down the gate, what did the people of Troy do? Idea: poured boiling water on them
18. Why couldn't the Greek army starve the people of Troy? Idea: They had lots of food and water.

═══ GO TO PART C IN YOUR TEXTBOOK. ═══

40   Lesson 72   © SRA/McGraw-Hill. All rights reserved.

TEXTBOOK

1. The│soldiers│protected│their equipment.
2. │Lawyers│with│talent│normally│succeed│.

C Number your paper from 1 through 16.
Skill Items

Use the words in the box to write complete sentences.

fail	succeed	starve	talent	faded
protected	slivers	soldiers	lawyers	equipment

1. The ▮▮▮ ▮▮▮ their ▮▮▮.
2. ▮▮▮ with ▮▮▮ normally ▮▮▮.

Review Items

3. Palm trees cannot live in places that get ▮▮▮. cold
4. What are the branches of palm trees called?
5. Name 2 things that grow on different palm trees.

6. Which letter shows the trunk? C
7. Which letter shows the fronds? A
8. Which letter shows the coconuts? B
9. Which letter shows the roots? D

4. fronds
5. coconuts, dates

Lesson 72   **185**

95

10. How many shells does a coconut have? **2**
11. What is the juice inside a coconut called?
12. Name **2** kinds of wells.

13. Which letter shows the crude oil? **B**
14. Which letter shows the fresh water? **A**
15. Which letter shows the salt water? **C**

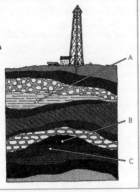

A
B
C

16. Gasoline comes from a liquid called ▓▓▓▓▓. **(crude) oil**

11. coconut milk
12. (fresh) water, (crude) oil

186   Lesson 72

Name _____

Story Items

1. On what floor of building C were Maria and Bertha at the beginning of today's story? **fifth floor** _____

2. Name two people that Maria and Bertha talked to on the fifth floor.
   Donna, Mr. Daniels _____

3. **Underline** 2 things that were in the first office.
   • <u>huge windows</u>   • a fireplace   • thick walls   • <u>thick rugs</u>

4. Which office was bigger, the office Donna was in or Mr. Daniels' office?
   Mr. Daniels' office _____

5. Was Mr. Daniels happy to see Maria? **no** _____

6. Where was Donna going to take Maria and Bertha at the end of the story?
   • Building 7   • Building B   • <u>Building 9</u>
7. What were they going to see there? **water** _____

8. Who said that the refinery uses the water in building 9?
   Donna _____

9. Was that person telling the truth?
   no _____

Lesson 73   **41**

Review Items

Write the years where they belong on the time line.
• 1993   • 1998   • 1991   • 1994   • 1996

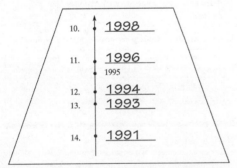

10. **1998**
11. **1996**
     1995
12. **1994**
13. **1993**
14. **1991**

Jar M is filled with ocean water. Jar P is filled with fresh water.

15. Which jar is heavier? **M**
16. Which jar will freeze at 32 degrees? **P**
17. Will the other jar freeze **above 32 degrees** or **below 32 degrees?**
    below 32 degrees

M   P

GO TO PART D IN YOUR TEXTBOOK.

42   Lesson 73

---

state, and we have always tried to be good to people from the state." His voice was quite loud.

"I'm sorry," Maria said. "I'm an investigator, and I have to do my job."

"Then **do** it," Mr. Daniels said sharply. Mr. Daniels walked from the office.

Before Bertha could ask, "What do we do now?" Donna came into the room. Bertha could tell that she felt very uneasy. "I'm to take you to building 9," she said. "You will see the water in that building."

"Is that where they use the water?" Maria asked.

"I think so," Donna said. She was lying. When people lie, they give off a special smell.

MORE NEXT TIME

D **Number your paper from 1 through 17.**

Review Items

1. Which arrow shows the way Linda's hand will move? **R**
2. Which arrow shows the way the crate will move? **S**

R
S

Lesson 73   191

3. Write the letter of each island on the map. **M, N, P**
4. L is not an island. Tell why.
   Idea: It is not surrounded by water.

5. Which letter shows the crude oil? **N**
6. Which letter shows the refinery? **L**
7. Which letter shows the pipeline? **M**

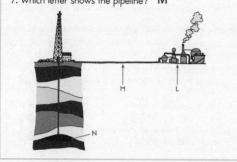

8. Which arrow shows the direction the crude oil is moving at A? **Z**
9. Which arrow shows the direction the crude oil is moving at B? **W**

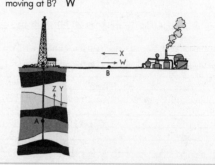

10. When a pot of water gets colder, which way does the temperature go? **down**
11. A sidewalk gets hotter. So what do you know about the temperature of the sidewalk?
12. What does ocean water taste like? **salt(y)**
13. If you drank lots of ocean water you would get ▮▮▮.

11. Idea: The temperature is higher/goes up.
13. thirsty

14. Which object is the hottest? **B**
15. What is the temperature of that object?
16. Which object is the coldest? **A**
17. What is the temperature of that object?

A
45 degrees

B
90 degrees

C
60 degrees

15. 90 degrees
17. 45 degrees

Name _____

Story Items

1. Did Donna act friendly in this story? **yes**
2. Bertha's nose told her that Donna felt very ▮▮▮.
   - happy   • uneasy   • scared
3. What kind of building was building 9?
   - an office   • a refinery   • a garage
4. Why did Maria and Bertha go to building 9?
   - to see oil   • to see water   • to see trucks
5. Where did Big Ted say the water came from? **a (refinery) well**
6. Was Big Ted telling the truth? **no**
7. Did Maria think that the Reef Oil Refinery was trying to trick her?
   yes
8. Maria wanted Mr. Daniels to take her to the ▮▮▮.
   - office buildings   • refinery buildings   • garages
9. Did Mr. Daniels want to do that? **no**

Review Items

10. Let's say you are outside when the temperature is 50 degrees. What is the temperature inside your body? **98 degrees**
11. Let's say you are outside when the temperature is 75 degrees. What is the temperature inside your body? **98 degrees**
12. Let's say a fly is outside when the temperature is 75 degrees. What is the temperature inside the fly's body? **75 degrees**

13. Would it be easier to catch a fly on a hot day or a cold day?
    <u>cold day</u>
14. Tell why. <u>Idea: The fly is slower when it is colder.</u>

15. A plane that flies from Italy to New York City goes in which direction?
    <u>west</u>
16. Where are the fuel tanks on a big jet? <u>on the wings</u>

17. Write the letter of the plane that is in the warmest air. <u>A</u>
18. Write the letter of the plane that is in the coldest air. <u>C</u>

C	5 miles high
B	4 miles high
	3 miles high
D	2 miles high
A	1 mile high

=========== GO TO PART C IN YOUR TEXTBOOK. ===========

44   Lesson 74   © SRA/McGraw-Hill. All rights reserved.

Mr. Daniels turned around and smiled faintly. He didn't say a word, but his expression was filled with hate. He ducked into Donna's car, and the car moved slowly down the road.

MORE NEXT TIME

C Number your paper from 1 through 17.
Skill Items

A dozen typists approached the stairs.
1. What word names people whose job is to type things neatly? **typists**
2. What word means **moved toward something?**
3. What word means **twelve?** **dozen**

Review Items

4. Write the letter of the animal that is facing into the wind. **P**
5. Which direction is that animal facing? **west**
6. So what's the **name** of that wind? **west wind**

2. approached   Lesson 74   199

7. When an object gets hotter, the temperature goes ▓▓▓. **up**

8. What place does the **A** show? **Turkey**
9. What place does the **B** show? **Italy**
10. What place does the **C** show? **New York (City)**

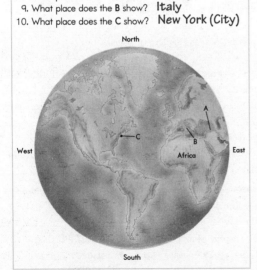

200   Lesson 74

15. **32 degrees**
17. **Idea: The water is frozen at 32 degrees, so it can't be ocean water.**

11. Write 2 letters that show bulkheads. **M, Q**
12. Write 2 letters that show decks. **R, S**
13. Which letter shows where the bow is? **P**
14. Which letter shows where the stern is? **N**

15. What is the temperature of the water in each jar?
16. Write the letter of each jar that is filled with ocean water. **B, D, F**
17. Jar E is not filled with ocean water. How do you know?

32 degrees 32 degrees 32 degrees 32 degrees 32 degrees 32 degrees

A   B   C   D   E   F

Lesson 74   201

75

Name _____

Story Items

1. Mr. Daniels got Maria in trouble with the chief by telling the chief ▓▓▓.

   • lies   • facts   • true stories

2. Maria didn't want the chief to see Bertha when they went to the refinery because ▓▓▓.

   • Bertha worked for the state   • <u>Bertha did not work for the state</u>

   • Bertha had an unusual talent

3. Bertha came up with a plan. Where did she hide?
   <u>Idea: under a blanket in Maria's van</u>

4. Where did Maria stop the van? <u>at the gate</u>

5. Who will bring the water near Bertha? <u>Maria</u>

6. How will Maria signal that it is all right for Bertha to talk?
   <u>Idea: Maria will tap on the back of the van.</u>

7. What will Bertha tell when Maria gives the signal?

   • Where the van is   • What time it is

   • <u>Where the water came from</u>

8. Maria and Bertha did not practice the plan before they left for the refinery because <u>Idea: Maria had been a little late.</u>

9. Who was sleepy in the van? <u>the chief</u>

10. Why did Bertha start feeling sick? <u>Idea: She was getting hot under the blanket.</u>

Lesson 75   **45**

Review Items

Fill in the blanks on the time line.

11. Write **now** next to the dot that shows the year now.
12. Write **3 thousand years ago** next to the right dot.
13. Write **1 thousand years ago** next to the right dot.
14. Write **1 hundred years ago** next to the right dot.
15. Write **2 hundred years ago** next to the right dot.

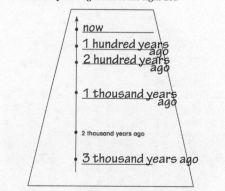

now
<u>1 hundred years ago</u>
<u>2 hundred years ago</u>
<u>1 thousand years ago</u>
2 thousand years ago
<u>3 thousand years ago</u>

16. During the war with Troy, what did the Greek army build to help them get inside Troy? <u>a big wooden horse</u>

17. What was inside this object? <u>3 Greek soldiers</u>

18. What did they do after they came out of the object?
    <u>Idea: opened the gate of Troy</u>

19. Who won the war, Troy or Greece? <u>Greece</u>

GO TO PART C IN YOUR TEXTBOOK.

46   Lesson 75

---

and she began to wonder how loudly she would have to talk for Maria to hear her. They probably should have practiced talking to each other when Bertha was under the blanket, but Maria had been a little late that morning so they had no time to practice.

The voice outside the van said something about Mr. Daniels. Did the voice say that Mr. Daniels would come to the gate? Bertha wasn't sure. She lifted her head and tried to hear better, but nobody was talking now.

As Maria's van waited at the gate, it began to fill with new smells, the smells of heat. The sun beat down on the van, and Bertha got hotter and hotter under the blanket. Bertha rolled over and tried to find a comfortable spot. It was getting so hot under the blanket that Bertha was starting to feel a little sick.

MORE NEXT TIME

C Number your paper from 1 through 18.

Skill Items

1. Lawyers with talent normally succeed.

Use the words in the box to write complete sentences.

| doctors | pretend | succeed | typists | talent |
| appeared | lawyers | approached | doubt |

1. ▓▓▓ with ▓▓▓ normally ▓▓▓.
2. A dozen ▓▓▓ ▓▓▓ the stairs.

2. A dozen typists approached the stairs.

Lesson 75   **205**

Review Items

3. How fast is car **A** going? <u>50 miles per hour</u>
4. How fast is car **B** going? <u>30 miles per hour</u>
5. Which car is going faster? <u>A</u>

   A   B

   50   30

6. Which eye can see <u>more</u> things at the same time, a human's eye or a fly's eye?
7. The United States is a ▓▓▓.   • city • state • <u>country</u>
8. Japan is a ▓▓▓. <u>country</u>
9. How many states are in the United States? <u>50</u>
10. Name a state in the United States that is bigger than Italy. <u>Alaska (or Texas)</u>
11. Italy is shaped something like a ▓▓▓. <u>boot</u>

206   Lesson 75

---

12. What place does the **A** show? China
13. What place does the **B** show? Italy
14. What place does the **C** show? Japan
15. What place does the **D** show? Turkey

The picture shows objects caught in a whirlpool.

16. Write the letter of the object that will go down the hole in the whirlpool first. **A**
17. Write the letter of the object that will go down the hole in the whirlpool next. **B**
18. Write the letter of the object that will go down the hole in the whirlpool last. **D**

76

Name _____

Story Items

1. What happened to the crude oil in building twenty-one?
   - • It became gasoline.   • It became darker.
   - • It became water.

2. There was a very strong smell at building twenty-one. What was that smell? **oil**

3. The inside of the van kept getting **hotter**

4. When Bertha smelled the water that the refinery was using, she knew where the water was from. Where was it from? **the creek**

5. Why did Bertha faint? **Idea: from the heat**

6. Make a **T** on the shadow of the tree.
7. Make a **C** on the shadow of the car.
8. Make an **H** on the shadow of the house.

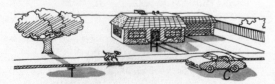

Review Items

9. Why didn't the people of Troy have cars?
   - • There were no cars yet.   • Cars cost too much.
   - • They liked horses better.

10. The people of Troy got in and out of the city through the great **gate**

11. How many ships sailed to Troy? **1 thousand**

12. How long did the war between Greece and Troy go on? **10 years**

13. If the Greek army could get a few men inside the wall of Troy, those men could **open the gate**

14. Name 2 kinds of wells. **(fresh) water, (crude) oil**

15. Gasoline comes from a liquid called **(crude) oil**

GO TO PART C IN YOUR TEXTBOOK.

Ideas: They are both dogs/same colors/facing right/have tails. A is standing, but B is sitting; A has a striped tail, but B has a white tail.

C Number your paper from 1 through 17.

Skill Item

1. Compare object A and object B. Remember, first tell how they're the same. Then tell how they're different.

Object A   Object B

Review Items

Each statement tells about how far something goes or how fast something goes. Write **how far** or **how fast** for each item.

2. He ran 5 miles per hour. **how fast**
3. He ran 5 miles. **how far**
4. The plane was 500 miles from New York City. **how far**
5. The plane was flying 500 miles per hour. **how fast**

6. What part of a car tells how fast the car is moving?
7. What's the boiling temperature of water?
   • 212 miles   • 212 degrees   • 112 degrees

6. speedometer

Lesson 76   213

Some of the objects in the picture are insects, and some are spiders.

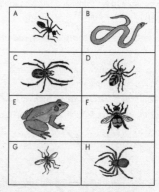

8. Write the letters of the spiders. **C, D, H**
9. Write the letters of the insects. **A, F, G**
10. When a glass gets colder, which way does the temperature go? **down**
11. A street gets hotter. So what do you know about the temperature of the street? **Idea: The temperature went up/got higher.**

214   *Lesson 76*

---

12. What liquid does the **A** show?
13. What liquid does the **B** show?
14. What liquid does the **C** show?

12. fresh water
13. crude oil
14. salt water

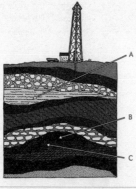

15. Which eye works like many drops, a human's eye or a fly's eye?
16. The biggest state in the United States is ____. Alaska
17. The second-biggest state in the United States is ____. Texas

Lesson 76   215

77

Name _____

Story Items

1. **Underline** 2 things that Bertha told about the chief to prove her talent.
   • He lived north of town.   • He had 3 dogs.
   • He had a dog.   • He lived near cottonwood trees.

2. How did Mr. Daniels act while the chief was asking Bertha questions?
   • angry   • nice   • quiet

3. What did Bertha tell the chief about the water that the refinery was using? **Idea: It was from the creek.**

4. The water had something in it that let Bertha know where the water was from. What was in the water? **(tiny) plants**

5. At the end of the story, the chief told Maria to get six jars of water. How many will come from the well? **3**

6. How many will come from the creek? **3**

7. What do you think the chief will do with the water?
   Ideas: have Bertha tell where the water came from; test her

Review Items

8. How many legs does an insect have? **6**
9. How many legs does a fly have? **6**
10. How many legs does a bee have? **6**
11. How many legs does a spider have? **8**
12. How many parts does a spider's body have? **2**
13. How many parts does a fly's body have? **3**

Lesson 77   49

14. How far is it from New York City to San Francisco?
    <u>25 hundred miles</u>

15. How far is it from San Francisco to Japan?
    <u>5 thousand miles</u>

16. What ocean do you cross to get from San Francisco to Japan?
    <u>Pacific (Ocean)</u>

Skill Item

17. Compare creek water and well water. Remember what you're going to tell first and what you're going to tell next.
    <u>Idea: They're both water. Creek water has tiny plants in it,</u>
    <u>but well water doesn't have tiny plants in it; etc.</u>

▬▬▬▬ GO TO PART C IN YOUR TEXTBOOK. ▬▬▬▬

C Number your paper from 1 through 15.

Review Items

1. Greece went to war with Troy because of a woman named ▇▇▇. Helen
2. The woman from Greece was important because she was a ▇▇▇. queen
3. The woman from Greece went away with a man from ▇▇▇. Troy

4. Which letter shows where Troy used to be? S
5. Which letter shows where Greece is? P
6. Which letter shows where Italy is? R

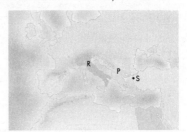

---

7. What place does **A** show?   Japan
8. What place does **B** show?   New York (City)
9. What place does **C** show?   San Francisco
10. What place does **D** show?   Pacific Ocean

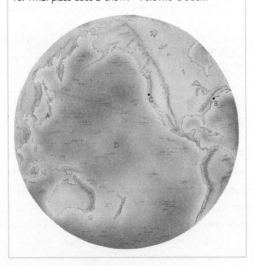

---

11. Which letter shows the crude oil?   F
12. Which letter shows the refinery?   E
13. Which letter shows the pipeline?   G

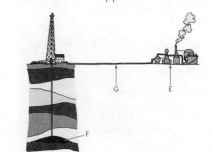

---

14. Which arrow shows the direction the crude oil is moving at A? **K**
15. Which arrow shows the direction the crude oil is moving at B? **P**

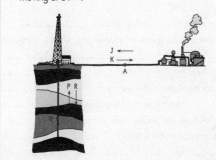

Name _____

Story Items

1. How many blindfolds did Bertha have on when she tested the water?
   3

2. **Underline** each blindfold.
   - a blue mask
   - a long cloth
   - tape
   - dark glasses
   - a leather belt
   - a hood

3. The chief put blindfolds on Bertha so she couldn't **see (the water)**

4. When Bertha tested the water, the chief didn't let her touch the jars of water so she wouldn't know the ▮▮▮.
   - temperature
   - weight
   - color

5. How many jars of water did Bertha test? **6**

6. How many jars did she get wrong? **0**

7. How did Mr. Daniels act after the test? **Idea: mad**

8. The chief ordered Mr. Daniels to ▮▮▮ the refinery.
   - sell
   - buy
   - close

9. When was Mr. Daniels to do that?
   - immediately
   - within a month
   - within a year

10. The chief wanted Bertha to be ▮▮▮.
    - a teacher
    - a special consultant
    - a driver

11. How much will Bertha earn each day? **$500**

Review Items

12. What do all living things need? **water**
13. What do all living things make? **babies**
14. Do all living things grow? **yes**
15. Are flies living things? **yes**
16. **Underline** 3 things you know about flies.
    - Flies make babies.
    - Flies need water.
    - Flies grow.
    - Flies need ants.
    - Flies need sugar.

17. Some of the lines in the box are one inch long and some are one centimeter long. Write the letter of every line that is one centimeter long. **C, D, E, F**

18. Write the letter of every line that is one inch long. **A, B, G, H**

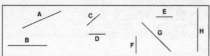

━━━ GO TO PART C IN YOUR TEXTBOOK. ━━━

C Number your paper from 1 through 17.

Skill Items

> **The job required a consultant.**
> 1. What word names a person who is hired for a special job? **consultant**
> 2. What word means **needed**? **required**

Review Items

3. When we weigh very small things, the unit we use is ▮▮▮. **gram(s)**

4. Write the letter of the ruler that will make the lowest sound. **D**

5. Write the letter of the ruler that will make the highest sound. **B**

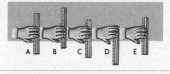

6. When we talk about miles per hour, we tell how ▮▮▮ something is moving. **fast**

7. When something tries to move in one direction, something else tries to move ▮▮▮. **in the opposite direction**

8. Arrow X shows the direction the boy will jump. Which arrow shows the direction the block of ice will move? **R**

9. A mile is a little more than ▮▮▮ feet.
   • I thousand   •⟦5 thousand⟧   • 5 hundred

10. How fast is truck **A** going? **55 miles per hour**
11. How fast is truck **B** going. **40 miles per hour**
12. Which truck is going faster? **A**

13. Airplanes land at airports. Ships land at ▮▮▮.
14. Airplanes are pulled by little trucks. Ships are pulled by ▮▮▮. **tugboats**
15. Airplanes unload at gates. Ships unload at ▮▮▮.
16. Which is longer, a centimeter or a meter?
17. How many centimeters long is a meter? **100**

13. harbors
15. docks
16. meter

Lesson 78   229

Name _____

A

FORM 50:
SPECIAL CONSULTANTS AND GROUP LEADERS

1. Have you been paid to work for the state before? _no_
2. How old are you? _15_
3. Print your full name. _Bertha Turner_
4. Do you want to be a **special consultant** or a **group leader**?
   special consultant
5. Do you have your own car? _no_
6. How much will you earn every day? _$500_
7. What is your special talent? _Idea: Using my nose_

If you are to be a group leader, answer these questions:

8. How many are in your group? _____
9. What is your special topic? _____

If you are to be a special consultant, answer this question:

10. What's the name of the investigator you work with?
    Maria Sanchez

B Story Items

11. Where did Achilles' mother take him when he was a baby?
    Idea: to a river with magic water

12. Why did she want to dip him in the river?
    • to clean him   • to make sure nothing could harm him
    • to teach him to swim

Lesson 79   53

---

13. **Finish the rule about the water in the river.** If the water touched a part of your body, **Idea: Nothing could hurt that part**

14. If you put your arm in the magic river, what would happen to your arm? **Idea: Nothing could hurt your arm.**

15. Achilles' mother held on to part of him when she dipped him in the river. What part? **his heel**

16. What part of Achilles did not get wet? **his heel**

17. What part of Achilles could get hurt? **his heel**

18. Achilles was in the army from ▮▮▮.
    • Italy   • Greece   • Troy

19. Why were all the soldiers afraid of Achilles?
    Idea: because nothing could hurt him

20. Is the story about Achilles a true story? **no**

▬▬▬▬ GO TO PART D IN YOUR TEXTBOOK. ▬▬▬▬

---

1. His left hand was his Achilles heel.
2. Their love of money was their Achilles heel.

D Number your paper from 1 through 14.
Write each sentence below using other words for the word **weakness**.
   1. His left hand was his **weakness**.
   2. Their love of money was their **weakness**.

Skill Items
3. A ⟦dozen⟧ typists ⟦approached⟧ the stairs.
Use the words in the box to write complete sentences.

friendly	approached	explained	guard	required
	dozen	fairly	complaint	consultant

3. A ▮▮▮ typists ▮▮▮ the stairs.
4. The job ▮▮▮ a ▮▮▮.
4. The job ⟦required⟧ a ⟦consultant⟧.

Review Items
5. When did the story of Troy take place?
   • 3 hundred years ago   •⟦3 thousand years ago⟧
   • 1 thousand years ago
6. Write the letters of the 4 kinds of weapons that soldiers used when they had battles with Troy.
   ⟦a.⟧ spears   ⟦b.⟧ bows   c. rockets   d. tanks
   ⟦e.⟧ arrows   f. planes   ⟦g.⟧ swords   h. guns

234   Lesson 79

Some things in the picture weigh **1 gram.** Some weigh **2 grams.** Some weigh **5 grams.** Write how much each object weighs.

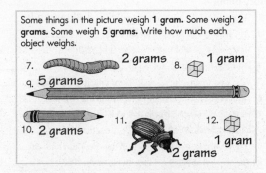

7. 2 grams   8. 1 gram

9. 5 grams

10. 2 grams   11. 2 grams   12. 1 gram

13. Which is longer, a centimeter or a meter?
14. How many centimeters long is a meter? 100

===== END OF LESSON 79 INDEPENDENT WORK =====

Number your paper from 1 through 19.
1. Name 2 kinds of wells. (fresh) water, (crude) oil

2. What liquid does the D show? crude oil
3. What liquid does the E show? fresh water
4. What liquid does the F show? salt water

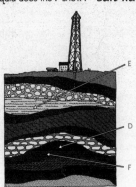

---

5. Which letter shows the crude oil? J
6. Which letter shows the refinery? H
7. Which letter shows the pipeline? K

---

8. Which arrow shows the direction the crude oil is moving at A? M
9. Which arrow shows the direction the crude oil is moving at B? P

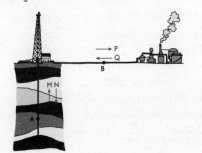

10. Gasoline comes from a liquid called ▆▆▆.
11. Write the sentence using other words for the word **weakness.**

   His love of money was his **weakness.**

10. (crude) oil
11. His love of money was his Achilles heel.

105

TEXTBOOK

For each item, write the underlined word from the sentences in the box.

> <u>Lawyers</u> with <u>talent</u> <u>normally</u> <u>succeed</u>.
> A <u>dozen</u> <u>typists</u> <u>approached</u> the stairs.
> The job <u>required</u> a <u>consultant</u>.

12. What underlining means **needed**?   required
13. What underlining names people whose job is to type things neatly?   typists
14. What underlining names a person who is hired for a special job?   consultant
15. What underlining names people who help us when we have questions about the law?   lawyers
16. What underlining means **usually**?   normally
17. What underlining means **twelve**?   dozen
18. What underlining means the opposite of **fail**?   succeed
19. What underlining refers to special skills?   talent

━━━━━━━━━ END OF TEST 8 ━━━━━━━━━

WORKBOOK

Name _____

Story Items

1. How many ships went to war with Troy? 1 thousand
2. Which army was Achilles in? Greek
3. How long was Achilles in the war? 10 years
4. Who was the greatest soldier of Troy? Hector
5. Who won when Achilles and Hector fought? Achilles
6. Achilles rode around the wall of Troy in a chariot
7. How did the people of Troy feel when Achilles killed Hector? Ideas: sad, mad, etc.
8. Did the arrows that hit Achilles in the chest hurt him? no
9. The arrow that killed Achilles hit him in the heel
10. The arrow had something on it that killed Achilles. What did it have on it?

   • powder   • <u>poison</u>   • paint

Review Items

11. The temperature inside your body is about 98 degrees when you are healthy.
12. Most fevers don't go over 101 degrees.
13. The place that is called Troy is now part of what country?

   • Greece   • <u>Turkey</u>   • Italy

WORKBOOK

Review Items

Here are the facts you need to fill out the form below: Your name is Sam Lee and you want to work as a group leader. You are 22 years old and you have your own car. You have worked for the state before and you will earn $300 per day. Your special topic is "Safe Driving." There are 50 people in your group.

> **FORM 50**
>
> **SPECIAL CONSULTANTS AND GROUP LEADERS**
>
> 14. Print your full name. Sam Lee
> 15. How old are you? 22
> 16. Have you worked for the state before? yes
> 17. Do you have your own car? yes
> 18. How much will you earn every day? $300
> 19. Do you want to be a **special consultant** or a **group leader**? group leader
>
> If you are to be a group leader, answer these questions:
>
> 20. How many are in your group? 50
> 21. What is your special topic? safe driving
>
> If you are to be a special consultant, answer this question:
>
> 22. What's the name of the investigator you work with? (no response)

━━━━━━━━━ GO TO PART D IN YOUR TEXTBOOK. ━━━━━━━━━

TEXTBOOK

4. Idea: shooting an arrow
5. Idea: steering the chariot

D Number your paper from 1 through 19.

1. What is the name of the vehicle in the picture?   chariot
2. How many wheels does the vehicle have?   2
3. What is pulling the vehicle?   (4) horses
4. What is soldier A doing?
5. What is soldier B doing?

Soldier A   Soldier B

Review Items

Write **W** for warm-blooded animals and **C** for cold-blooded animals.
6. ant C   8. dog W
7. cow W   9. spider C

11. Idea: Because she is higher.

10. Lee is 10 miles high. Jean is 15 miles high. Who is colder? Jean

11. Tell why.

The ship in the picture is sinking. It is making currents as it sinks.

12. Write the letter of the object that will go down the whirlpool first. B

13. Write the letter of the object that will go down the whirlpool last. D

14. The temperature inside your body is about ▮▮▮▮ degrees when you are healthy. 98

15. Most fevers don't go over ▮▮▮▮ degrees. 101

16. The place that is called Troy is now part of what country?
    • Greece   • Turkey   • Italy

17. Write the letter of the sun you see at sunset. R

18. Write the letter of the sun you see at noon. T

19. Write the letter of the sun you see early in the morning. V

SPECIAL PROJECT

Some of the stories that you have read are called **myths.** They are fiction, but they tell about famous heroes. The myth about Achilles is a Greek myth.

Here are the names of other heroes of Greek myths: Athena, Zeus, Poseidon, Hermes, Hercules, Jason. Select 2 names and find out what those characters did.

82

Name _____

Story Items

1. People who lived 80 thousand years ago did not have many things that we have today. **Underline** 4 things they did not have.

   • TV sets   • bones   • phones   • refrigerators
   • food   • rocks   • dogs   • books

2. What clue could tell you that someone ate chicken? Ideas: chicken bones, chicken guts, etc.

3. What clue could tell you that someone ate a coconut? coconut shells

4. What's a good place to look for clues about people who lived long ago? Ideas: caves, garbage piles

5. Some people who lived 80 thousand years ago lived in caves.

6. Name 2 clues that tell us that dogs may have lived with people 8 thousand years ago. Idea: bones with dog teeth marks; bones of dogs

7. Name one clue that tells us how people may have hunted large animals like buffalo. broken buffalo bones found at the bottom of a cliff

8. Name 2 clues that tell us that people used fire to cook their food. Any 2: ashes; burn marks on bones; rocks with smoke and heat marks

9. Did the first people who lived in caves cook their food? no

10. Did the people who lived in caves many years later cook their food? yes

11. Was the author's purpose to **persuade, inform,** or **entertain**? inform

Review Items

Here's how fast different things can go:

   • 200 miles per hour   • 500 miles per hour
   • 20 miles per hour   • 35 miles per hour

12. Which speed tells how fast a fast dog can run? 35 miles per hour

13. Which speed tells how fast a jet can fly? 500 miles per hour

14. Which speed tells how fast a fast man can run? 20 miles per hour

15. Which army was Achilles in during the war between Troy and Greece? Greek

16. How long was Achilles in the war? 10 years

17. Who was the greatest soldier of Troy? Hector

18. Who won when Hector and Achilles fought? Achilles

19. Achilles rode around the wall of Troy in a chariot

20. The arrow that killed Achilles hit him in the heel

21. That arrow had something on it that killed Achilles. What did it have on it? poison

GO TO PART C IN YOUR TEXTBOOK.

do not find any burn marks on bones. These clues tell us something about how the people ate their food.

If we look at a garbage pile in a cave that people have used for hundreds of years, we can tell how things changed. We can tell if the people began to eat different things. Let's say we find that some of the garbage in a pile was not cooked. These things are near the bottom of the garbage pile. Let's say the things near the top of the pile were cooked. By looking at the pile, we can tell that people who lived in the cave first did not cook their food. They ate things raw. The people who lived in the same cave many, many years later began to cook food. In the next story, you'll learn the rule for getting clues from a pile.

MORE NEXT TIME

C Number your paper from 1 through 17.

Review Items a, c, e, g, i, j, k, l, m

1. Write the letter of each place that is in the United States.
   a. Denver   f. Italy   j. Texas
   b. Turkey   g. Lake Michigan k. San Francisco
   c. Chicago   h. Japan   l. Ohio
   d. China   i. New York City m. California
   e. Alaska

Lesson 82   253

2. Write the letter of the animal that is facing into the wind. **H**
3. Which direction is that animal facing? **south**
4. So what's the **name** of that wind? **south wind**

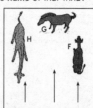

5. What is the temperature of the water in each jar?
6. Write the letter of each jar that is filled with ocean water. **B, D, E**
7. Jar C is not filled with ocean water. How do you know? **Idea: It's frozen.**

5. **32 degrees**

254   Lesson 82

8. Which letter shows where Troy used to be? **E**
9. Which letter shows where Greece is? **F**
10. Which letter shows where Italy is? **D**

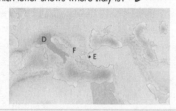

11. What is the name of the vehicle in the picture? **chariot**
12. How many wheels does the vehicle have? **2**
13. What is pulling the vehicle? **(4) horses**
14. What is soldier X doing? **Idea: shooting arrows**
15. What is soldier Y doing? **Idea: steering, the chair**

Lesson 82   255

16. You would have the least amount of power if you pushed against one of the handles. Which handle is that? **S**
17. Which handle would give you the most power? **R**

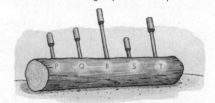

256   Lesson 82

Name _____

1. Things closer to the bottom of the pile went into the pile **earlier**.
2. Things closer to the top of the pile went into the pile **later**.

The picture below shows a pile of garbage.

3. Write the words **earlier** and **later** in the right boxes.
4. Which thing went into the pile earlier, thing M or thing B? **B**
5. Which thing went into the pile earlier, thing A or thing S? **S**
6. Which thing went into the pile later, thing A or thing B? **A**
7. Which thing went into the pile later, thing M or thing R? **M**

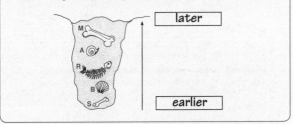

later

earlier

8. What clues would tell us that people used fire to cook their food?
Ideas: smoke marks on stones; burn marks on bones; ashes

9. Did the first people who lived in caves cook their food? **no**

10. How do we know? **Ideas: no ashes, no burn marks on bones, no heat or smoke marks on stones**

The picture below shows a hole dug near a beach.

11. When we dig into the pile, what's the first thing we find?
small stones
12. What's the next thing we find? **sand**
13. What's the next thing we find? **shells**
14. What's the next thing we find? **large stones**
15. What's the last thing we find? **mud**

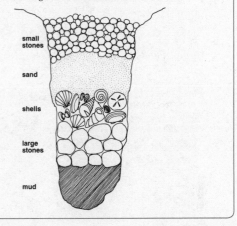

small stones

sand

shells

large stones

mud

GO TO PART C IN YOUR TEXTBOOK.

C Number your paper from 1 through 21.

Skill Items

The adults huddled around the fire. **huddled**
1. What word tells that the adults crowded together?
2. What word means **grown-ups**? **adults**

Review Items

Jar A is filled with ocean water. Jar B is filled with fresh water.
3. Which jar is heavier? **A**
4. Which jar will freeze at 32 degrees? **B**
5. Will the other jar freeze **above 32 degrees** or **below 32 degrees**?

A   B

6. During the war with Troy, what did the Greek army build to help them get inside Troy?
7. What was inside this object? **(Greek) soldiers**
8. What did they do after they came out of the object?
9. Who won the war, Troy or Greece? **Greece**

6. **Idea: large wooden horse**
8. **opened the gate**

---

10. What part does the A show? **outer shell**
11. What part does the B show? **inner shell**
12. What part does the C show? **coconut meat**
13. What part does the D show? **(coconut) milk**

A   B   C   D

14. When people have very high fevers, how do they feel? **sick**
15. They may see and hear things that are not ▨▨. **real**
16. People who lived 80 thousand years ago did not have many things that we have today. Write the letters of 4 things they did not have. **c, f, g, h**
   a. bones   b. trees   c. computers   d. food
   e. rocks   f. stoves   g. cars   h. movies
17. Name 2 clues that tell us that dogs may have lived with people 8 thousand years ago.
18. Name one clue that tells us how people may have hunted large animals like buffalo. **Idea: broken buffalo bones**

17. **Ideas: bones with dog teeth marks; dog bones in caves**

TEXTBOOK

19. Write the letter that shows a tugboat. N
20. Write two letters that show ships. J, L
21. Write two letters that show docks. K, M

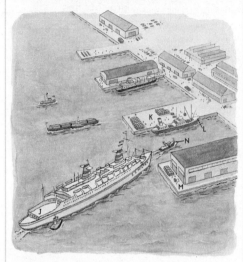

Lesson 83   265

WORKBOOK

Name _____

A

1. Which picture shows how you should hold a burning branch if you don't want to get burned?
   X _____

2. Draw an arrow from each dot to show which way the heat will move.

   X   Y

3. How does fire like to move, up or down? up _____

B   Story Items

4. Write **north**, **south**, **east**, and **west** in the right boxes.
5. The wind blows from the north. Draw an arrow from the dot to show that wind.

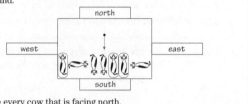

north

west   east

south

6. **Circle** every cow that is facing north.

WORKBOOK

Review Items

7. Write the words **earlier** and **later** in the right boxes.
8. Which thing went into the pile earlier, thing M or thing A? A
9. Which thing went into the pile earlier, thing B or thing R? B
10. Which thing went into the pile later, thing S or thing B? B
11. Which thing went into the pile later, thing A or thing R? A

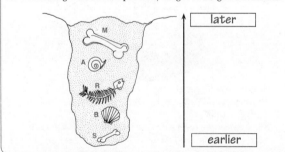

later

earlier

GO TO PART D IN YOUR TEXTBOOK.

TEXTBOOK

D   Number your paper from 1 through 26.

Story Items

1. The people who lived 80 thousand years ago did not live like we do. Where did the people live? in caves
2. The adults who lived in the cave didn't like winter because it was too ████.
   • slow   • <u>cold</u>   • hot
3. Let's say that Jack stands up. What would you do to imitate Jack? stand up
4. Let's say that Jean hops on one foot. What would you do to imitate Jean? hop on one foot
5. During a storm, which comes first, lightning or thunder?

6. What happened when the child in the story held the burning branch with the burning part pointed down?
7. A man held the burning branch with the burning part pointed ████. up
8. Did the man get burned? no
9. How did the people in the cave feel about the fire? happy

The cave people learned two rules about fire.
10. If you put things in the fire, those things will get ████.
11. The fire makes the cave ████. warm

6. Idea: The child got burned.
10. hot

---

12. Ideas: They are both places to live; you can live in both of them. A house has walls/windows/roof but a cave doesn't.

Skill Items

12. Compare a house and a cave. Remember, first tell how they're the same. Then tell how they're different.

Use the words in the box to write complete sentences.

realized   adventure   skeletons   permitted   consultant
continued   required   expression   adults   huddled

13. The job ▮▮▮▮ a ▮▮▮▮.   **required, consultant**
14. The ▮▮▮▮ ▮▮▮▮ around the fire.   **adults, huddled**

Review Items

15. Arrow B shows the direction the girl will jump. Which arrow shows the direction the boat will move?   **A**

Lesson 84   **273**

16. What does ocean water taste like?   **salt**
17. If you drank lots of ocean water you would get ▮▮▮▮.
18. How many shells does a coconut have?   **2**
19. What is the juice inside a coconut called?
20. What year is it now?   **(current year)**
21. In what year were you born?
22. In what year was the first airplane made?   **1903**
23. What was the year 1 hundred years ago?
24. In what year did the United States become a country?
25. Things closer to the bottom of the pile went into the pile ▮▮▮▮.   **earlier**
26. Things closer to the top of the pile went into the pile ▮▮▮▮.   **later**

17. thirsty
19. coconut milk
21. (student's birth year)
23. (appropriate year)
24. 1776

274   *Lesson 84*

85

Name _____

A

1. The people who lived in caves drew pictures on the cave walls. **Underline** 3 things they made pictures of.

• <u>cows</u>   • fish   • birds   • <u>hands</u>   • <u>horses</u>

2. Hand A is the hand of ▮▮▮▮.   • a child   • <u>an adult</u>   • an ape
3. Name one thing you can tell about hand B.
   <u>Ideas: It is small; it belongs to a child.</u>
4. Name 2 ways that hand A is different from hand C.
   <u>Ideas (any 2): Hand A is an outline, but hand C is not.</u>
   <u>Hand A is missing part of a finger, but hand C is not.</u>
   Hand A is big, but hand C is bigger.

A   B   C

5. **Underline** 3 things that cave people used to make paint.

• <u>fat</u>   • hair   • <u>earth</u>   • salt   • <u>blood</u>

The picture shows the outline of a hand on a cave wall.

6. Make an **X** on the part of the wall that was covered with paint.
7. Make a **Y** on the part of the wall that was not covered with paint.

8. Cave people painted pictures of horses on cave walls. How are those horses different from horses that live today?

   <u>Idea: Those horses are much smaller.</u>

Lesson 85   **63**

9. Some kinds of animals that lived thousands of years ago are not alive today. We know what those animals looked like because we have found ▮▮▮▮.

• hair   • <u>bones</u>   • living animals

Review Items

Fill in the blanks on the time line.

10. Write **now** next to the dot that shows the year now.
11. Write **3 thousand years ago** next to the right dot.
12. Write **1 thousand years ago** next to the right dot.
13. Write **1 hundred years ago** next to the right dot.
14. Write **2 thousand years ago** next to the right dot.

• <u>now</u>
• <u>1 hundred years ago</u>
• 2 hundred years ago
• <u>1 thousand years ago</u>
• <u>2 thousand years ago</u>
• <u>3 thousand years ago</u>

▮▮▮▮ GO TO PART C IN YOUR TEXTBOOK. ▮▮▮▮

1. Ideas: ashes; burn marks on bones; smoke marks on rocks

C Number your paper from 1 through 23.
Review Items

1. What clues would tell us that people used fire to cook their food?

2. Did the people who first lived in caves cook their food? **no**

3. How do we know?

4. Which letter shows the trunk? **M**
5. Which letter shows the fronds? **K**
6. Which letter shows the coconuts? **N**
7. Which letter shows the roots? **L**

K
N
M
L

3. Idea: They left no clues that would tell that they cooked food.

---

8. do work

8. All machines make it easier for someone to ▢.

9. When did the story of Troy take place?
   • 1 thousand years ago   • 1 hundred years ago
   • 3 thousand years ago
10. Why didn't the people of Troy have cars?
    • Cars were too much trouble.
    • There were no cars yet.
    • They didn't like cars.
11. The people of Troy got in and out of the city through the great ▢. **gate**

12. Write the letters of the 4 kinds of weapons that soldiers used when they had battles with Troy. **b, d, f, g**
    a. planes   c. rockets   e. guns   g. spears
    b. swords   d. arrows   f. bows   h. tanks
13. Name **2** kinds of wells.
14. During a storm, which comes first, lightning or thunder?
15. How does fire like to move, up or down?
16. Let's say that Tony sits down. What would you do to imitate Tony? **sit down**
17. The cave people learned two rules about fire: If you put things in the fire, those things will get ▢. **hot**
18. The fire makes the cave ▢. **warm**

13. (fresh) water well, (crude) oil well

---

19. When we dig into the pile in the picture, what's the first thing we find? **small stones**
20. What's the next thing we find? **sand**
21. What's the next thing we find? **shells**
22. What's the next thing we find? **large stones**
23. What's the last thing we find? **mud**

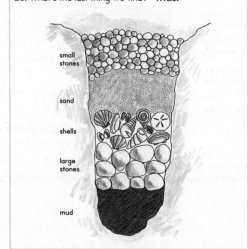

small stones

sand

shells

large stones

mud

Name _____

Under each horse, write what kind of horse is shown.
• Mongolian horse   • racehorse   • pony   • draft horse   • quarter horse

1. <u>draft horse</u>   2. <u>racehorse</u>

3. <u>quarter horse</u>   4. <u>Mongolian horse</u>   5. <u>pony</u>

6. What 3 things are quarter horses good at doing?
   • <u>turning</u>   • <u>running fast</u>   • <u>stopping</u>
   • starting fast   • pulling heavy loads

7. How many third-graders weigh as much as a quarter horse?
   <u>15</u>

8. What are draft horses good at doing?
   • turning   • running fast   • stopping
   • starting fast   • <u>pulling heavy loads</u>

9. How many third-graders weigh as much as a draft horse? <u>30</u>

10. The Mongolian horse was the kind of horse that lived <u>30</u> thousand years ago.

12. Ideas: racing; running fast

11. How many third-graders weigh as much as a Mongolian horse?

    8

12. What are racehorses good at doing? _____

13. How tall is a racehorse at the head? (about) 2 meters

14. How many third-graders weigh as much as a racehorse?

    15

15. How tall is a pony at the shoulder? (a little over) 1 meter

16. How many third-graders weigh as much as a pony? 4

17. Which horse has thin legs, a racehorse or a draft horse?

    racehorse

18. Which horse has a shorter back, a racehorse or a quarter horse?

    quarter horse

Review Items

19. A speedometer tells about ▇▇▇.

    • hours   • <u>miles per hour</u>   • miles

20. The people who lived in caves drew pictures on the cave walls. Write
    the letters of 4 things they made pictures of. a, e, f, h

    a. hands   b. fish   c. bears   d. dogs

    e. horses   f. cows   g. birds   h. elephants

21. Cave people painted pictures of horses on cave walls. How are those
    horses different from horses that live today?

    Idea: They are smaller.

GO TO PART C IN YOUR TEXTBOOK.

C Number your paper from 1 through 15.
Review Items

1. Which letter shows where New York City is? P
2. Which letter shows where San Francisco is? R

3. Palm trees cannot live in places that get ▇▇▇. cold
4. What are the branches of palm trees called? fronds
5. Name **2** things that grow on different palm trees. dates, coconuts

---

7. Idea: It is not entirely surrounded by water.

6. Write the letter of each island on the map. A, C, D
7. **B** is not an island. Tell why.

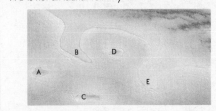

8. Greece went to war with Troy because of a woman
   named ▇▇▇. Helen
9. The woman from Greece was important because she
   was a ▇▇▇. queen
10. The woman from Greece went away with a man from
    ▇▇▇. Troy
11. Which army was Achilles in during the war between
    Troy and Greece? Greek
12. How long was Achilles in the war? 10 years
13. Who was the greatest soldier of Troy? Hector
14. Who won when Hector and Achilles fought? Achilles
15. Achilles rode around the wall of Troy in a ▇▇▇. chariot

Name _____

Story Items

1. Write the words **earlier** and **later**
   in the right boxes.

2. How many years ago did layer
   A go into the pile?

   38 million years ago

3. How many years ago did layer
   B go into the pile?

   28 million years ago

4. How many years ago did layer
   C go into the pile?

   11 million years ago

5. How many years ago did layer
   D go into the pile?

   1 million years ago

6. How many years ago did layer
   E go into the pile?

   30 thousand years ago

| later |

NOW
Story of Troy
30 thousand
years ago

1 million
years ago

11 million
years ago

28 million
years ago

38 million
years ago

| earlier |

7. The horse skeleton in layer A
   is no bigger than a ▇▇▇.

   • <u>small dog</u>   • pony   • big dog

8. The horse skeleton in layer B is about as big as a ▇▇▇.

   • small dog   • pony   • <u>big dog</u>

9. The horse skeleton in layer C is about as big as a ▇▇▇.

   • small dog   • <u>pony</u>   • big dog

WORKBOOK

10. The people who lived in caves drew pictures on the cave walls. **Underline** 4 things they made pictures of.

• hands • feet • cats • elephants • horses • dogs • birds • cows

11. Things closer to the bottom of the pile
went into the pile earlier
12. Things closer to the top of the pile
went into the pile later
13. How was the earliest horse different from horses that live today?
Idea: It was much smaller.
14. The earliest horses on Earth are not alive today. How long ago did the earliest horses live?
   - 38 thousand years ago
   - 28 years ago
   - 38 million years ago
   - 30 thousand years ago

Review Items

Write what kind of horse each picture shows.

• racehorse • quarter horse • pony • Mongolian horse • draft horse

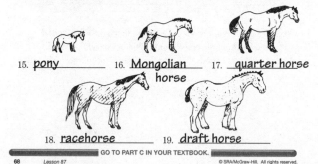

15. pony 16. Mongolian horse 17. quarter horse

18. racehorse 19. draft horse

GO TO PART C IN YOUR TEXTBOOK.

 © SRA/McGraw-Hill. All rights reserved.

TEXTBOOK

C Number your paper from 1 through 20.

Skill Item

1. Compare the way people ate 80 thousand years ago and the way we eat today. The people who lived 80 thousand years ago ____.

Review Items

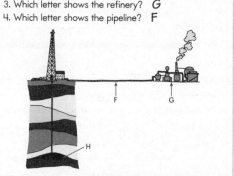

2. Which letter shows the crude oil? H
3. Which letter shows the refinery? G
4. Which letter shows the pipeline? F

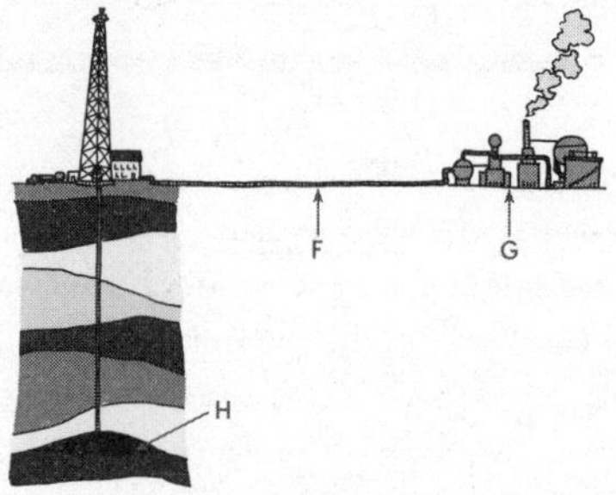

1. Ideas: The people who lived 80 thousand years ago did not cook their meat, but we do; the people who lived 80 thousand years ago ate inside caves, but we eat inside houses.

TEXTBOOK

5. Which arrow shows the direction the crude oil is moving at A? C
6. Which arrow shows the direction the crude oil is moving at B? F

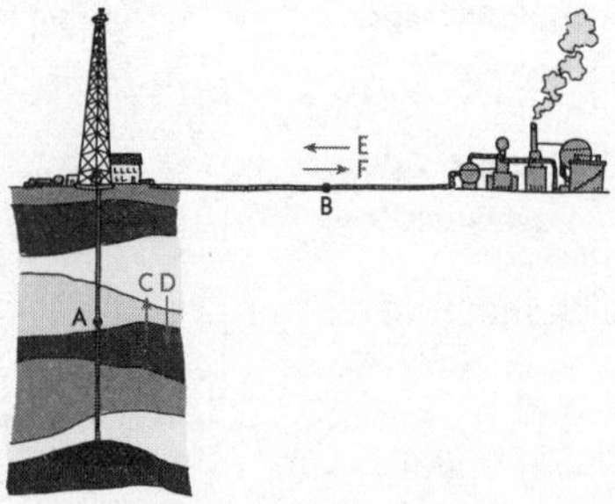

Write each sentence using other words for the word **weakness.**

7. Her **weakness** was her weak knees.
8. His anger was his **weakness.**

7. Her Achilles heel was her weak knees.
8. His anger was his Achilles heel.

TEXTBOOK

12. Idea: bones with dog teeth marks and the bones of dogs in their piles

9. The arrow that killed Achilles hit him in the ____. heel
10. That arrow had something on it that killed Achilles. What did it have on it? poison
11. People who lived 80 thousand years ago did not have many things that we have today. Write the letters of 4 things they did not have. c, e, g, h

a. dogs	d. trees	g. telephones
b. bones	e. TV sets	h. books
c. refrigerators	f. food	i. dirt

12. Name 1 clue that tells us that dogs may have lived with people 8 thousand years ago.
13. Name one clue that tells us how people may have hunted large animals like buffalo.
14. Name 2 clues that tell us that people used fire to cook their food.
15. How many third-graders weigh as much as a Mongolian horse? 8
16. How many third-graders weigh as much as a draft horse? 30
17. How many third-graders weigh as much as a racehorse? 15
18. Which horse has a shorter back, a racehorse or a quarter horse?

13. Idea: broken buffalo bones (at bottom of cliff)
14. Any 2: ashes; burn marks on bones; smoke marks on rocks

19. The picture shows the outline of a hand on a cave wall. Which letter shows the part of the wall that was covered with paint? **C**
20. Which letter shows the part of the wall that was not covered with paint? **B**

Name _____

Story Items

1. Eohippus lived __38__ million years ago.
2. **Underline** 2 ways that the front legs of eohippus were different from the front legs of a horse that lives today.

   - <u>They were smaller.</u>   • They had smaller hooves.
   - <u>They didn't have hooves.</u>   • They were faster.

3. The changes in the legs made horses __faster__
4. Who was faster, eohippus or large cats? __large cats__
5. Over millions of years, what happened to the size of horses?
   __Idea: They got bigger.__
6. Bigger animals are safer because ▓▓▓▓.

   • not as many animals run faster
   • not as many animals are smaller
   • <u>not as many animals hunt bigger animals</u>

7. Which animal is safer, an elephant or a mouse? __elephant__
8. Tell why. __Idea: Not many animals hunt bigger animals.__
9. Was the author's purpose to **persuade, inform,** or **entertain?**
   __inform__

Review Items

10. The horse skeleton in layer A is no bigger than a ▓▓▓.

    • big dog   • <u>small dog</u>   • pony
11. The horse skeleton in layer B is about as big as a ▓▓▓.

    • <u>big dog</u>   • small dog   • pony
12. The horse skeleton in layer C is about as big as a ▓▓▓.

    • big dog   • small dog   • <u>pony</u>
13. Write the words **earlier** and **later** in the right boxes.
14. How many years ago did layer A go into the pile?
    __38 million years ago__
15. How many years ago did layer B go into the pile?
    __28 million years ago__
16. How many years ago did layer C go into the pile?
    __11 million years ago__
17. How many years ago did layer D go into the pile?
    __1 million years ago__
18. How many years ago did layer E go into the pile?
    __30 thousand years ago__

	later
E	NOW Story of Troy 30 thousand years ago
D	1 million years ago
C	11 million years ago
B	28 million years ago
A	38 million years ago
	earlier

GO TO PART C IN YOUR TEXTBOOK.

Not many animals hunt elephants. A rabbit is a very small animal. Many animals hunt rabbits.

When horses were very small, many animals hunted them. When horses got bigger, not as many animals hunted them. So the bigger horses could go out into the open more than smaller horses. Large cats hunted big horses, but if a large cat came along, the big horse could run away from the cat.

Here's the last rule about horses: **Animals are safer when they run together in a herd.** Wild horses run together in herds.

So horses changed in three ways. They became bigger. They became faster. They ran in herds.

THE END

C Number your paper from 1 through 20.

Story Items

1. Horses changed in 3 ways. **Write the letters** of those 3 ways. c, f, g
   a. They became slower.   e. They lived alone.
   b. They lived in caves.   f. They became bigger.
   c. They became faster.   g. They ran in herds.
   d. They became smaller.

2. Idea: poured boiling water into the holes

Review Items

2. When the Greek army dug holes under the wall, what did the people of Troy do?
3. When the Greek army put ladders against the wall of Troy, what did the people of Troy do?
4. Why couldn't the Greek army starve the people of Troy?
5. When the Greek army tried to knock down the gate, what did the people of Troy do?

6. What is the name of the vehicle in the picture? *chariot*
7. How many wheels does the vehicle have? **2**
8. What is pulling the vehicle? **horses**
9. What is soldier R doing? *steering the chariot*
10. What is soldier S doing? *shooting an arrow*

Soldier S   Soldier R

3. Idea: pushed them off
4. Idea: The people of Troy had lots of food and water.
5. Idea: poured boiling water on them

304   Lesson 88

---

11. Ideas: caves; garbage piles

11. What's a good place to look for clues about people who lived long ago?
12. Some people who lived 80 thousand years ago lived in ▓▓▓▓. **caves**
13. Did the first people who lived in caves cook their food? **no**
14. Did the people who lived in caves many years later cook their food? **yes**

15. When we dig into the pile in the picture, what's the first thing we find?
16. What's the next thing we find? **sand**
17. What's the next thing we find? **shells**
18. What's the next thing we find?
19. What's the last thing we find? **mud**
15. **small stones**
18. **large stones**

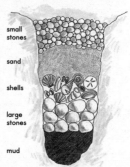

small stones
sand
shells
large stones
mud

20. The earliest horses on Earth are not alive today. How long ago did the earliest horses live?
• 38 million years ago • 38 thousand years ago
• 38 years ago

Lesson 88   305

89

Name _____

A

Pretend you are Bertha and fill out the form below. The facts that you need are in Part B on page 307 of your textbook.

1. Last Name **Turner**   2. First Name **Bertha**
3. Street Address **2233 Forest Street**
4. City **San Francisco**   5. State **California**
6. Phone Number **345-1101**
7. How much money are you putting in the bank? $ **500**

B Story Items

8. What do people keep in banks? **money**
9. What kind of job did Andrew Dexter have? **bank teller**
10. When Andrew was young, was he very strong? **no**
11. In high school, Andrew went out for 3 teams. **Underline** those 3 teams.
• soccer • basketball • hockey • baseball • golf • tennis • football
12. Was Andrew good enough for the teams? **no**
13. Andrew spent lots of time doing 2 things. Name those 2 things.
Idea: He watched and he daydreamed.
14. In real life, did many people love Andrew? **no**
15. In Andrew's dreams, how did people feel about him?
Ideas: They loved him; they thought he was a star.

Lesson 89   71

---

16. What kind of place is in this picture? **bank**
17. **Circle** the teller.
18. Write **C** on the counter.
19. Write **P** on the person who is giving money to the teller.
20. Write **L** on the person who is leaving.

GO TO PART D IN YOUR TEXTBOOK.

72   Lesson 89

The crowd cheers. "That guy is great," they yell.

Then Andrew has a turn at bat. BLAM—he blasts the ball completely out of sight.

The crowd goes wild. "We love Andrew," they yell. "We love him. He's the greatest player in the world."

And Andrew becomes a star: a super, super, super star.

Andrew's dreams were just like the dreams that you may have. In Andrew's dreams, people loved him. But Andrew's dreams were just dreams. In real life, not many people loved him. In fact, not many people noticed that he was around.

Get a picture of Andrew. There he was, working in the bank. He did his job, but his mind was often far from the bank. He dreamed about being important. He wanted to be the star. He wanted people to love him.

MORE NEXT TIME

D Number your paper from 1 through 16.

Skill Items

The customer bought a valuable gift.
1. What word tells that something is worth a lot?
2. What word names a person who buys things?

1. valuable
2. customer

Review Items
3. During a storm, which comes first, lightning or thunder?
4. How does fire like to move, up or down?
5. Let's say that Sally claps her hands. What would you do to imitate Sally? **clap my hands**

6. The cave people learned two rules about fire: If you put things in the fire, those things will get ▇▇▇. **hot**
7. The fire makes the cave ▇▇▇. **warm**

8. The people who lived in caves drew pictures on the cave walls. Write the letters of 4 things they made pictures of. **a, b, d, f**
   a. cows   b. horses   c. birds   d. elephants
   e. fish   f. hands   g. bears   h. dogs
9. Cave people painted pictures of horses on cave walls. How are those horses different from horses that live today? **Idea: They were smaller.**

10. Eohippus lived ▇▇▇ million years ago. **38**
11. The front legs of eohippus were different from the front legs of a horse that lives today. Write the letters of 2 ways that they were different. **b, d**
   a. They were faster.   b. They were smaller.
   c. They had smaller hooves. d. They didn't have hooves.

---

12. Over millions of years, horses changed in size. What happened to the size of horses? **They got bigger.**
13. Bigger animals are safer because ▇▇▇.
    • not as many animals are smaller
    • not as many animals hunt bigger animals
    • not as many animals run faster

14. Which animal is safer, a horse or a mouse?
15. Why? **Idea: because it is bigger**

16. Horses changed in 3 ways. Write the letters of those 3 ways.
    a. They became slower.   e. They lived in caves.
    b. They ran in herds.   f. They became faster.
    c. They lived alone.   g. They became smaller.
    d. They became bigger.

TEST 9   90

Number your paper from 1 through 30.
1. Which army was Achilles in during the war between Troy and Greece? **Greek**
2. How long was Achilles in the war? **10 years**
3. Who was the greatest soldier of Troy? **Hector**
4. Who won when Hector and Achilles fought? **Achilles**
5. Achilles rode around the wall of Troy in a ▇▇▇. **chariot**
6. What's a good place to look for clues about people who lived long ago? **Ideas: in their garbage; in caves**
7. Some people who lived 80 thousand years ago lived in ▇▇▇. **caves**
8. Things closer to the bottom of the pile went into the pile ▇▇▇. **earlier**
9. Things closer to the top of the pile went into the pile ▇▇▇. **later**

10. Which thing went into the pile earlier, thing R or thing X? **R**
11. Which thing went into the pile later, thing R or thing T? **R**

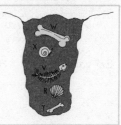

12. When we dig into the pile in the picture, what's the first thing we find? **small stones**
13. What's the next thing we find? **sand**
14. What's the last thing we find? **mud**

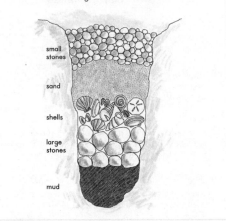

small stones

sand

shells

large stones

mud

15. During a storm, which comes first,  or thunder?
16. How does fire like to move, or down?
17. The people who lived in caves drew pictures on the cave walls. Write the letters of 4 things they made pictures of. **d, e, f, g**

    a. dogs   e. cows
    b. bears   f. horses
    c. fish   g. elephants
    d. hands   h. birds

Write what kind of horse each picture shows.
- racehorse   • quarter horse   • pony
- Mongolian horse   • draft horse

18. **Mongolian horse**   19. **quarter horse**   20. **draft horse**   21. **pony**

22. How many third-graders weigh as much as a draft horse? **30**
23. How many third-graders weigh as much as a Mongolian horse? **8**
24. How many third-graders weigh as much as a racehorse? **15**
25. Eohippus lived ▯▯▯▯ million years ago. **38**

26. Horses changed in 3 ways. Write the letters of those 3 ways. **b, c, f**
    a. They lived in caves.   e. They became smaller.
    b. They became bigger.   f. They became faster.
    c. They ran in herds.   g. They became slower.
    d. They lived alone.

Skill Items

For each item, write the underlined word from the sentences in the box.

> The adults huddled around the fire.
> The customer bought a valuable gift.

27. What underlining means **grown-ups**? **adults**
28. What underlining tells that something is worth a lot?
29. What underlining tells that the adults crowded together? **huddled**
30. What underlining names a person who buys things?

28. valuable   30. customer

━━━ END OF TEST 9 ━━━

Name _____

Ⓐ

1. When was the check below written? **March 10, 2006**
2. Who should the bank pay? **Tom Lee**
3. How much should the bank pay? **$10 (ten dollars)**
4. Whose money should the bank use to pay Tom Lee?
   Rod Mack's

	March 10, 2006
Pay to ___Tom Lee___	$10
___Ten___	**dollars**
	Rod Mack

Ⓑ Story Items

5. When Andrew said, "Thank you" to the first customer, what did the first customer say? **nothing**
6. When the second customer came to Andrew, Andrew was daydreaming. What was he daydreaming about?
   - football   • baseball   • basketball

WORKBOOK

7. Andrew noticed something on the counter when he finished with the second customer. What was on the counter? a package

8. Where did Mr. Franks want Andrew to take the package?
   - to Magnetic Research Company
   - to Magnetic Tape Company
   - to Magnetic Refill Company

9. Did Andrew know what was in the package? no

10. Was the package **heavy** or **light?** heavy

11. As Andrew drove to Magnetic Research Company, what was he thinking about? basketball

12. Why did a woman in a car yell at Andrew?
    Idea: He was in her lane.

13. After the woman yelled at him, he told himself to pay attention to
    his driving.

GO TO PART D IN YOUR TEXTBOOK.

TEXTBOOK

jumps up and shoots. The ball slowly sails toward the basket. Then it slowly drops—right through the basket.

The sound of the crowd is so loud that the floor shakes. The fans are yelling, screaming, leaping from their seats. People are lifting Andrew onto their shoulders. They are carrying him from . . .

"Watch where you're driving," yelled the woman in the car next to Andrew's car. "Stay in your own lane."

"Sorry," Andrew said softly. He told himself to pay attention to his driving.

MORE NEXT TIME

D **Number your paper from 1 through 21.**

Skill Items

Use the words in the box to write complete sentences.

valuable	dollars	hollow	adults	dozen
noticed	huddled	enough	customer	million

1. The ___ ___ around the fire.
2. The ___ bought a ___ gift.

1. The adults huddled around the fire.
2. The customer bought a valuable gift.

TEXTBOOK

Review Items

3. Which letter shows where the ground gets warm first? J
4. Which letter shows where the ground gets warm last? S

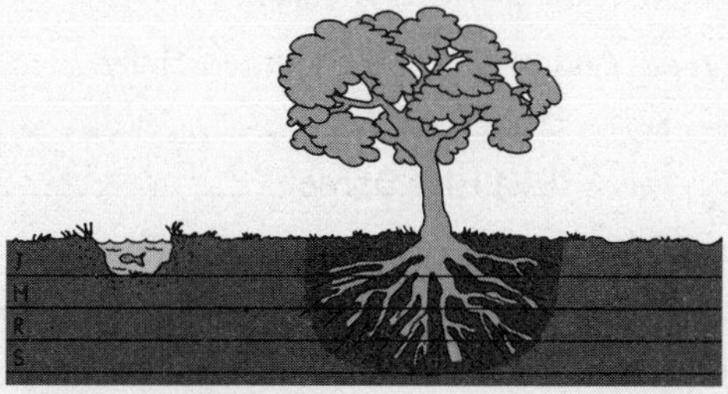

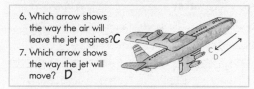

5. In which season is the danger of forest fires greatest? fall

6. Which arrow shows the way the air will leave the jet engines? C
7. Which arrow shows the way the jet will move? D

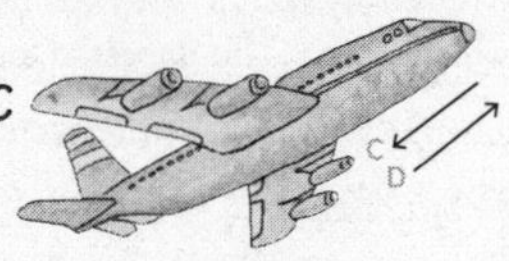

8. You can see drops of water on grass early in the morning. What are those drops called? dew

TEXTBOOK

9. The picture shows objects caught in a giant whirlpool. The path is shown for object A. Will the path for object B go around **more times** or **fewer times?** (more times)
10. Which path will go around the fewest times, the path for A, B, or C? (A)

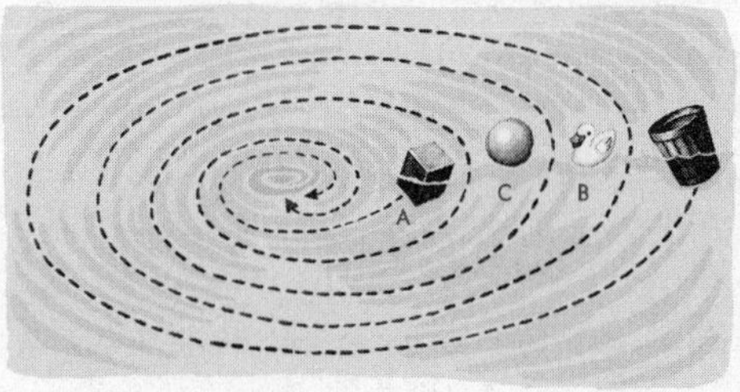

11. Airplanes unload at gates. Ships unload at ___. docks
12. Airplanes are pulled by little trucks. Ships are pulled by ___. tugboats
13. Airplanes land at airports. Ships land at ___. harbors
14. How many ships sailed to Troy? 1 thousand
15. How long did the war between Greece and Troy go on? 10 years

16. If the Greek army could get a few men inside the wall of Troy, these men could ▓▓▓. **open the gate**

17. What kind of place is in the picture? **bank**
18. What do we call the person who stands behind the counter and takes people's money? **bank teller**

19. What part of the world is shown on the map?
20. How far is it from H to G? **25 hundred miles**
21. How far is it from T to S? **13 hundred miles**

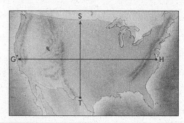

19. **United States**

92

Name _____

Story Items

1. Name 2 things that a strong magnet can pick up.
   (Any 2 metal objects:) nails, paper clips, etc.

2. Electricity can turn any steel bar into a magnet. What are these magnets called? **electromagnets**

3. **Underline** a place where these magnets are used.
   • schools   • <u>wrecking yards</u>   • parks   • banks

4. Andrew walked into a room that was filled with something. What was it filled with?
   • garbage   • fish   • <u>electricity</u>

5. What made the motor in the package run? **electricity**

6. Magnetic Research Company planned to put this kind of motor in ▓▓▓.
   • toasters   • refrigerators   • parks   • <u>cars</u>

7. When Andrew walked into the room, the motor melted and burned Andrew's **hands**

8. Did Andrew know what had happened to him? **no**

9. How did Andrew's legs and arms feel when he left Magnetic Research Company? **Idea: tingly**

10. What happened when Andrew tugged at his car door? _____
    Idea: It came off.

Review Items

Fill out the bank form below using these facts.

   • Your name is Sally Andrews.
   • You're going to put $100 in the bank.
   • You live at 144 High Street, Redding, California.
   • Your phone number is 555-3434.

11. Last name **Andrews**   12. First name **Sally**
13. Phone number **555-3434**
14. Street address **144 High Street**
15. City **Redding**   16. State **California**
17. How much money are you putting in the bank? **$100 (100 dollars)**

18. What do people keep in banks? **money**

19. Roots keep a tree from **falling over**

20. Roots carry **water** to all parts of the tree.

21. In which season is the danger of forest fires greatest? **fall**

22. **Underline** the 4 names that tell about time.
    • <u>week</u>   • inch   • centimeter   • <u>second</u>
    • <u>minute</u>   • meter   • <u>hour</u>

23. A mile is a little more than ▓▓▓ feet.
    • 1 thousand   • <u>5 thousand</u>   • 5 hundred

▬▬▬▬▬ GO TO PART C IN YOUR TEXTBOOK. ▬▬▬▬▬

The man touched the package again. This time he didn't get a shock. He pulled Andrew's fingers from the package. Then he opened the package. "Oh no," he said. "Look at it. It's completely wrecked."

The woman shook her head. "Two years. It took us two years to make that machine. And look at it now."

Before Andrew left the building, a doctor examined him. The doctor put some oily stuff on Andrew's hands. He asked, "How do you feel?"

Andrew said, "I'm all right," but he felt very strange. His hands and arms tingled. His legs tingled. Even his eyes had a kind of tingling feeling. "I'm all right," he repeated.

But Andrew was not the same person that he had been. Andrew started to find out just how different he was when he left the Magnetic Research Company. His car door was stuck. So he gave it a tug. He pulled the door completely off the car.

MORE NEXT TIME

C Number your paper from 1 through 11.
1. Write the letters of the 5 names that tell about length.
   - a. minute
   - b. hour
   - c. day
   - d. centimeter
   - e. second
   - f. yard
   - g. mile
   - h. meter
   - i. year
   - j. inch
   - k. week

Lesson 92   331

Review Items

2. Which liquid does the A show? crude oil
3. Which liquid does the B show? fresh water
4. Which liquid does the C show? salt water

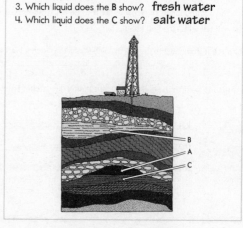

5. What do all living things need? water
6. What do all living things make? babies
7. Do all living things grow? yes
8. Gasoline comes from a liquid called ▓▓▓. crude oil

332   Lesson 92

9. What place does the A show? Italy
10. What place does the B show? Greece
11. What place does the C show? Troy

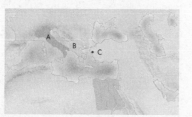

Lesson 92   333

93

Name _____

A

1. About how much does a leopard weigh?
   - • <u>100 pounds</u>   • 150 pounds   • 500 pounds
2. About how much weight can a leopard carry? 150 pounds
3. About how much does a chimpanzee weigh? 100
4. About how much force can a chimpanzee pull with? 500 pounds

B Story Items

5. Andrew is now as strong as ▓▓▓.
   - • an alligator   • <u>an African elephant</u>   • a leopard
6. Andrew knew that Mr. Franks was mad by looking at his
   eyebrows
7. Andrew didn't ring the bell by the front door at Magnetic Research Company. Tell why.
   Idea: He didn't see the bell.
8. What happened to Andrew after Mr. Franks had a talk with him?
   - • Andrew was fried.   • Andrew was tired.   • <u>Andrew was fired.</u>
9. How high did Andrew jump to catch the baseball? 3 yards
10. Had anybody ever jumped that high before Andrew did? no
11. Andrew threw the ball to the catcher. How fast did that ball move?
    (over) 100 miles per hour

Lesson 93   77

The catcher is going to catch three different balls. Look at the speed of the three baseballs flying through the air. One ball will knock the catcher over. One ball will knock the catcher back a little bit, but it won't knock him over. One ball will do nothing.

12. Write **knock over** next to the ball that will knock the catcher over.

13. Start at the dot and make an arrow under the catcher to show which way he will fall when the ball knocks him over.

14. Write **knock a little** next to the ball that will knock the catcher back a little.

15. Write **nothing** next to the ball that will not knock the catcher back at all.

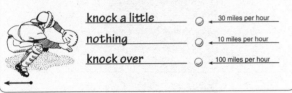

knock a little _____ ○← 30 miles per hour

nothing _____ ○← 10 miles per hour

knock over _____ ○← 100 miles per hour

←

GO TO PART D IN YOUR TEXTBOOK.

D Number your paper from 1 through 18.

Skill Items

> They had reasons for interrupting her talk.
> 1. What word tells about why they interrupted her talk?
> 2. What word tells that they didn't let her finish talking?

Review Items
3. Name 2 things that a strong magnet can pick up.
4. Electricity can turn any steel bar into a magnet. What are these magnets called? electromagnets
5. Name a place where these magnets are used.

1. reasons
2. interrupting
3. Any 2 things made of metal: paper clips, nails, etc.
4. Idea: wrecking yard

---

6. A forest fire may burn for ▮▮▮.
 • hours   • weeks   • minutes
7. A forest fire kills both ▮▮▮ and ▮▮▮.
 • plants   • whales   • fish   • animals
8. About how many years could it take for the forest to grow back?
 • 20 years   • 200 years   • 100 years

Each statement tells about how far something goes or how fast something goes. Write **how far** or **how fast** for each item.
 9. He ran 5 miles. how far
10. He ran 5 miles per hour. how fast
11. The plane was 500 miles from New York City. how far
12. The plane was flying 500 miles per hour. how fast

13. Write the letter of the tree that has deeper roots. A
14. Write the letter of the tree that begins to grow first every year. B

A   B

---

15. When was the check below written?
16. Who should the bank pay? Kim Johns
17. How much should the bank pay?
18. Whose money should the bank use to pay Kim Johns?

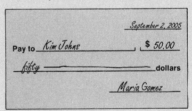

September 2, 2005

Pay to Kim Johns _____ $ 50.00

fifty _____ dollars

Maria Gomez

15. September 2, 2005
17. fifty dollars ($ 50)
18. Maria Gomez's

WORKBOOK

Name _____

A

> **Write the name of each part of a football player's uniform.**
>
> • shoulders • hat • shoulder pads • knee pads • helmet
>
>
>
> 1. <u>helmet</u> 2. <u>shoulder pads</u>

3. How long is a football field? **100 yards**

4. **Underline** 2 ways that a football team can move the ball down the field.

• slide • <u>pass</u> • roll • <u>run</u>

5. If a team moves the ball all the way to the other end of the field, that team gets points. How many points? **6**

6. If team A has the ball, team B tries to ▮▮▮.

• kick the ball • catch the passes
• <u>tackle the player with the ball</u> • kick the player with the ball

B Story Items

7. Andrew did two impossible things at the playground. How high did he jump? **3 yards**

8. How fast did he throw the ball? **100 miles per hour**

9. Denny Brock was a ▮▮▮.

• player • guard • <u>coach</u>

Lesson 94 79

WORKBOOK

10. Denny Brock was almost always mad because his team was **Ideas: the worst; very bad; etc.**

11. The people who owned the Titans were unhappy. Who did they say they might fire? **(coach) Denny Brock**

12. How many fans came to the ball park to watch most professional teams? **50 thousand**

13. How many fans came to the ball park to watch the Titans? **15 thousand**

14. Why did Andrew lie to the guard? **Idea: because he wanted to meet Denny**

15. Did Denny want to talk to Andrew? **no**

16. What did Denny say he would do if Andrew didn't leave? **Idea: have Andrew thrown out**

Skill Items

> Here's the rule: **The more fans that come to a game, the more money the team gets from tickets.**

17. **Circle** the name of the team that gets the most money from tickets.

18. **Underline** the name of the team that gets the least money from tickets.

> • Rams .... 50 thousand fans
> • (Wildcats) .... 60 thousand fans
> • Jets .... 40 thousand fans
> • Chargers .... 50 thousand fans
> • <u>Spartans</u> .... 30 thousand fans
> • Bulls .... 50 thousand fans

GO TO PART D IN YOUR TEXTBOOK.

80 Lesson 94

TEXTBOOK

1. The [customer] bought a [valuable] gift.
2. They had [reasons] for [interrupting] her talk.

Denny yelled, "That guard should know better than that. Now get out of here. We're having a practice."

"I can help your team," Andrew said. "I'm very good at . . . "

"Are you deaf?" Denny yelled. "I said get out of here."

"But I can help your . . . "

"Listen, buddy, get out of here or I'll have you thrown out."

MORE NEXT TIME

D Number your paper from 1 through 19.

Skill Items

> **Use the words in the box to write complete sentences.**
>
> | | | | |
> |---|---|---|---|
> | interrupting | power | tingling | company |
> | customer | magnetic | valuable | reasons |

1. The ▮▮▮ bought a ▮▮▮ gift.
2. They had ▮▮▮ for ▮▮▮ her talk.

Review Items

3. When do trees begin to grow?

• in the winter • [in the spring]

4. Trees begin to grow when their roots get ▮▮▮. **warm(er)**

350 Lesson 94

TEXTBOOK

5. Write the letter of the tree that has deeper roots. **R**
6. Write the letter of the tree that begins to grow first every year. **M**

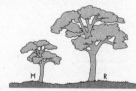

7. A forest fire may burn for ▮▮▮.
• hours • minutes • [weeks]
8. A forest fire kills both ▮▮▮ and ▮▮▮.
• whales • [plants] • fish • [animals]
9. About how many years could it take for the forest to grow back?
• 20 years • 100 years • [200 years]

10. The names in one box tell about time. Write the letter of that box. **B**
11. The names in one box tell about length. Write the letter of that box. **A**

A	yard	centimeter	inch	meter	mile
B	week	year	second	month	minute	hour

Lesson 94 351

123

12. Does a housefly weigh **more than a gram** or less than a gram?

13. Does a long pencil weigh more than a gram or less than a gram?

14. If you get smaller, your voice gets ▉▉▉. **Idea: higher**

15. Jean got smaller. So what do you know about Jean's voice? **Idea: It got higher.**

Use these answers:
- 100 pounds   - 150 pounds   - 500 pounds

16. About how much does a chimpanzee weigh?
17. About how much force can a chimpanzee pull with?
18. About how much does a leopard weigh?
19. About how much weight can a leopard carry?

16. **100 pounds**
17. **500 pounds**
18. **100 pounds**
19. **150 pounds**

352   *Lesson 94*

Name _____

Ⓐ

1. A second is a unit of ▉▉▉.
   - weight   - length   - **time**

2. Which stopwatch shows that 2 seconds have passed? **C**
3. Which stopwatch shows that 6 seconds have passed? **D**
4. Which stopwatch shows that 8 seconds have passed? **B**

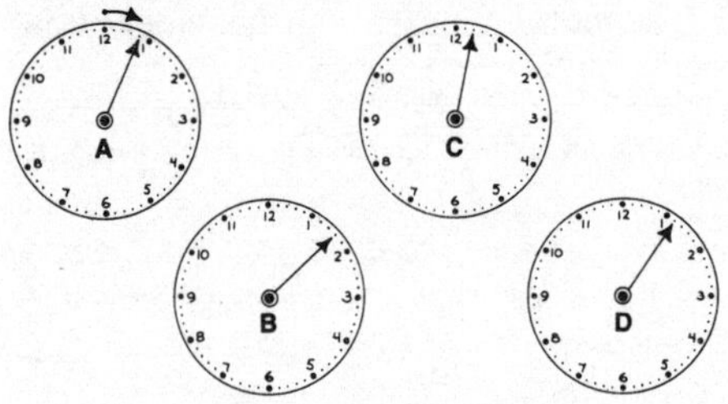

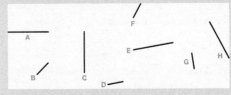

Ⓑ Story Items

5. The player who pulled his leg muscle was the ▉▉▉ for the Titans.
   - passer   - **kicker**   - runner

6. How did Denny feel about that player getting hurt? **Ideas: mad; upset**
7. Did Denny believe that Andrew could kick? **no**
8. Did Andrew know what hang-time is? **yes**
9. Andrew didn't tell what hang-time is because he was ▉▉▉.
   - **uneasy**   - sweating   - smiling

Lesson 95   **81**

---

10. If the hang-time for a kick is 4 seconds, how long does the ball stay in the air? **4 seconds**

11. Andrew was standing on the field holding the football. Who was watching him? **Idea: (all) the players and coaches**

12. Denny told Andrew, "I want to see a **four**-second hang-time."

13. **Circle** the longest hang-time.

14. **Underline** the shortest hang-time.
   - 3 seconds   - (7 seconds)   - 5 seconds   - 2 seconds

Review Items

Write the name of each part of a football player's uniform.
- knee pads   - hat   - shoulders   - helmet   - shoulder pads

15. **shoulder pads**    16. **helmet**

═══ GO TO PART D IN YOUR TEXTBOOK. ═══

82   *Lesson 95*

He heard a couple of the players yelling, "Look at that. He's holding the ball all wrong." They laughed louder.
MORE NEXT TIME

Ⓓ Number your paper from 1 through 18.
Review Items

Some of the lines in the box are one inch long and some are one centimeter long.

1. Write the letter of every line that is one centimeter long. **B, D, F, G**
2. Write the letter of every line that is one inch long.

[Diagram with lines labeled A, B, C, D, E, F, G, H]

3. When we weigh very small things, the unit we use is ▉▉▉. **gram(s)**
4. If you get smaller, your voice gets ▉▉▉. **Idea: higher**
5. Lynn got smaller. So what do you know about Lynn's voice? **Idea: It got higher.**

2. **A, C, E, H**

358   *Lesson 95*

TEXTBOOK

Each statement tells about how far something goes or how fast something goes. Write **how far** or **how fast** for each item.
6. Jean walked 4 miles per hour. **how fast**
7. Jean walked 4 miles. **how far**
8. The train was going 100 miles per hour. **how fast**
9. The train was 100 miles from Denver. **how far**

Here's how fast different things can go:
 • 20 miles per hour • 35 miles per hour
 • 200 miles per hour • 500 miles per hour
10. Which speed tells how fast a jet can fly?
11. Which speed tells how fast a fast man can run?
12. Which speed tells how fast a fast dog can run?

13. How long is a football field? **100 yards**
14. Write 2 ways that a football team can move the ball down the field.
 • roll • slide • <u>pass</u> • <u>run</u>
15. How many parts does the body of an insect have? **3**
16. How many legs does an insect have? **6**
17. How many legs does a spider have? **8**
18. How many parts does a spider's body have? **2**

10. **500 miles per hour**
11. **20 miles per hour**
12. **35 miles per hour**

Lesson 95 **359**

WORKBOOK

Name _____

Story Items

1. Andrew kicked the football two times. Why was it hard to see the ball when Andrew kicked it?
 • <u>It moved so fast.</u> • It moved so slowly.
  • It made so much noise.

2. The coaches and players were silent right after Andrew kicked the ball the first time because they were ▓▓▓.
 • watching Andrew • <u>watching the ball</u> • making jokes

3. When the first ball stopped rolling, the players began to yell at Andrew. What did they want Andrew to do? **Idea: kick the ball again**

4. What was Andrew's hang-time the first time he kicked the ball? **9 seconds**

5. What was Andrew's hang-time the second time he kicked the ball? **11 seconds**

6. How many people in the world besides Andrew could kick a ball with a hang-time of more than 9 seconds? **none**

7. After his second kick how did the players treat Andrew? **Idea: like a star**

8. Denny was being nice to Andrew at the end of the story because he wanted Andrew to **Idea: play for the Titans**.

9. Was the author's purpose to **persuade, inform** or **entertain**? **entertain**

Lesson 96 **83**

96

WORKBOOK

Review Items

10. Did the first people who lived in caves cook their food? **no**

11. Did the people who lived in caves many years later cook their food? **yes**

12. The picture shows the outline of a hand on a cave wall. Which letter shows the part of the wall that was covered with paint? **R**

13. Which letter shows the part of the wall that was not covered with paint? **M**

_____ GO TO PART C IN YOUR TEXTBOOK. _____

TEXTBOOK

C Number your paper from 1 through 21.
Review Items
1. Which is longer, a yard or a meter?
2. Which is longer, a centimeter or a meter?
3. How many centimeters long is a meter? **100**

4. How fast is truck **A** going? **50 miles per hour**
5. How fast is truck **B** going. **35 miles per hour**
6. Which truck is going faster? **A**

A
50

B
35

Write what kind of horse each picture shows.
 • racehorse • quarter horse • pony
  • Mongolian horse • draft horse

7. **pony** 8. **racehorse** 9. **draft horse**

10. A second is a unit of ▓▓▓.
 • length • weight • time • distance

364 *Lesson 96*

125

TEXTBOOK

chariot

11. What is the name of the vehicle in the picture?
12. How many wheels does the vehicle have? **2**
13. What is pulling the vehicle? **horses**
14. What is soldier P doing? **steering**
15. What is soldier J doing? **shooting arrow**

Soldier J   Soldier P

16. Which stopwatch shows that 3 seconds have passed? **D**
17. Which stopwatch shows that 9 seconds have passed? **A**
18. Which stopwatch shows that 5 seconds have passed? **C**

TEXTBOOK

19. Write the letter of the sun you see at noon. **N**
20. Write the letter of the sun you see at sunset. **L**
21. Write the letter of the sun you see early in the morning. **P**

West   East

WORKBOOK

97

Name _____

A

1. Who makes more money, a professional football player or a bank teller?
   <u>a professional football player</u>

2. Which football players are worth the most money?
   - the worst players
   - <u>the players that fans want to see</u>
   - the fastest players

3. A football player who is very good at running with the ball may earn 3 <u>million dollars</u> a year.

B Story Items

4. When Andrew said that he would play for the Titans, Denny didn't jump up and down with joy. What did Denny think Andrew was trying to do?
   - be friendly   • work hard   • <u>trick him</u>

5. When Denny wants a player for the Titans, he makes an offer to the player. Does the player usually take that offer? <u>no</u>

6. So Denny makes a new offer. For this offer Denny offers ▨▨▨.
   - less money   • the same money   • <u>more money</u>

7. Denny knew that if Andrew was on the team, fans would come to the games even if the Titans lost. Why would they come?
   <u>Idea: to see Andrew kick the ball</u>

WORKBOOK

8. How much was Andrew worth for each game that he played?
   - <u>more than 1 million dollars</u>   • less than 1 million dollars
   - 200 thousand dollars   • 2 hundred dollars each month
   - 2 thousand dollars each month   • 20 thousand dollars each month

9. How much money did Andrew ask for?
   <u>2 thousand dollars each month</u>

10. How much money per month did Denny say he would pay Andrew?
    <u>20 thousand dollars each month</u>

11. How much money is that per year?
    - 100 thousand dollars   • 240 dollars   • <u>240 thousand dollars</u>

12. After the men shook hands, both men were happy. Denny was happy because he <u>Idea: He didn't have to pay Andrew very much money</u>

13. Andrew was happy because he <u>Idea: never thought that he would earn so much money ($ 20,000 a month)</u>

Review Items

14. What part of a car tells how fast the car is moving?
    <u>speedometer</u>

15. Which army was Achilles in during the war between Troy and Greece? <u>Greek</u>

16. How long was Achilles in the war? <u>10 years</u>

17. Who was the greatest soldier of Troy? <u>Hector</u>

18. Who won when Hector and Achilles fought? <u>Achilles</u>

19. Achilles rode around the wall of Troy in a <u>chariot</u>

▨▨▨ GO TO PART D IN YOUR TEXTBOOK. ▨▨▨

what you're doing. No player of mine is going to work for only 2 thousand dollars a month. I'll pay you 20 thousand dollars a month. That's 240 thousand dollars a year."

Andrew had seen a lot of money when he worked in the bank. He had counted piles of money worth more than 20 thousand dollars, but he never thought that he would earn 20 thousand dollars a month. "That's great," Andrew said, smiling. "That's really great."

The men shook hands again. Denny was very happy because he didn't pay Andrew very much. Andrew was very happy because he was going to make more money than he ever thought he'd make.

MORE NEXT TIME

D Number your paper from 1 through 19.
Skill Items

> He frequently argued about the championship.

1. What word names a contest between the two best teams? **championship**
2. What word means **often**? **frequently**
3. What word tells what he did that showed he didn't agree? **argued**

Review Items

4. Things closer to the top of the pile went into the pile ▨▨. **later**
5. Things closer to the bottom of the pile went into the pile ▨▨. **earlier**
6. The people who lived in caves drew pictures on the cave walls. Write the letters of 4 things they made pictures of.
   |a.|cows |b.|horses |c.|elephants   d. birds
   e. fish |f.|hands   g. dogs   h. bears
7. If the hang-time for a kick is 7 seconds, how long does the ball stay in the air? **7 seconds**

8. Write the letter of the shortest hang-time. **d**
9. Write the letter of the longest hang-time. **a**
   a. 9 seconds   b. 4 seconds
   c. 6 seconds   d. 3 seconds

10. The temperature inside your body is about ▨▨ degrees when you are healthy. **98**
11. Most fevers don't go over ▨▨ degrees. **101**

---

12. 38 million years ago
13. 28 million years ago

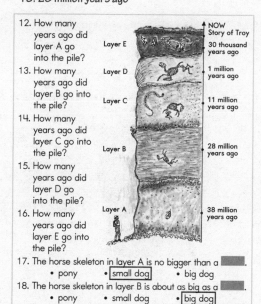

12. How many years ago did layer A go into the pile?
13. How many years ago did layer B go into the pile?
14. How many years ago did layer C go into the pile?
15. How many years ago did layer D go into the pile?
16. How many years ago did layer E go into the pile?

Layer E — NOW Story of Troy — 30 thousand years ago
Layer D — 1 million years ago
Layer C — 11 million years ago
Layer B — 28 million years ago
Layer A — 38 million years ago

17. The horse skeleton in layer A is no bigger than a ▨▨.
    • pony   • small dog   • big dog
18. The horse skeleton in layer B is about as big as a ▨▨.
    • pony   • small dog   • big dog
19. The horse skeleton in layer C is about as big as a ▨▨.
    • pony   • small dog   • big dog

14. 11 million years ago
15. 1 million years ago
16. 30 thousand years ago

Name _____
Story Items

1. Before Andrew's first game, announcements appeared in the newspapers. The announcements gave the impression that Andrew could turn the Titans into ▨▨.
   • a baseball team   • a winning team   • a losing team
2. Did the announcements tell what Andrew could do? **no**
3. How many fans came to Andrew's first game?
   (over) 50 thousand
4. Who were the fans talking about?
   Andrew
5. The fans didn't think the Titans would win because they were playing
   Idea: the best team in the league (the Wildcats)
6. How did the players feel just before the game started?
   • sleepy   • nervous   • happy
7. Andrew was more frightened than the other players because he had never ▨▨.
   • seen 50 thousand people   • played in front of 50 thousand people
8. Who kicked the ball at the beginning of the game? **Andrew**
9. Which team caught the ball? **Titans**
10. How far was the ball from the goal line? **10 yards**
11. How far did the Titans need to go to score their first touchdown?
    10 yards

12. The Wildcats got the ball. Tell **2** ways they moved the ball down the field. **Idea: passing and running**

13. How did the Titans get the ball back?
    - A Wildcat passed the ball.   • <u>A Wildcat fumbled the ball.</u>
        - A Wildcat ran with the ball.

14. What did the crowd do when the Titans began to lose yards?
    Idea: booed

15. Did the crowd laugh when they heard that Andrew was going to kick an 80-yard goal? **no**

━━━━━━━━━━ GO TO PART C IN YOUR TEXTBOOK. ━━━━━━━━━━

---

1. reasons, interrupting
2. frequently, argued, championship

C Number your paper from 1 through 19.

Skill Items

Use the words in the box to write complete sentences.

uniform	interesting	frequently	scolded	interrupting
arranged	reasons	championship	mistake	argued

1. They had ▓▓▓ for ▓▓▓ her talk.
2. He ▓▓▓ ▓▓▓ about the ▓▓▓.

Review Items

3. During a storm, which comes first, lightning or thunder?
4. How does fire like to move, up or down?
5. Cave people painted pictures of horses on cave walls. How are those horses different from horses that live today? **Idea: They are smaller.**
6. Which horse has a longer back, a racehorse or a quarter horse?
7. Eohippus lived ▓▓▓ million years ago. **38**
8. The front legs of eohippus were different from the front legs of a horse that lives today. Write the letters of 2 ways that they were different.
    - a. They didn't have hooves.   b. They had smaller hooves.
    - c. They were smaller.   d. They were faster.

---

9. Which animal is safer, a bear or a rabbit?
10. Why? **Idea: because a bear is bigger**

11. How fast is car **A** going? **15 miles per hour**
12. How fast is car **B** going? **50 miles per hour**
13. Which car is going faster? **B**

14. The arrow that killed Achilles hit him in the ▓▓▓. **heel**
15. That arrow had something on it that killed Achilles. What did it have on it? **poison**

---

16. Which thing went into the pile earlier, thing R or thing T?
17. Which thing went into the pile earlier, thing Y or thing J?
18. Which thing went into the pile later, thing R or thing X?
19. Which thing went into the pile later, thing J or thing T?

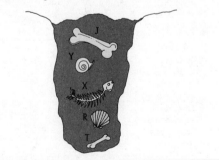

Name _____

Story Items

1. How far did Andrew kick the ball?
   - 100 yards   • 200 yards   • <u>180 yards</u>

2. It wasn't a field goal because it didn't **Idea: go through the upright poles**

3. The Wildcats were winning, and the Titans were getting hurt. Name the player who was hurting the Titans. **Smiling Sam**

4. **Underline** 3 things that tell what Smiling Sam looked like.
   - small
   - had no hair
   - had a friendly smile
   - old
   - fast
   - <u>had missing teeth</u>
   - <u>had a mean smile</u>
   - <u>big</u>

5. The coach didn't want Andrew to talk to Smiling Sam because he thought **Idea: Smiling Sam would hurt Andrew**

6. Andrew talked to Smiling Sam anyway. Did Andrew scare Smiling Sam? **no**

7. When the ball came to Andrew, he waited for somebody. Who? **Smiling Sam**

8. **Underline** 3 things that happened to Smiling Sam when Andrew hit him.
   - Sam tackled Andrew.
   - <u>Sam was knocked out.</u>
   - <u>Sam's teeth were loose.</u>
   - Sam's shirt was torn.
   - <u>Sam flew backwards.</u>

   Lesson 99   89

---

9. Why were the Titans surprised when Andrew ran with the ball? **Idea: They didn't know he could run with the ball.**

10. In the game with the Wildcats, Andrew scored **4** touchdowns.

11. Which team won the game? **Titans**

Review Items

Fill out the bank form below using these facts.
- Your name is Zack Morris.
- You're going to put $50 in the bank.
- You live at 1252 Main Street, Fort Worth, Texas.
- Your phone number is 651-1222.

12. Last name **Morris**   13. First name **Zack**

14. Phone number **651-1222**

15. Street address **1252 Main Street**

16. City **Fort Worth**   17. State **Texas**

18. How much money are you putting in the bank? **$50**

GO TO PART C IN YOUR TEXTBOOK.

90   Lesson 99

TEXTBOOK

Titan players crowded around Andrew. "Wow," one of them said. "You're the greatest."

"Yeah," another one said. "I didn't know you could run with the ball."

Andrew ran with the ball three more times during that game and he made three more touchdowns. The Titans won the game, 35 to 21.

MORE NEXT TIME

C Number your paper from 1 through 14.

Review Items

1. People who lived 80 thousand years ago did not have many things that we have today. Write the letters of **6** things they did not have.
   - a. dogs
   - e. bones
   - <u>i.</u> refrigerators
   - <u>b.</u> computers
   - <u>f.</u> TV sets
   - j. dirt
   - c. food
   - g. rocks
   - k. trees
   - <u>d.</u> stoves
   - <u>h.</u> cars
   - <u>l.</u> telephones

2. Name 2 things that a strong magnet can pick up.

3. Electricity can turn any steel bar into a magnet. What are these magnets called? **electromagnets**

4. Name a place where these magnets are used. **wrecking yard**

2. Any 2 items made of metal: nails, paper clips, etc.

386   Lesson 99

TEXTBOOK

5. When was the check below written? **June 3, 2006**
6. Who should the bank pay? **Ann Rogers**
7. How much should the bank pay? **twelve dollars ($12)**
8. Whose money should the bank use to pay Ann Rogers? **Alice Kapp's**

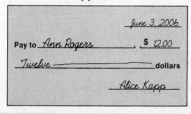

June 3, 2006

Pay to _Ann Rogers_ , $ _12.00_

Twelve _____ dollars

Alice Kapp

Use these answers:
   100 pounds   150 pounds   500 pounds

9. About how much does a leopard weigh?
10. About how much weight can a leopard carry?
11. About how much does a chimpanzee weigh?
12. About how much force can a chimpanzee pull with?

13. How long is a football field? **100 yards**
14. Write 2 ways that a football team can move the ball down the field.
   - <u>run</u>
   - <u>pass</u>
   - slide
   - roll

9. **100 pounds**   10. **150 pounds**   Lesson 99   387
11. **100 pounds**   12. **500 pounds**

100 | TEST 10

Number your paper from 1 through 27.

1. When was the check below written?
2. Who should the bank pay? **Sally Daniels**
3. How much should the bank pay?
4. Whose money should the bank use to pay Sally Daniels? **Chase Edwards'**

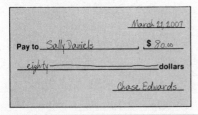

Pay to _Sally Daniels_ $ _80.00_

eighty ——————————dollars

Chase Edwards

March 21, 2007

5. Name **2** things that a strong magnet can pick up.
6. Electricity can turn any steel bar into a magnet. What are these magnets called? **electromagnets**
7. Name a place where these magnets are used.

1. March 21, 2007
3. eighty dollars ($80)
5. Any 2 items made of metal: nails, paper clips, etc.
7. Idea: wrecking yard

388   Lesson 100

Use these answers:

500 pounds   150 pounds   100 pounds

8. About how much weight can a leopard carry?
9. About how much does a leopard weigh?
10. About how much force can a chimpanzee pull with?
11. About how much does a chimpanzee weigh?

Write the name of each part of a football player's uniform.
- shoulders   • shoulder pads   • knee pads
- helmet   • hat

12. **helmet**   13. **shoulder pads**

14. How long is a football field? **100 yards**
15. Write 2 ways that a football team can move the ball down the field.
• run   • pass   • slide   • roll
16. A second is a unit of ▭.
• distance   • time   • length   • weight

8. 150 pounds
9. 100 pounds
10. 500 pounds
11. 100 pounds

Lesson 100   389

---

17. Which stopwatch shows that 8 seconds have passed?   **D**
18. Which stopwatch shows that 4 seconds have passed?   **B**
19. Which stopwatch shows that 6 seconds have passed?   **C**

A   B   C   D

20. If the hang-time for a kick is 4 seconds, how long does the ball stay in the air? **4 seconds**

21. Write the letter of the longest hang-time.   **b**
22. Write the letter of the shortest hang-time.   **a**
a. 3 seconds   b. 8 seconds   c. 5 seconds   d. 6 seconds

390   Lesson 100

Skill Items

They had reasons for interrupting her talk.
He frequently argued about the championship.

23. What underlining means **often**?   **frequently**
24. What underlining tells that they didn't let her finish talking?   **interrupting**
25. What underlining names a contest between the two best teams?   **championship**
26. What underlining tells about why they interrupted her talk?   **reasons**
27. What underlining tells what he did that showed he didn't agree?   **argued**

━━━━━━ END OF TEST 10 ━━━━━━

Lesson 100   391

101

Name _____

Story Items

1. The newspapers made up a name for Andrew. What name?
   Handy Andy

2. **Underline** 2 reasons why Andrew didn't daydream anymore.
   - He was too tired.
   - He was too busy.
   - His life was like his daydreams.
   - He was losing his strength.

3. Everything changed when Andrew started playing with the Titans. How did the players change?
   - They complained more.
   - They played better.

4. How did the coaches change?
   - They yelled less.
   - They yelled more.
   - They practiced less.

5. How did the owners of the team change?
   - They didn't talk about firing Denny.
   - They didn't talk about winning.
   - They didn't go to the games.

6. When a player ran into Andrew it felt like running into
   Idea: the side of a truck

7. On the sixth Sunday, Andrew felt strange. When he was getting dressed for the game, he noticed that his hands and feet

   Idea: were tingling

8. Andrew used to be as strong as an African elephant. He was now as strong as Ideas: a quarter horse; 5 or 6 strong men

9. How did Andrew feel when he realized he was losing his strength?
   - frightened
   - angry
   - happy

Review Items

10. The biggest state in the United States is Alaska

11. The second-biggest state in the United States is Texas

12. **Underline** the names of 2 states in the United States that are bigger than Japan.
    - Ohio
    - Canada
    - Texas
    - Alaska

13. All machines make it easier for someone to do work

Fill in the blanks on the time line.

14. Write **now** next to the dot that shows the year now.

15. Write **3 thousand years ago** next to the right dot.

16. Write **1 hundred years ago** next to the right dot.

17. Write **2 thousand years ago** next to the right dot.

18. Write **2 hundred years ago** next to the right dot.

now
1 hundred years ago
2 hundred years ago
1,000 years ago
2 thousand years ago
3 thousand years ago

═══ GO TO PART C IN YOUR TEXTBOOK. ═══

"What's the matter, man?" George said and sat next to Andrew. The bench bent down under the weight of Mean George. "Andy, you look sick."

Andrew said, "You guys are going to have to help me out. I don't think I'll be able to run or kick as well today."

"You've got to," George said. "Without you, we're just a bunch of bums."

"No," Andrew shouted. "Don't you say that. You guys are great. You just don't know it. You can do it without me. You just have to tell yourselves that you can."
                    MORE NEXT TIME

═══════

C Number your paper from 1 through 15.

Review Items

1. When we talk about how hot or cold something is, we tell about the ▆▆▆ of the thing. temperature

2. How fast does a jumbo jet fly?
   - 5 miles per hour
   - 50 miles per hour
   - 500 miles per hour

---

3. New York (City)   4. San Francisco

3. Write the name of the city that's on the east coast.
4. Write the name of the city that's on the west coast.
5. Which letter shows where Denver is? C
6. Which letter shows where Chicago is? D

7. Let's say you are outside when the temperature is 40 degrees. What is the temperature inside your body?

8. Let's say a fly is outside when the temperature is 40 degrees. What is the temperature inside the fly's body? 40 degrees

9. Let's say you are outside when the temperature is 85 degrees. What is the temperature inside your body?
   98 degrees

7. 98 degrees

131

10. Write the letter of the animal that is facing into the wind. **C**
11. Which direction is that animal facing? **west**
12. So what's the **name** of that wind? **west wind**

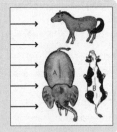

13. What is the temperature of the water in each jar?
14. Write the letter of each jar that is filled with ocean water. **A, D, E**
15. Jar B is not filled with ocean water. How do you know? **Idea: It's frozen.**

32 degrees 32 degrees 32 degrees 32 degrees 32 degrees 32 degrees

A   B   C   D   E   F

13. 32 degrees

Lesson 101   7

Name _____
Story Items

1. When Andrew was as strong as an elephant, he didn't play as hard as he could have because he didn't want to **Idea: hurt the other players**

2. Andrew was tackled in the first game he played after his strength faded. Had Andrew ever been tackled before? **no**

3. How many times did Andrew get tackled in that game? **4**

4. How many touchdowns did Andrew make? **4**

5. Did Mean George think that Andrew did a **good job** or a **bad job** in the game? **a good job**

6. When the game was over, Andrew sat in the locker room. How did his arms and legs feel? **They were tingling.**

7. What was happening to him? **Idea: He was losing his strength.**

8. Andrew imagined what the fans would do when he lost all his strength. Andrew thought the fans would ▆▆. Underline 2 things.

   • cheer   • <u>boo</u>   • clap   • <u>throw things onto the field</u>

9. The Titans were different during the practices. Underline 2 ways they were different.

   • They took it easy.   • They blamed each other.

   • <u>They ran faster.</u>   • <u>They tried harder.</u>

10. How strong was Andrew at the end of the story? **Ideas: as strong as a Mongolian horse; stronger than the strongest man**

Lesson 102   **3**

Andrew was getting weaker. The stopwatches below show some of his hang-times.

11. **Cross out** the stopwatch that shows his hang-time when he was weakest.

12. **Circle** the stopwatch that shows the best hang-time.

13. How many seconds are shown on the stopwatch that you crossed out? **3 seconds**

14. How many seconds are shown on the stopwatch that you circled? **6 seconds**

A   B   C

Review Items

15. What's the boiling temperature of water?

   • 212 miles   • <u>212 degrees</u>   • 112 degrees

16. When a glass of water gets hotter, which way does the temperature go? **up**

17. An oven gets colder. So what do you know about the temperature of the oven? **Idea: It went down.**

18. When the temperature goes up, the number of ▆▆ gets bigger.

   • miles   • <u>degrees</u>   • hours   • miles per hour

▆▆▆▆▆ GO TO PART C IN YOUR TEXTBOOK. ▆▆▆▆▆

C Number your paper from 1 through 17.
Review Items   2. west

1. Which letter shows where San Francisco is? **X**
2. If you were in San Francisco, which direction would you face if you wanted the wind to blow in your face?

Y

X

3. The United States is a ▆▆▆.   • city • state • <u>country</u>
4. Japan is a ▆▆▆.   **country**
5. How many states are in the United States? **50**

6. Would it be easier to catch a fly on **a hot day** or <u>**a cold day**</u>?
7. Tell why. **Idea: A fly is slower when it's colder.**

Lesson 102   13

---

8. Which letter shows where Italy is? W
9. Which letter shows where China is? Y
10. Which letter shows where Turkey is? X
11. Which letter shows where Japan is? Z

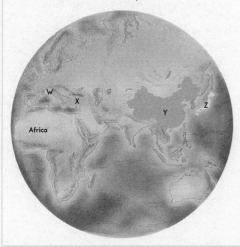

12. do work   13. heel

12. All machines make it easier for someone to ▮▮▮.
13. The arrow that killed Achilles hit him in the ▮▮▮.
14. That arrow had something on it that killed Achilles.
    What did it have on it? poison

Here's how fast different things can go:
  • 20 miles per hour
  • 35 miles per hour
  • 200 miles per hour
  • 500 miles per hour
15. Which speed tells how fast a fast man can run?
16. Which speed tells how fast a jet can fly?
17. Which speed tells how fast a fast dog can run?

15. 20 miles per hour
16. 500 miles per hour
17. 35 miles per hour

103

Name _____

Story Items

1. Were Andrew's hang-times getting **longer** or **shorter**? <u>shorter</u>

2. What did Andrew do to stay away from the players on the other team?
   • <u>ran faster</u>   • ran over them   • kicked the ball

3. What would happen to the Titans if they won the game in today's story?
   • They'd win the championship.
   • <u>They'd play in the championship game.</u>
   • They'd play 3 more games.

4. When Andrew kicked the field goal, how far did he kick it?
   • 90 yards   • <u>50 yards</u>   • 40 yards   • 60 yards

5. How did the Titans feel after the game? <u>Ideas: very happy; wild</u>

6. How long was it before the championship game?
   • 1 week   • <u>2 weeks</u>   • 3 weeks

7. Andrew squeezed the handle of his locker. What was he trying to find out? <u>Idea: how strong he was</u>

8. What happened when he squeezed it? <u>Ideas: nothing; no dent</u>

9. What did Andrew want for the team? <u>Idea: for them to win the championship</u>

10. When Andrew first played with the Titans, he was as strong as <u>an elephant</u>

11. In today's story, Andrew was as strong as <u>Ideas: a small horse; a Mongolian horse</u>

Review Items

12. Which weighs more, one gram or one water strider?
    <u>one gram</u>

13. How many ants would it take to weigh one gram?
    • about 10   • <u>about 100</u>   • about 1000

14. What's the boiling temperature of water? <u>212 degrees</u>

15. Which object is the hottest? <u>C</u>
16. What is the temperature of that object? <u>60 degrees</u>
17. Which object is the coldest? <u>B</u>
18. What is the temperature of that object? <u>30 degrees</u>

A
45 degrees

B
30 degrees

C
60 degrees

GO TO PART C IN YOUR TEXTBOOK.

C Number your paper from 1 through 17.

Skill Items

She commented about the still water.
1. What word means **silent** or **peaceful**? still
2. What word means quickly **told** about something? commented

Review Items
Write **W** for warm-blooded animals and **C** for cold-blooded animals.
3. beetle C
4. spider C
5. horse W
6. cow W
7. bee C
8. When a plane flies from New York City to San Francisco, is it flying in the **same direction** or the **opposite direction** as the wind?
9. How far is it from New York City to San Francisco?
10. How far is it from San Francisco to Japan?
11. What ocean do you cross to get from San Francisco to Japan? Pacific (ocean)

8. opposite direction (as the wind)
9. 25 hundred miles
10. 5 thousand miles

12. Write the letter of each place that is in the United States. a, c, d, e, i, j, k, l, m
    a. Alaska   f. Turkey   j. California
    b. Italy   g. China   k. Ohio
    c. New York City   h. Japan   l. San Francisco
    d. Lake Michigan   i. Chicago   m. Texas
    e. Denver
13. Write the letters of the 5 names that tell about length.
    a. minute   g. mile   b, d, g, h, j
    b. meter   h. yard
    c. day   i. year
    d. centimeter   j. inch
    e. second   k. hour
    f. week
14. A mile is a little more than ▮▮▮ feet.
    • 1 thousand   • 5 thousand   • 5 hundred
15. You can see drops of water on grass early in the morning. What are those drops called? dew

16. You would have the most power if you pushed against one of the handles. Which handle is that? E
17. Which handle would give you the least amount of power? B

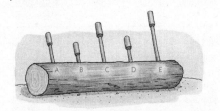

Name _____

Story Items
1. Why couldn't Andrew play in the championship game? _____
   Idea: because he had lost his strength
2. Andrew told Denny he'd lost his strength. What did Denny tell Andrew to do? Idea: rest for a few days
3. When Andrew went to the locker room who followed him?
   • nobody   • Denny   • some teammates
4. When Mean George slapped Andrew on the back, it hurt Andrew. Would that slap hurt Handy Andy? no
5. Did Andrew go to the ball park for the championship game? no
6. Who did he think would win the championship game? Wildcats
7. What did Andrew want to watch on TV? the championship game
8. What happened when he turned on his TV set?
   • nothing   • the set worked   • the doorbell rang
9. What did Andrew wiggle? the plug
10. What was wrong with the electric cord? Idea: It was worn out.
11. When Andrew wiggled the plug, his finger touched bare metal and Andrew got a (terrible/electric) shock
12. How did the shock make Andrew's feet and legs feel? Idea: They tingled.

Review Items

13. Are beetles living things? _yes_

14. **Underline** 3 things you know about beetles.
    - Beetles need ants.
    - Beetles grow.
    - Beetles need sugar.
    - Beetles need water.
    - Beetles make babies.

15. Write **north, south, east,** and **west** in the right boxes on the map.

16. An arrow goes from the **X**. Which direction is that arrow going?
    east

17. An arrow goes from the **Y**. Which direction is that arrow going?
    south

18. An arrow goes from the **Z**. Which direction is that arrow going?
    west

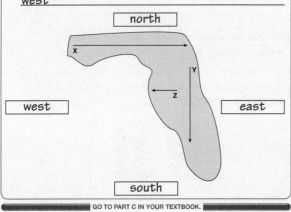

GO TO PART C IN YOUR TEXTBOOK.

C Number your paper from 1 through 18.

Skill Items

Use the words in the box to write complete sentences.

| received | argued | still | realized | commented |
| championship | unusual | frequently | chances |

1. He ▨▨▨ ▨▨▨ about the ▨▨▨.
2. She ▨▨▨ about the ▨▨▨ water.

Review Items

3. When we talk about miles per hour, we tell how ▨▨▨ something is moving. _fast_

4. Which arrow shows the way the air leaves the balloon? _B_
5. Which arrow shows the way the balloon will move? _A_

1. He |frequently| |argued| about the |championship.|
2. She |commented| about the |still| water.

---

6. Tom is 4 miles high. Jack is 20 miles high. Who is colder? _Jack_
7. Tell why. _Idea: Jack is higher._

8. The arrows show that the temperature is going up on thermometer **A** and going down on thermometer **B**. In which picture is the water getting colder, **A** or **B**? _B_
9. In which picture is the water getting hotter, **A** or **B**? _A_

10. Write the letter of the plane in each picture that will go the fastest. _A, N_

---

11. The names in one box tell about time. Write the letter of that box. _B_
12. The names in one box tell about length. Write the letter of that box. _A_

| A | centimeter | inch | yard | meter | mile |
| B | week | year | second | month | minute | hour |

13. When we weigh very small things, the unit we use is ▨▨▨. _gram(s)_
14. If you get smaller, your voice gets ▨▨▨. _Idea: higher_
15. Jean got smaller. So what do you know about Jean's voice? _Idea: It got higher._
16. Airplanes land at airports. Ships land at ▨▨▨. _harbors_
17. Airplanes are pulled by little trucks. Ships are pulled by ▨▨▨. _(little) tugboats_
18. Airplanes unload at gates. Ships unload at ▨▨▨. _docks_

10. Ideas: They cheered; they went wild.

105

Name _____

Story Items

1. Andrew got an electric shock from ▮▮▮▮.
   - • the TV plug   • the toaster   • the radio

2. The electric shock changed Andrew. How did it change him?
   Idea: It made him stronger.

3. What was Andrew trying to find out when he squeezed the doorknob?
   Idea: how strong he was

4. What happened when Andrew squeezed the doorknob?
   Ideas: nothing; he didn't dent it.

5. What happened when he pulled on the door?
   - • He pulled the door open.   • nothing
   - • He pulled the door off its hinges.

6. How strong was Andrew now?
   - • as strong as an elephant   • as strong as a horse
   - • as strong as a super strong man

7. Did Andrew run to the ball park or go in a car?
   Idea: ran

8. As Andrew ran to the ball park, did many people recognize him?
   yes

9. When Andrew got to the locker room, the game had already started.
   Which team was winning? **Wildcats**

10. What did the fans do when they saw Andrew? _____

11. Andrew had a plan to fool the Wildcats. What was that plan?
    Ideas: to pass the ball; to throw the ball (instead of kicking or running with it)

Lesson 105   9

12. What did Andrew do with the ball at the end of the story?
    Idea: dropped it

Review Items

13. A speedometer tells about ▮▮▮▮.
    - • miles   • miles per hour   • hours

14. Write the letter of the plane that is in the coldest air. **D**
15. Write the letter of the plane that is in the warmest air. **E**

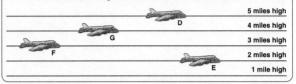

```
                                    5 miles high
                        D
              G                     4 miles high
                                    3 miles high
     F                              2 miles high
                            E       1 mile high
```

Jar **J** is filled with ocean water. Jar **K** is filled with fresh water.

16. Which jar is lighter? **K**
17. Which jar will freeze at 32 degrees? **K**
18. Will the other jar freeze **above 32 degrees** or **below 32 degrees**?
    below 32 degrees

J   K

GO TO PART C IN YOUR TEXTBOOK.

10   *Lesson 105*

C Number your paper from 1 through 19.

Review Items

Things that are this far apart ◄——► on the map are 2 miles apart.
Things that are this far apart ◄————————► on the map are 4 miles apart.

1. How far is it from the park to the hill? **2 miles**
2. How far is it from the forest to the field? **2 miles**

FIELD
FOREST
SCHOOL
HILL
POOL   PARK

34   *Lesson 105*

3. You would have the least amount of power if you pushed against one of the handles. Which handle is that? **I**
4. Which handle would give you the most power? **J**

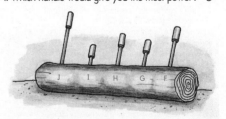

J   I   H   G   F

10. (*correct answer*)   11. (*correct answer*)

5. The place that is called Troy is now part of what country?
   - • Greece   • Turkey   • Italy

6. In what year was the first airplane made? **1903**
7. In what year were you born? (*student's birth year*)
8. What year is it now? (*correct answer*)
9. In what year did the United States become a country? **1776**
10. What was the year 2 hundred years ago?
11. What was the year 1 hundred years ago?
12. What was the year 3 hundred years ago?
13. When did the story of Troy take place?

12. (*correct answer*)   13. **3 thousand years ago**   *Lesson 105*   35

Each statement tells about how far something goes or how fast something goes. Write **how far** or **how fast** for each item.

14. He ran 5 miles per hour. how fast
15. He ran 5 miles. how far
16. The plane was 500 miles from New York City.
17. The plane was flying 500 miles per hour.

18. Did the first people who lived in caves cook their food? no
19. Did the people who lived in caves many years later cook their food? yes

16. how far
17. how fast

36   Lesson 105

Name _____

Story Items

1. How long is a football field? 100 yards

2. How long was the pass that Andrew made?
   • 30 yards   • 60 yards   • <u>80 yards</u>

3. A Titan caught Andrew's pass. Did that Titan score a touchdown?
   yes

4. What was the score after the Titans scored a field goal?
   • 14 to 14   • <u>14 to 10</u>   • 14 to 7

5. Who was winning? Wildcats

6. Andrew made the winning score by ▉.
   • <u>running</u>   • kicking   • passing

7. The fans started leaving before the game was over because they thought the Titans Idea: would lose

8. When Andrew finally made the winning score, how many seconds were left in the game? 10

9. When did Andrew quit playing for the Titans?
   • during the championship game
   • <u>after the championship game</u>
   • during the spring

10. What kind of job did Andrew get?
    • working with the owners
    • <u>working with the coaches</u>
    • working with the kids

11. Why didn't Andrew daydream as much after the Titans won the championship? Ideas: He liked his job; he had lived a great daydream.

Lesson 106   11

---

12. What happens when Andrew goes for walks?
    Idea: Lots of kids join him.

Review Items

13. The tube is filled with water. Draw the skin that covers the top of the water.

Write the years where they belong on the time line.

•1997   •1991   •1995   •1992   •1999

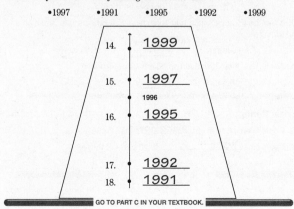

14. 1999
15. 1997
    1996
16. 1995
17. 1992
18. 1991

GO TO PART C IN YOUR TEXTBOOK.

12   Lesson 106

C Number your paper from 1 through 15.
Review Items

1. What's the boiling temperature of water? 212 degrees

2. Write the letters of the 4 kinds of weapons that soldiers used when they had battles with Troy. a, b, d, e
   a. bows   b. spears   c. planes   d. arrows
   e. swords   f. rockets   g. guns   h. tanks

3. During the war with Troy, what did the Greek army build to help them get inside Troy?
4. What was inside this object? Idea: (Greek) soldiers; men
5. What did they do after they came out of the object?
6. Who won the war, Troy or Greece? Greece

7. Name 2 kinds of wells. oil (well), water (well)
8. The temperature inside your body is about ▉ degrees when you are healthy. 98
9. Most fevers don't go over ▉ degrees. 101

3. (large wooden) horse
5. opened the gate

42   Lesson 106

137

10. Which letter shows the crude oil? K
11. Which letter shows the refinery? H
12. Which letter shows the pipeline? J

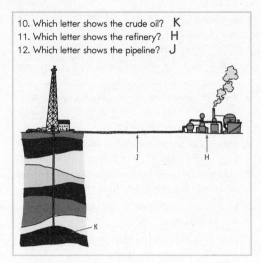

13. How fast is truck **A** going? *15 miles per hour*
14. How fast is truck **B** going? *30 miles per hour*
15. Which truck is going faster? B

107

Name _____

A

1. Find place **A** on map 1. What ocean is that? <u>Pacific (Ocean)</u>
2. What's the name of country **B**? <u>United States</u>
3. Name 2 cities in country **B**.
   <u>(Accept any 2 U.S. cities.)</u>
4. Find **F** on map 2. What's the name of country **F**? <u>Turkey</u>
5. What happened in country **F** about 3 thousand years ago?
   <u>Idea: war between Greece and Troy</u>
6. What's the name of country **G**? <u>Italy</u>
7. What's the name of country **H**? <u>Japan</u>
8. Name 2 girls who went to country **H**. <u>Linda, Kathy</u>

Map 1   Map 2

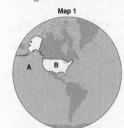 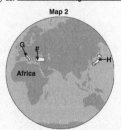

B Story Items

9. **Underline** 3 ways that people traveled 2 hundred years ago.
   - by car
   - by jet
   - <u>by horse</u>
   - by train
   - <u>by walking</u>
   - <u>by water</u>

10. About how long would it take to go from New York City to San Francisco on a good horse?
    - 3 days
    - 3 weeks
    - <u>3 months</u>
11. How long does that trip take on a jet?
    - <u>6 hours</u>
    - 6 days
    - 6 weeks

12. How fast can an ocean liner go?
    - 20 miles per hour
    - <u>40 miles per hour</u>
    - 4 miles per hour

13. About how long would it take to go from San Francisco to Japan on a sailing ship?
    - 30 hours
    - <u>30 days</u>
    - 30 weeks
14. About how long does that trip take on an ocean liner?
    - 5 hours
    - <u>5 days</u>
    - 5 weeks

Review Items

15. Roots keep a tree from <u>falling down</u>
16. Roots carry <u>water</u> to all parts of the tree.

GO TO PART D IN YOUR TEXTBOOK.

D Number your paper from 1 through 16.
Review Items

1. Which letter shows where the ground gets warm first? D
2. Which letter shows where the ground gets warm last? P

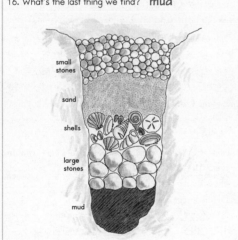

3. In which season is the danger of forest fires greatest? fall
4. What do people keep in banks? money

---

5. B, C, D, F   6. A, E, G

Some of the lines in the box are one inch long and some are one centimeter long.
    5. Write the letter of every line that is one centimeter long.
    6. Write the letter of every line that is one inch long.

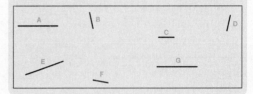

7. Greece went to war with Troy because of a woman named ▨▨▨. Helen
8. The woman from Greece was important because she was a ▨▨▨. queen
9. The woman from Greece went away with a man from ▨▨▨. Troy

10. What's a good place to look for clues about people who lived long ago? Ideas: garbage piles; caves
11. Some people who lived 80 thousand years ago lived in ▨▨▨. caves

---

12. When we dig into the pile in the picture, what's the first thing we find? small stones
13. What's the next thing we find? sand
14. What's the next thing we find? shells
15. What's the next thing we find? large stones
16. What's the last thing we find? mud

small
stones

sand

shells

large
stones

mud

Name _____

Story Items

1. The picture shows the first two rows of the word bank. Three words do not belong in this part of the word bank. **Circle** the words that do not belong.

FRONT

2. The people in Hohoboho only did one thing. What was that?
   talked

3. All the words in Hohoboho stayed in a strange place called
   the word bank

Skill Items

4. Compare object A and object B. Remember, first tell how they're the same. Then tell how they're different.
   Ideas: They're both pickup trucks/old/facing
   right. A is empty, but B has a load of rocks, etc.

Object A   Object B

WORKBOOK

Review Items

5. When do trees begin to grow?   • in the winter   • <u>in the spring</u>

6. Trees begin to grow when their roots get <u>warm</u>

7. A forest fire may burn for ▮▮.

      • minutes   • hours   • <u>weeks</u>

8. A forest fire kills both ▮▮ and ▮▮.

      • <u>plants</u>   • whales   • fish   • <u>animals</u>

9. About how many years could it take for the forest to grow back?

      •100 years   •20 years   •<u>200 years</u>

10. **Underline** 4 names that tell about time.

      • <u>week</u>   • inch   • centimeter   • <u>second</u>

      • <u>minute</u>   • meter   • <u>hour</u>   • yard

11. Which is shorter, a meter or a yard? <u>yard</u>

12. Which is longer, a meter or a centimeter? <u>meter</u>

13. How many centimeters long is a meter? <u>100</u>

14. How many ships sailed to Troy? <u>1 thousand</u>

15. How long did the war between Greece and Troy go on?
<u>10 years</u>

16. If the Greek army could get a few men inside the wall of Troy, these men could <u>Idea: open the gate</u>

17. **Underline** 3 ways that people traveled 2 hundred years ago.

      • <u>by water</u>   • by jet   • by train

      • by walking   • by car   • <u>by horse</u>

▬▬▬▬▬ GO TO PART D IN YOUR TEXTBOOK. ▬▬▬▬▬

TEXTBOOK

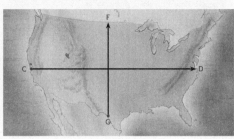

D Number your paper from 1 through 13.
Review Items

United States

1. What part of the world is shown on the map?
2. The map shows how far apart some places are. How far is it from **G** to **F**? 13 hundred miles
3. How far is it from **C** to **D**? 25 hundred miles

TEXTBOOK

United States

4. Find **F** on map 1. What place does the **F** show?
5. What place does the **E** show? Pacific Ocean
6. Find **C** on map 2. What place does the **C** show? Turkey
7. What happened in place **C** about 3 thousand years ago? Idea: war between Greece and Troy
8. What's the name of place **D**? Greece
9. What's the name of place **B**? Italy
10. What's the name of place **A**? Japan

Map 1   Map 2

   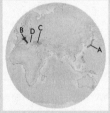

11. How fast is car **A** going? 50 miles per hour
12. How fast is car **B** going? 30 miles per hour
13. Which car is going faster? A

A
50

B
30

WORKBOOK

109

Name _____

Story Items

1. Why were the words in the back of the word bank so sad? _____
<u>Idea: because they weren't said very often</u>

2. Which word sat closer to the front of the word bank, **run** or
temperature? <u>temperature</u>

3. **Circle** all the words that belong to the **sit** family.
4. **Cross out** all the words that belong to the **run** family.

      • jump   • hiding   • ~~runner~~   • (sat)   • glass
      • book   • see   • cup   • rider   • hot
      • eats   • ~~ran~~   • (sits)   • (sitting)   • ~~running~~
      • (sitter)   • flying   • ~~runs~~   • talked   • (sit)

5. **Underline** 3 relatives of the word. **walk**.

      • washer   • climbing   • <u>walks</u>   • wheeling
      • <u>walking</u>   • weaver   • <u>walker</u>

6. Which word sat closer to the front of the word bank, **running** or
maggot? <u>maggot</u>

7. So which word was happier? <u>maggot</u>

8. **Underline** 3 relatives of the word **jump**.

      • <u>jumper</u>   • leaper   • happen   • sits
      • <u>jumps</u>   • hops   • <u>jumping</u>

9. **Underline** the 6 words that do **not** tell about doing something.

      • <u>hot</u>   • <u>hats</u>   • hops   • running
      • <u>only</u>   • jump   • look   • <u>blue</u>
      • <u>and</u>   • sits   • <u>tall</u>

WORKBOOK

Skill Items

Here's the rule: **All the words in the front row were happy.**

10. The word **run** was not in the front row. So what else do you know about the word **run?** <u>nothing</u>

11. The word **eat** was in the back row. So what else do you know about the word **eat?** <u>nothing</u>

12. The word **me** was in the front row. So what else do you know about the word **me?** <u>Idea: It was happy.</u>

Review Items

Use these answers: • 100 pounds   • 150 pounds   • 500 pounds

13. About how much does a chimpanzee weigh? <u>100 pounds</u>

14. About how much force can a chimpanzee pull with? <u>500 pounds</u>

15. About how much does a leopard weigh? <u>100 pounds</u>

16. About how much weight can a leopard carry? <u>150 pounds</u>

17. How long is a football field? <u>100 yards</u>

18. **Underline 2** ways that a football team can move the ball down the field.

    • bounce   • slide   • <u>pass</u>   • <u>run</u>

19. A second is a unit of ▨.

    • distance   • weight   • length   • <u>time</u>

──── GO TO PART D IN YOUR TEXTBOOK. ────

TEXTBOOK

"It will happen again," **runner** would reply. "You'll see. One of these days, they're going to start saying my name all the time. I'll bet I get to move up five rows. You'll see."

"Oh, be quiet."

Then the sad words would sit back and feel sad. Long day after long day, they would sit and try not to listen to those words in the front of the bank whooping and howling.

MORE NEXT TIME

──────────

D Number your paper from 1 through 18.

Skill Items

Their amazing effort surprised the neighbors.

1. What word names people who live near you?
2. What word means **strength**?
3. What word means that something is hard to believe?

1. neighbors
2. effort
3. amazing

TEXTBOOK

Review Items

4. Write the letter of the tree that has deeper roots. R
5. Write the letter of the tree that begins to grow first every year. E

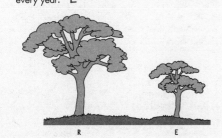

TEXTBOOK

6. Which letter shows the crude oil? B
7. Which letter shows the fresh water? A
8. Which letter shows the salt water? C

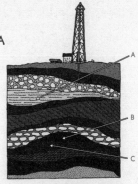

9. Gasoline comes from a liquid called ▨. crude oil

13. Yoko Tanaka

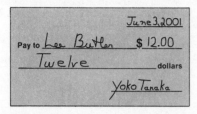

10. When was the check below written? June 3, 2001
11. Who should the bank pay? Lee Butler
12. How much should the bank pay? twelve dollars ($12)
13. Whose money should the bank use to pay Lee Butler?

> June 3, 2001
> Pay to Lee Butler $12.00
> Twelve _____ dollars
> Yoko Tanaka

14. Name 2 things that a strong magnet can pick up.
15. How many parts does the body of an insect have? 3
16. How many legs does an insect have? 6
17. How many legs does a spider have? 8
18. How many parts does a spider's body have? 2

14. Any 2 metal items: paper clips, nails, etc.

Lesson 109   69

---

110 [TEST 11]

Number your paper from 1 through 18. 1. Pacific Ocean

1. Find **A** on map 1. What place does the **A** show?
2. What place does the **B** show? United States
3. Find **C** on map 2. What place does the **C** show?
4. What happened in place **C** about 3 thousand years ago?
5. What's the name of place **D**? Italy
6. What's the name of place **E**? Japan

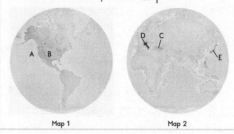

Map 1   Map 2

7. Write the letters of 3 ways that people traveled 2 hundred years ago. b, d, e

    a. by jet   d. by walking
    b. by water   e. by horse
    c. by train   f. by car

3. Turkey
4. Idea: war between Greece and Troy.

70   *Lesson 110*

---

8. Write the letters of all the words that belong to the **jump** family. b, i, l, o, s
9. Write the letters of all the words that belong to the **ride** family. a, e, f, j, q

a. ride	f. rider	k. chair	p. flying
b. jumping	g. sitting	l. jumper	q. riding
c. hot	h. talked	m. hiding	r. eats
d. book	i. jumps	n. see	s. jump
e. rode	j. rides	o. jumped	t. run

10. commented   11. neighbors

Skill Items

> For each item, write the underlined word from the sentences in the box.
>
> > She commented about the still water.
> > Their amazing effort surprised the neighbors.

10. What underlining means **quickly told about something**?
11. What underlining names **people who live near you**?
12. What underlining means that something is **hard to believe**? amazing
13. What underlining means **silent** or **peaceful**? still
14. What underlining means **strength**? effort

Lesson 110   71

Copy the words in the box. After each word, write the guide words for the page where you would find that word in a glossary.

	Guide Words
15. bucket	bed — breakfast
16. bridge	breeze — bumble
17. begun	bunny — by
18. busy	

15. breeze, bumble
16. breeze, bumble
17. bed, breakfast
18. bunny, by

═══ **END OF TEST 11** ═══

72   *Lesson 110*

WORKBOOK

111

Name _____

A

1. The country to the north of the United States is <u>Canada</u> .

2. Which country is bigger, Japan or the United States?
   <u>United States</u>

3. Which country is bigger, the United States or Canada?
   <u>Canada</u>

4. Is the United States **bigger** than most other countries or **smaller** than most other countries? <u>bigger</u>

5. Which letter shows Alaska? <u>D</u>
6. Which letter shows the rest of the United States? <u>F</u>
7. Which letter shows Canada? <u>E</u>

Lesson 111   19

WORKBOOK

B Story Items

8. On what day did the words in the word bank get moved?
   <u>Friday</u>

9. Let's say that the word **paper** was said more often during the week. Would **paper** get moved **toward the front** or **toward the back** of the word bank? <u>toward the front</u>

10. Let's say the word **passenger** was moved toward the back of the word bank. Was **passenger** said **more often** or **less often**?
    <u>less often</u>

11. When a word got moved up in the word bank, how did the word feel?
    <u>Ideas: happy; excited; etc.</u>

12. What was the only thing that the people in Hohoboho did before the big change? <u>talk</u>

13. The people in Hohoboho started to swim after the big change. Name 3 more things they started to do. **1** <u>(Any 3: walk; wander;</u> **2** <u>eat; run; sing; climb;</u> **3** <u>dance; look at things; kick</u> <u>things; sit on things; etc.)</u>

14. They started to do these things on ▮▮.
    • Sunday   • <u>Thursday</u>   • Friday

GO TO PART D IN YOUR TEXTBOOK.

20   Lesson 111

TEXTBOOK

"Twenty times," the word **hop** said. "They said my name twenty times and the day isn't even over yet."

"That's nothing," **run** said, "I'm already up to 56."

Two words in the front row, **we** and **us,** were talking. **We** said, "Tomorrow is Friday. What do you think will happen to those words in the back row?"

"I don't know," **us** said. "We'll have to wait and see."
MORE NEXT TIME

D Number your paper from 1 through 26.
Skill Items

Use the words in the box to write complete sentences.

| effort | noticed | neighbors | still | awful |
| world | commented | special | amazing | |

1. She ▮▮▮ about the ▮▮▮ water.
2. Their ▮▮▮ ▮▮▮ surprised the ▮▮▮.

1. She [commented] about the [still] water.
2. Their [amazing] [effort] surprised the [neighbors].

Lesson 111   77

TEXTBOOK

Review Items
Write what kind of horse each picture shows.
• Mongolian horse   • draft horse   • pony
   • racehorse   • quarter horse

 3. pony   4. Mongolian horse   5. quarter horse

 6. racehorse   7. draft horse

8. Which animal is safer, a cow or a cat? <u>cow</u>
9. Why? <u>Idea: because it's bigger</u>

10. Electricity can turn any steel bar into a magnet. What are these magnets called? <u>electromagnets</u>
11. Name a place where these magnets are used.
    <u>wrecking yards</u>

78   Lesson 111

143

Write the name of each part of a football player's uniform.
• shoulders   • shoulder pads   • knee pads
        • helmet   • hats

12. **helmet**   13. **shoulder pads**

14. Which stopwatch shows that 3 seconds have passed?
15. Which stopwatch shows that 9 seconds have passed?
16. Which stopwatch shows that 5 seconds have passed?

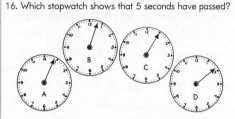

17. If the hang-time for a kick is 2 seconds, how long does the ball stay in the air? **2 seconds**

14. B   15. D   16. C

Some of Andrew's hang-times are shown on the stopwatches.
18. Write the letter of the watch that shows his best hang-time. **C**
19. How many seconds are shown on that watch? **6**
20. Write the letter of the watch that shows his worst hang-time. **B**
21. How many seconds are shown on that watch? **3**

A   B   C

22. Write the letters of 3 relatives of the word **sit.**
   [a.]sits   b. talked   [c.]sat   d. hopped   e. walker   [f.]sitter
23. Eohippus lived ▇ million years ago. **38**
24. The front legs of eohippus were different from the front legs of a horse that lives today. Write the letters of 2 ways that they were different.
   a. They had smaller hooves.   [b.]They didn't have hooves.
   c. They were faster.   [d.]They were smaller.

25. Write the letter of the shortest hang-time. **b**
26. Write the letter of the longest hang-time. **a**
   a. 8 seconds b. 4 seconds c. 6 seconds d. 5 seconds

112

Name _____
Story Items

1. How long did the announcements in the word bank usually take?
   • <u>30 minutes</u>   • 1 hour   • all day

2. Did the announcements take **more time** or **less time** on the Friday after the big change? **more time**

3. Name **3** words that got moved over 100 rows.
   ① run   ② walk   ② jump

4. **Underline** the 2 words that had to leave row 1.
   • some   • none   • <u>only</u>   • have
   • did   • <u>were</u>   • run   • Mom

5. Let's say the word **and** got moved from row 1 to row 30. Was **and** said **more often** or **less often**? **less often**

6. Here are facts about how often some words were said each day. Some words sit in row 20. Some words sit in row 1. **Circle** the words that sit in row 1.
   • (Is) was said 120 times.   • (Run) was said 100 times.
   • (Had) was said 110 times.   • Book was said 4 times.
   • Good was said 3 times.   • (Me) was said 109 times.
   • Other was said 2 times.   • Glass was said 6 times.
   • None was said 5 times.   • (He) was said 98 times.
   • (Sit) was said 105 times.   • (Climb) was said 104 times.

Review Items

7. Which army was Achilles in during the war between Troy and Greece? **Greek**
8. How long was Achilles in the war? **10 years**
9. Who was the greatest soldier of Troy? **Hector**
10. Who won when Hector and Achilles fought? **Achilles**
11. Achilles rode around the wall of Troy in a **chariot**.
12. People who lived 80 thousand years ago did not have many things that we have today. **Underline** 9 things they did not have.
   • sky   • bones   • <u>refrigerators</u>   • trees   • <u>computers</u>
   • <u>TV sets</u>   • <u>trains</u>   • <u>telephones</u>   • food   • rocks
   • <u>books</u>   • <u>movies</u>   • <u>stoves</u>   • <u>cars</u>   • dirt

Fill out the bank form below using these facts.
   • Your name is Zack Turner.
   • You're going to put $200 in the bank.
   • You live at 222 York Street, Fort Worth, Texas.
   • Your phone number is 555-6121.

13. Last name **Turner**   14. First name **Zack**
15. Phone number **555-6121**
16. Street address **222 York Street**
17. City **Fort Worth**   18. State **Texas**
19. How much money are you putting in the bank? $**200**

 GO TO PART C IN YOUR TEXTBOOK.

Run laughed and said, "I don't care. I'll remember this forever. This is great."

By the end of that Friday, run could turn around and talk to some of its relatives that were in row two. The words running, runs, and ran were in row 2. Runner was in row five, but runner was very happy. "I never thought I would even see this part of the word bank," runner said.

When the next Friday came around, the words like run and walk and jump and the others kept their seats near the front of the word bank. In fact, they're still there. And run is no longer sad. In fact, run is happy all day and all night. Run yells and shouts and says, "That's me. I'm number one." And the other words that had been in the last row are happier than they ever thought they would be.

THE END

C Number your paper from 1 through 18.

Skill Item

1. Compare object A and object B. Remember, first tell how they're the same. Then tell how they're different.

Object A

Object B

1. Ideas: They are both yellow/vehicles/ have wheels. A is a cab, but B is a car. A has a top, but B does not.

84   Lesson 112

Review Items

2. What is the name of the vehicle in the picture? **chariot**
3. How many wheels does the vehicle have? **2**
4. What is pulling the vehicle? **horses**
5. What is soldier A doing? **shooting arrow**
6. What is soldier B doing? **steering**

Soldier A   Soldier B

7. The country to the north of the United States is ▨.
8. Is the United States **bigger** than most other countries or **smaller** than most other countries? **bigger**
9. Which country is bigger, Japan or the United States?
10. Which country is bigger, the United States or Canada?

7. Canada

Lesson 112   85

Write what kind of horse each picture shows.
- racehorse
- quarter horse
- pony
- Mongolian horse
- draft horse

11. draft horse

12. racehorse

13. quarter horse

14. Mongolian horse

15. pony

86   Lesson 112

16. What place does the A show? **United States**
17. What place does the B show? **Canada**
18. What place does the C show? **Alaska**

C
B
A

Lesson 112   87

Name _____

A

1. If you go east from Australia, what ocean do you go through?
   Pacific (Ocean)

2. If you go west from the United States, what ocean do you go
   through? Pacific (Ocean)

B Story Items

3. Name the country where this part of the story takes place.
   Australia

4. What is a group of kangaroos called? mob

5. The mob moved from place to place when the mob ran out
   of ████.
   • grass and weeds   • water and grass   • gas and food

6. How do you know Toby wasn't very important in the mob?
   • He was at the front of the mob.
   • He was not in a mob.
   • He was at the back of the mob.

7. What is a baby kangaroo called?
   • mob   • joey   • cry baby

8. Name the only 2 things Toby liked to do.
   eat and sleep

9. Did Toby's mother like Toby? yes

Lesson 113   23

WORKBOOK

10. Did Toby like to be called a joey? no

11. Write the letter of the most important kangaroo in the mob. R

12. Write the letter of Toby. U

13. Write the letter of a kangaroo that is almost as important as the
    leader. S

GO TO PART D IN YOUR TEXTBOOK.

24   Lesson 113

TEXTBOOK

D Number your paper from 1 through 26.

1. Which letter shows where Australia is?   G
2. Which letter shows where the United States is?   H
3. Which letter shows where Canada is?   I
4. Which letter shows where the Pacific Ocean is?   E

5. Which letter shows a kangaroo?   B
6. Which letter shows a platypus?   A
7. Which letter shows a koala?   C

Lesson 113   93

TEXTBOOK

Skill Items

    Police officers checked the ship's cargo.
8. What words mean **cops**?   police officers
9. What word refers to the things that a ship carries?   cargo

Review Items

10. Jean is 16 miles high. Sue is 8 miles high. Who is
    colder?   Jean
11. Tell why.   Idea: because she is higher

12. Write 2 letters that show bulkheads.   A, D
13. Write 2 letters that show decks.   C, F
14. Which letter shows where the bow is?   E
15. Which letter shows where the stern is?   B

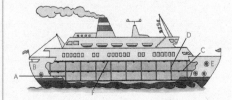

94   Lesson 113

16. 32 degrees

16. What is the temperature of the water in each jar?
17. Write the letter of each jar that is filled with ocean water. **D, F**
18. Jar E is not filled with ocean water. How do you know? **Idea: It is frozen.**

32 degrees 32 degrees 32 degrees 32 degrees 32 degrees 32 degrees

A   B   C   D   E   F

19. Write the letter of the one name that tells about temperature. **f**
20. Write the letters of the 6 names that tell about distance or length. **c, e, h, i, k, n**
21. Write the letters of the 5 names that tell about time.
22. Write the letters of the 2 names that tell about speed.

   a. meters per week   h. miles   **a, l**
   b. years   i. meters
   c. inches   j. days
   d. minutes   k. centimeters
   e. feet   l. miles per hour
   f. degrees   m. hours
   g. weeks   n. yards

21. **b, d, g, j, m**

---

23. Three thousand years ago, part of Greece went to war with ▨▨▨. **Troy**
24. The war began because a queen from ▨▨▨ ran away with a man from ▨▨▨. **Greece, Troy**
25. ▨▨▨ ships went to war with Troy.
   • 5 thousand   • 1 thousand   • 1 hundred
26. How long did the war last? **10 years**

Name _____

A

1. What is the only country that has wild kangaroos?
   • America   • Canada   • <u>Australia</u>

2. Big kangaroos grow to be as big as a **man**

3. Small kangaroos grow to be not much bigger than a ▨▨▨.
   • cow   • <u>rabbit</u>   • moose

4. How long is a kangaroo when it is born? **3 centimeters**

5. Where does a baby kangaroo live right after it is born?
   Idea: in its mother's pouch

6. How long does it live there? **half a year**

7. How far can a kangaroo go in one jump? **(over) 10 feet**

B Story Items

8. A kangaroo that sits on a hill and warns the mob when trouble is coming is called a **lookout**

9. What does that animal do if there's trouble?
   • waves its tail   • <u>stamps its foot</u>   • screams

10. Who told Toby he had to be a lookout? **the leader (of the mob)**

11. Where did Toby go to be a lookout? **Idea: at the top of a high hill**

---

12. When Toby was a tiny kangaroo, hunters caught his father. What job did his father have when he was caught?
   lookout

13. Why did Toby's father get caught? **Idea: He fell asleep.**

14. Where did some kangaroos think Toby's father was now?
   • on the other side of Australia
   • <u>on the other side of the Pacific Ocean</u>
   • on the other side of Turkey

15. Toby's father had a tail that was different from any other kangaroo's tail. Name 2 ways that his father's tail was different.
   Ideas: the longest tail (that any kangaroo ever had); it had 3 large white spots on it.

16. After Toby got to the top of the hill, he did something he didn't mean to do. What was that? **Idea: He fell asleep.**

17. Who did Toby hear at the end of the story? **a hunter**

▬▬▬▬▬ GO TO PART D IN YOUR TEXTBOOK. ▬▬▬▬▬

that lookout. He'll warn the others." Suddenly, Toby realized that the voice was not part of a dream. He opened his eyes and looked around. Five hunters were sneaking past him on their way down the hill to the mob.

MORE NEXT TIME

D 1. Idea: They are both fruit/have a skin/have a stem.
Number your paper from 1 through 21.

Skill Items

A is red, but B is yellow. A is an apple, but B is a banana.

1. Compare object A and object B. Remember, first tell how they're the same. Then tell how they're different.

Object A   Object B

Use the words in the box to write complete sentences.

neighbors	cargo	flight attendants	police officers
puzzled	effort	dashboard	amazing	double

2. Their ▢ ▢ surprised the ▢.
3. ▢ checked the ship's ▢.

2. Their amazing effort surprised the neighbors.
3. Police officers checked the ship's cargo.

Lesson 114   101

Review Items

4. During the war between part of Greece and Troy, what kept the soldiers from getting inside Troy?
5. At last, the Greek army built a ▢.
6. What was inside this object?
7. What did the men do at night?   Idea: opened the gate

8. **Write the letters** of the 9 places that are in the United States.

a. Australia   g. Lake Michigan   m. San Francisco
b. New York City   h. Japan   n. California
c. Chicago   i. Turkey   o. Canada
d. Alaska   j. Texas   p. Denver
e. China   k. Italy
f. Ohio   l. Greece

9. If you go east from Australia, what ocean do you go through?   Pacific (Ocean)
10. If you go west from the United States, what ocean do you go through?   Pacific (Ocean)
11. What is a group of kangaroos called?   mob
12. What is a baby kangaroo called?   joey

4. Idea: the walls around Troy
5. (large wooden) horse
6. Idea: men; (Greek) soldiers

102   Lesson 114

---

13. Write the letters of the 5 lines that are one inch long.   A, D, F, H, J
14. Write the letters of the 5 lines that are one centimeter long.   B, C, E, G, I

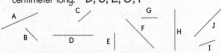

15. Which letter shows where Australia is?   P
16. Which letter shows where the United States is?   M
17. Which letter shows where Canada is?   O
18. Which letter shows where the Pacific Ocean is?   N

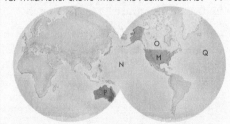

19. Which is longer, a yard or a meter?   yard
20. Which is longer, a centimeter or a meter?   meter
21. How many centimeters long is a meter?   100

Lesson 114   103

115

Name _____

A

1. A peacock is a large ▢.
   • fish   • dog   • <u>bird</u>

2. The feathers of a male peacock are different from the feathers of other birds. **Underline** 2 ways they are different.
   • <u>longer</u>   • stronger   • <u>more colorful</u>
                  • older   • shorter

3. Do peacocks live as wild animals in Australia?   no

4. Which is more beautiful—a peacock's feathers or a peacock's voice?   feathers

5. What does a male peacock spread when it shows off?   (its) tail feathers

6. How long is a full-grown peacock from its head to the end of its tail?   2 meters

B Story Items

7. Name the leader of the hunters.   Mabel

8. About how far was it from the mob to the ship?   10 miles

9. What country was Mabel from?   Canada

10. In that country, Mabel ran a large   circus

Lesson 115   27

11. **Underline** 2 kinds of animals Mabel wanted to catch in Australia.

- peacocks
- <u>koalas</u>
- platypuses
- camels
- elephants
- <u>kangaroos</u>
- cuckoos

12. Mabel didn't plan to keep all the animals she caught. What was she going to do with the animals she didn't keep?
<u>Idea: sell them to zoos or circuses</u>

13. What did Toby do to signal the mob about the hunters?
- smacked his tail
- <u>smacked his foot</u>
- smacked his lips

14. After Toby's first signal, the mob stood still. What did the mob do after Toby's second signal? <u>moved fast</u>

15. What happened to Toby at the end of the story? <u>Ideas: He got caught; a sailor tackled him.</u>

16. The hunters hoped to get 5 kangaroos. How many did they catch? <u>one</u>

17. Who saved the other kangaroos? <u>Toby</u>

━━━━━ GO TO PART D IN YOUR TEXTBOOK. ━━━━━

D Number your paper from 1 through 21.

Skill Items

Write the word from the box that means the same thing as the underlined part of each sentence.

important	although	confused	foul
motioning	constructing	opposite	normal

1. They finished <u>building</u> the house last week.   constructing
2. The garbage smelled <u>bad</u>.   foul
3. She went to school, <u>but</u> she was sick.   although

4. Compare the word **two** and the word **to**. Remember, first tell how they're the same. Then tell how they're different.

Review Items   1776
5. In what year did the United States become a country?
6. What is the only country that has wild kangaroos?
7. How far can a kangaroo go in one jump?   (over) 10 feet
8. A kangaroo is ▨ centimeters long when it is born.   3
9. Big kangaroos grow to be as big as a ▨.   man

4. Ideas: They both sound the same.
Two has a w, but to does not.
6. Australia

---

10. Which letter shows a kangaroo?   Y
11. Which letter shows a platypus?   X
12. Which letter shows a koala?   Z

13. Where does a baby kangaroo live right after it is born?   mother's pouch
14. How long does it live there?   half a year

15. Toby's father had a tail that was different from any other kangaroo's tail. Name 2 ways that his father's tail was different.
16. What part of a car tells how fast the car is moving?
17. When a plane flies from New York City to San Francisco, is it flying in the **same direction** or the **opposite direction** as the wind?   opposite direction

15. Ideas: It was very large; it had 3 white spots on it.
16. speedometer

---

18. Which thing went into the pile earlier, thing R or thing X?   X
19. Which thing went into the pile earlier, thing J or thing T?   T
20. Which thing went into the pile later, thing R or thing T?   R
21. Which thing went into the pile later, thing Y or thing J?   J

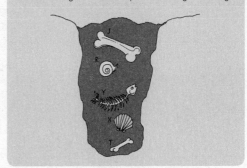

WORKBOOK

116

Name ____________________

A

1. How many seconds are in one minute? 60
2. Some clocks have a hand that moves fast. When that hand goes all the way around the clock, how much time has passed?
   - one hour
   - <u>one minute</u>
   - one second
3. The hand that moves fast went around 2 times. How much time passed? two minutes

B

4. What do we call the things that a ship carries? cargo

Look at the picture of the ship. Write one of these names on each line:

- stern
- hold
- deck
- bulkhead
- bow

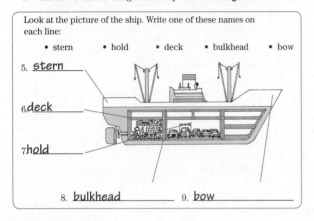

5. stern

6. deck

7. hold

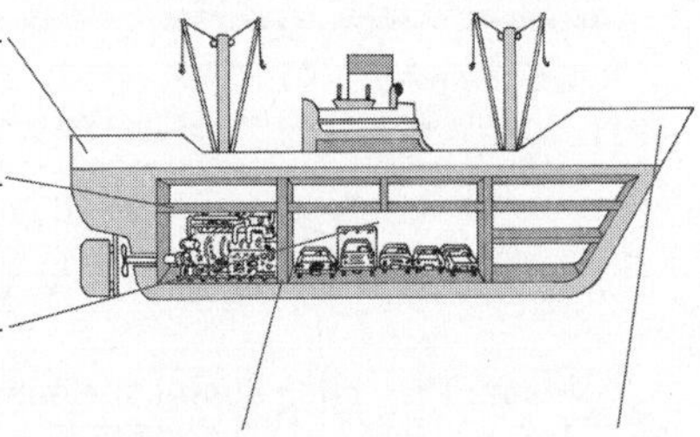

8. bulkhead 9. bow

WORKBOOK

10. What do we call the part of the ship where the cargo is carried? hold

C Story Items

11. About how far did the sailors have to carry Toby? 10 miles
12. What time of day was it when Toby reached the ship?
    - morning
    - noon
    - <u>evening</u>
13. Name the part of the ship where the sailors threw Toby. the hold
14. Why couldn't Toby see when he first got there? Idea: because it was dark
15. What did Toby smell? other animals
16. Name the country that is just north of the United States. Canada
17. **Underline** 2 kinds of animals that were locked up with Toby.
    - snake
    - <u>peacock</u>
    - duck
    - <u>kangaroo</u>
    - turkey
18. Which animal was showing off? the peacock
19. Where did that animal come from?
    - China
    - Turkey
    - <u>India</u>
20. Name the country the ship is going to. Canada

GO TO PART E IN YOUR TEXTBOOK.

TEXTBOOK

2. An oak tree is a living thing.

E Number your paper from 1 through 19.

Skill Items

Here's a rule: **Every plant is a living thing.**

1. A duck is not a plant. So what else do you know about a duck? nothing
2. An oak tree is a plant. So what else do you know about an oak tree?
3. A boy is not a plant. So what else do you know about a boy? nothing

4. Compare object A and object B. Remember, first tell how they're the same. Then tell how they're different.

4. Idea: They are both (pickup) trucks/have wheels. A is older/green/empty, but B is newer/brown/has a dog in the back.

TEXTBOOK

Review Items

5. A kangaroo that sits on a hill and warns the mob when trouble is coming is called a ▬. lookout
6. What's the name of the large, beautiful bird of India with a colorful tail? peacock
7. How many meters long is that bird from its head to the end of its tail? 2 meters
8. What does a male peacock spread when it shows off? (its tail) feathers
9. Which is more beautiful, a peacock's feathers or a peacock's voice? feathers
10. A kangaroo is ▬ centimeters long when it is born. 3
11. Big kangaroos grow to be as big as a ▬. man
12. Where does a baby kangaroo live right after it is born? Idea: in its mother's pouch
13. How long does it live there? half a year

Write **W** for warm-blooded animals and **C** for cold-blooded animals.

14. beetle   C
15. cow   W
16. horse   W
17. spider   C
18. bee   C

19. The people who lived in caves drew pictures on the cave walls. Write the letters of 4 things they made pictures of.

a. hands
b. fish
c. bears
d. dogs
e. horses
f. cows
g. birds
h. elephants

Lesson 116   **119**

Name _____

A Skill Items

Here are three events that happened in the story:
a. The police boat left and one of the sailors untied the animals.
b. Pip told the other animals that the trip to Canada would take 10 days.
c. The sailors tied up the animals and covered them with blankets.

1. Write the letter of the event that happened near the beginning of the story. **b**

2. Write the letter of the event that happened in the middle of the story. **c**

3. Write the letter of the event that happened near the end of the story. **a**

B Story Items

4. In what country are peacocks wild animals?
   • Turkey   • Pacific   • India   • Japan   • Canada   • Australia

5. Where was the ship when Toby got on it? **Australia**

6. Name the country the ship was going to. **Canada**

7. How long would that trip take? **10 days**

8. What ocean was the ship crossing? **Pacific (Ocean)**

Lesson 117   **31**

---

9. How did Mabel and the captain break the law in Australia?
   • hunting peacocks   • hunting lions
   • <u>hunting on a game preserve</u>

10. Pip wanted the captain to stand behind him so that Pip would look ███.
    • ugly   • old   • <u>beautiful</u>

11. What did the captain drop over Pip? **a net**

12. Why was Toby happy when he saw the police boat?
    • <u>He thought he would be saved.</u>
    • He thought Mabel was coming.
    • He thought the captain was leaving.

13. Did the peacock think that the police would help the animals? **no**

14. What was the police officer supposed to look at?
    • the stern   • <u>the cargo</u>   • the captain

15. What was the real cargo? **animals**

16. What did Mabel say their cargo was? **Idea: sacks of grain**

17. Did Mabel lie about the cargo? **yes**

███████ GO TO PART C IN YOUR TEXTBOOK. ██████

"As you can see," Mabel said, "we're just carrying sacks of grain."

"Yeah," the captain said. "Sacks of grain."

Footsteps moved into the hold. Toby tried to make some sound by wiggling around.

The officer said, "Sounds as if you have rats in here. Better be careful or they'll get into your grain."

"Thank you, Officer," Mabel said. "We'll take care of the rats."

"Yeah," another voice said. "We'll take care of the rats."

Then the footsteps moved up the stairs. There was the sound of a door closing. A minute or two later, there was the sound of a motor that moved farther and farther from the ship Toby was on.

When one of the sailors untied the animals, Pip said, "What did I tell you? Mabel may be a crook, but she is very smart."

Things looked bad for Toby.

MORE NEXT TIME

C Number your paper from 1 through 21.
Skill Items

The champions performed perfectly.
1. What word means **without any mistakes**? **perfectly**
2. What word means **put on a show**? **performed**
3. What word means **they won the championship**? **champions**

Lesson 117   **123**

151

Review Items
4. If you go east from Australia, what ocean do you go through? **Pacific (Ocean)**
5. What does a male peacock spread when it shows off? **(its) tail feathers**
6. Which is more beautiful, a peacock's feathers or a peacock's voice? **feathers**
7. What is a group of kangaroos called? **mob**
8. What is a baby kangaroo called? **joey**

9. Which letter shows the stern? **U**
10. Which letter shows the hold? **S**
11. Which letter shows a deck? **V**
12. Which letter shows the bow? **R**
13. Which letter shows a bulkhead? **T**

14. What do we call the part of a ship where the cargo is carried? **hold**
15. Name the country that is just north of the United States. **Canada**
16. How many seconds are in one minute? **60**

17. Some clocks have a hand that moves fast. When that hand goes all the way around the clock, how much time has passed? **60 seconds**
18. The hand that moves fast went around 6 times. How much time passed? **6 minutes**

19. A mile is more than ▮▮▮ feet. **5000**
20. Things closer to the bottom of the pile went into the pile ▮▮▮. **earlier**
21. Things closer to the top of the pile went into the pile ▮▮▮. **later**

118

Name _____

A Skill Items

Here are three events that happened in the story:
  a. The sailors put Toby on a cart.   b. The ship docked in Canada.
        c. Mabel took Toby to a circus.

1. Write the letter of the event that happened near the beginning of the story. **b**

2. Write the letter of the event that happened in the middle of the story. **a**

3. Write the letter of the event that happened near the end of the story. **c**

B

4. Which direction would you go to get from the main part of the United States to Canada? **north**

5. Which country is **larger**—Canada or the United States? **Canada**

6. Where do **more** people live—in Canada or in the United States? **United States**

7. Which country is **warmer**—Canada or the United States? **United States**

8. Write **north, south, east,** and **west** in the right boxes.
9. Make an **A** on Canada.
10. Make a **T** on the main part of the United States.

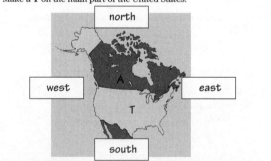

north

west   A   east

T

south

C Story Items

11. Name the country where the ship docked. **Canada**
12. What time was it when they docked?
    • afternoon   • evening   • <u>night</u>
13. Where did the truck take Toby? **to a circus**
14. What will he do there?
    • shoot a cannon   • drive a truck
        • <u>get shot from a cannon</u>
15. How did Toby feel at the end of the story? **Ideas: sad; unhappy; homesick**

GO TO PART D IN YOUR TEXTBOOK.

about the dust. The dust didn't seem very bad to him now. He missed the thumping sound of the mob. He missed the leader. Toby missed his mother and the other kangaroos. He missed the smell of grass and the sound of the wind.

As he sat there in his cage, he felt a large tear run down the side of his nose and fall off. "Oh, very bad," he said to himself and tried to go to sleep. Poor Toby even missed Pip.

MORE NEXT TIME

D Number your paper from 1 through 23.
Skill Items

Use the words in the box to write complete sentences.

perfectly	finest	cargo	pouch
champions	pilots	tough	police officers

1. ▭ checked the ship's ▭.
2. The ▭ performed ▭.

1. ⟨Police officers⟩ checked the ship's ⟨cargo⟩.
2. The ⟨champions⟩ performed ⟨perfectly⟩.

130   *Lesson 118*

Review Items

Write the letter that shows where each place is.
3. Italy   H   7. Canada   B
4. Greece   K   8. United States   D
5. Turkey   J   9. New York City   C
6. San Francisco   A

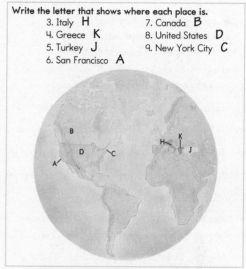

10. What is the only country that has wild kangaroos?
11. How far can a kangaroo go in one jump?
12. A kangaroo is ▭ centimeters long when it is born. 3
13. Big kangaroos grow to be as big as a ▭. man

10. Australia   11. (over) 10 feet

Lesson 118   131

---

14. Where does a baby kangaroo live right after it is born? Idea: in its mother's pouch
15. How long does it live there? half a year

16. How many seconds are in one minute? 60

17. Some clocks have a hand that moves fast. When that hand goes all the way around the clock, how much time has passed? 60 seconds
18. The hand that moves fast went around 8 times. How much time passed? 8 minutes

For items 19–23, write the correct years.
• 1985   • 1982   • 1987   • 1981   • 1989

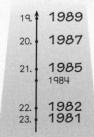

19.   1989
20.   1987
21.   1985
      1984
22.   1982
23.   1981

132   *Lesson 118*

119

Name _____

A Skill Items

Here are three events that happened in the story:
    a. The owner took Toby into a tent.
    b. Two boys threw papers at Toby.
    c. The owner told Toby to ride a bicycle backward on the high wire.

1. Write the letter of the event that happened near the beginning of the story. a

2. Write the letter of the event that happened in the middle of the story. c

3. Write the letter of the event that happened near the end of the story. b

B

4. **Underline** the place where a circus is sometimes held.
        • a train   • a tent   • a store

5. Are all the acts on the ground? no

C Story Items

6. The owner told Toby that he had to do tricks if he wanted
   Ideas: to eat; to get fed

Lesson 119   35

7. Was Toby part of a good circus? **no**

8. Was Toby the only animal in the circus? **yes**

9. About how many people were in the stands? **20**

Here are the announcements the owner made:
   a. Toby will ride a bicycle backward on the floor.
   b. Toby will ride a bicycle forward on the floor.
   c. Toby will ride a bicycle backward on the high wire.
   d. Toby will walk with the bicycle on the floor.

10. Write the letter of the first announcement the owner made. **c**

11. Write the letter of the second announcement the owner made. **a**

12. Write the letter of the third announcement the owner made. **b**

13. Write the letter of the fourth announcement the owner made. **d**

14. Write the letter of the easiest trick. **d**

15. The owner told Toby to do different tricks. Which was easier, the first trick or the second trick? **second trick**

16. Did Toby do any tricks? **no**

17. Will Toby get any food from the circus owner? **no**

GO TO PART D IN YOUR TEXTBOOK.

The owner said, "One moment, ladies and gentlemen. Before Toby rides the bicycle backward on the floor, Toby will ride it forward on the floor."

The owner looked at Toby and said, "Do it." Toby shook his head, no.

People were now yelling, "I want my money back," and "Let's call a cop."

The owner held up his hands and said, "Before Toby rides the bicycle forward on the floor, Toby will walk with the bicycle on the floor."

Toby looked at the owner and shook his head no again.

"This is the worst show in the world," people were yelling. A woman was shaking her umbrella at the owner. Two boys were throwing papers at Toby. Toby was saying, "Oh, worse than bad."

MORE NEXT TIME

D Number your paper from 1 through 21.
Review Items
1. Which direction would you go to get **from Canada** to the main part of the United States? **south**
2. Which country is **smaller**, Canada or the United States?
3. Which country is **colder**, Canada or the United States?
4. Where do **more** people live, in Canada or in the United States?

---

5. Which letter shows Canada? **E**
6. Which letter shows the United States? **F**

E

F

7. Tom is 4 miles high. Jack is 20 miles high. Who is colder? **Jack**
8. Tell why. **Idea: because he's higher**

9. What year is it now? **(current year)**
10. In what year were you born? **(student's birth year)**
11. In what year was the first airplane made? **1903**
12. What was the year 1 hundred years ago? **(correct answer)**
13. What was the year 2 hundred years ago? **(correct answer)**

---

14. In what year did the United States become a country? **1776**
15. What was the year 3 hundred years ago? **(correct answer)**
16. During a storm, which comes first, lightning or thunder? **lightning**
17. How does fire like to move, up or down? **up**

18. The picture shows the outline of a hand on a cave wall. Which letter shows the part of the wall that was covered with paint? **B**
19. Which letter shows the part of the wall that was not covered with paint? **R**

20. Cave people painted pictures of horses on cave walls. How are those horses different from horses that live today? **Idea: They're smaller.**
21. Which horse has a shorter back, a racehorse or a quarter horse?

TEST 12 **120**

Number your paper from 1 through 32.

1. Which direction would you go to get from the main part of the United States to Canada? **north**
2. Which country is **larger,** Canada or the United States?
3. Which country is **warmer,** Canada or the United States?
4. Where do **more** people live, in Canada or in the United States?
5. Is the United States **bigger** than most other countries or **smaller** than most other countries? **bigger**
6. In what country are peacocks wild animals? **India**
7. What is the only country that has wild kangaroos?
8. How far can a kangaroo go in one jump?
9. A kangaroo is ▆▆ centimeters long when it is born. **3**

10. Where does a baby kangaroo live right after it is born?
11. How long does it live there?
   • half a month   • half a year   • half a week

7. Australia
8. (over) 10 feet
10. in its mother's pouch

Lesson 120   **141**

---

12. What place does the **A** show? **United States**
13. What place does the **S** show? **Pacific Ocean**
14. What place does the **J** show? **Alaska**
15. What place does the **Z** show? **Australia**
16. What place does the **P** show? **Canada**

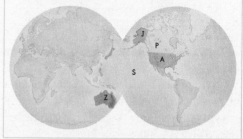

17. What's the name of the large, beautiful bird of India with a colorful tail? **peacock**
18. How long is that bird from its head to the end of its tail? **2 meters**

19. What is a group of kangaroos called? **mob**
20. What is a baby kangaroo called? **joey**
21. How many seconds are in one minute? **60**

142   *Lesson 120*

---

22. Some clocks have a hand that moves fast. When that hand goes all the way around the clock, how much time has passed? **60 seconds**
23. The hand that moves fast went around 8 times. How much time passed? **8 minutes**

24. If you go east from Australia, what ocean do you go through? **Pacific (Ocean)**

Skill Items

For each item, write the underlined word or words from the sentences in the box.

Police officers checked the ship's cargo.
The champions performed perfectly.

25. What underlining means **put on a show?** **performed**
26. What underlining means **cops?** **police officers**
27. What underlining refers to the things that a ship carries? **cargo**
28. What underlining means **without any mistakes?**
29. What underlining means **they won the championship?** **champions**

28. perfectly

Lesson 120   **143**

Here are three things you did as part of the test:
   a. You answered questions about animals.
   b. You answered items about Canada and the United States.
   c. You answered questions about the meanings of words.
30. Write the letter of the thing you did near the beginning of the test. **b**
31. Write the letter of the thing you did near the middle of the test. **a**
32. Write the letter of the thing you did near the end of the test. **c**

━━━━━ END OF TEST 12 ━━━━━

144   *Lesson 120*

WORKBOOK

121

Name _____

A

1. Boxers wear large mittens when they box. What are those mittens called? <u>boxing gloves</u>

2. What do we call the place where boxers box?
   - a rink   • <u>a ring</u>   • a square

3. Is that place round? <u>no</u>

4. What do the boxers do with the gloves? <u>Idea: hit each other</u>

B Story Items

5. The circus owner told Toby that he had to do tricks if he wanted <u>Ideas: to eat food; not to be hungry</u>

6. Was Toby part of a good circus? <u>no</u>

7. Why did the owner refund the people's money?
   - because it rained   • because the circus closed
   - <u>because Toby did not do any tricks</u>

8. The owner didn't give Toby any food. Tell why. <u>Idea: because Toby did not do any tricks</u>

9. How much did the circus owner pay for Toby?
   - ten thousand dollars   • <u>a thousand dollars</u>   • a hundred dollars

Lesson 121   **37**

WORKBOOK

10. How much did Mabel pay the owner when she bought Toby back?
    - ten thousand dollars   • a thousand dollars   • <u>a hundred dollars</u>

11. Who made the best deal, Mabel or the owner? <u>Mabel</u>

12. Where did Mabel take Toby after she bought him back?
    - <u>Roadside Zoo</u>   • Roadside Cafe   • City Zoo

13. Did she make money when she sold Toby the second time? <u>yes</u>

14. Toby recognized his father by looking at his <u>tail</u>

Review Items

15. Write the letter **A** on Australia.
16. Write the letter **B** on the United States.
17. Write the letter **C** on Canada.
18. Write the letter **D** on the Pacific Ocean.

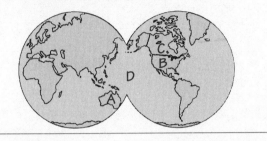

GO TO PART D IN YOUR TEXTBOOK.

38   Lesson 121

TEXTBOOK

and blue skies and the mob and Australia. They talked about Toby's mother and the leader and the other kangaroos from the mob. Then Toby's father said, "Son, we've got to get out of this terrible place and go home."
Toby said, "Double good."
                    MORE NEXT TIME

D Number your paper from 1 through 19.

Skill Items

Here are 3 events that happened in the story. Write **beginning, middle,** or **end** for each event.
1. Mabel and the captain took Toby to the Roadside Zoo.
2. Toby recognized his father. **end**
3. The owner talked to Mabel on the phone. **beginning**

She paid the correct amount.
4. What word tells how much there is? **amount**
5. What word means **right**? **correct**

1. middle

Lesson 121   **149**

TEXTBOOK

Review Items

6. Write the letters of the 5 names that tell about time.
7. Write the letter of the one name that tells about temperature. **a**
8. Write the letters of the 6 names that tell about distance or length. **d, e, h, i, l, o**
9. Write the letters of the 3 names that tell about speed.

   a. degrees   f. hours   k. miles per year
   b. minutes   g. weeks   l. yards
   c. miles per hour h. centimeters   m. years
   d. meters   i. miles   n. inches per week
   e. inches   j. days   o. feet

10. You can see drops of water on grass early in the morning. What are those drops called? **dew**
11. When we weigh very small things, the unit we use is ▓▓▓. **grams**
12. Name **2** kinds of wells.
13. Gasoline comes from a liquid called ▓▓▓. **(crude) oil**

   6. b, f, g, j, m
   9. c, k, n
   12. (fresh) water well, (crude) oil well

150   Lesson 121

---

14. The arrow that killed Achilles hit him in the ▓▓▓▓. **heel**
15. That arrow had something on it that killed Achilles. What did it have on it? **poison**

16. Some clocks have a hand that moves fast. When that hand goes all the way around the clock, how much time has passed? **60 seconds**
17. The hand that moves fast went around 3 times. How much time passed? **3 minutes**

18. In what country are peacocks wild animals? **India**
19. A mile is a little more than ▓▓▓▓ feet. **5 thousand**

Name _____
Story Items

1. The two boxing kangaroos in the story were **Toby and his father**.
2. Who did the kangaroos hit? **zoo owner**
3. Did the crowd like this act? **yes**
4. Why didn't the crowd listen to Toby?
   - • People were clapping and yelling. (underlined)
   - • People were sleeping.   • People were eating.
5. Who made the crowd become quiet? **Pip**
6. Who told the police where to find Mabel and the captain? **zoo owner**
7. What happened to Mabel and the captain? **Idea: They went to jail.**
8. Pip decided to stay in Canada so he could ▓▓▓▓.
   - • open a zoo   • entertain people (underlined)
   - • box with kangaroos
9. Name the country that Toby and his father went to at the end of the story. **Australia**
10. Why did the other kangaroos shout, "Hooray for Toby"? **Idea: because he had saved them**

---

11. Make an **L** on the leader of the mob.
12. Make a **T** on Toby.
13. Make an **F** on Toby's father.
14. Make an **M** on Toby's mother.

Review Items

15. Why did the circus owner refund the people's money? **Idea: because Toby hadn't performed**
16. How much did the circus owner pay for Toby? **1 thousand dollars**
17. How much did Mabel pay the circus owner when she bought Toby back? **1 hundred dollars**

GO TO PART C IN YOUR TEXTBOOK.

---

4. She paid the [correct] [amount].
5. The [champions] performed [perfectly].

C Number your paper from 1 through 21.
Skill Items

Here are three events that happened in the story.
Write **beginning**, **middle**, or **end** for each event.
1. Toby and his father were taken to a small tent. **beginning**
2. The police arrived. **middle**
3. The other kangaroos cheered when they saw Toby and his father. **end**

Use the words in the box to write complete sentences.

| sailors | perfectly | amount | colorful |
| correct | champions | surprise | loudly |

4. She paid the ▓▓▓▓ ▓▓▓▓.
5. The ▓▓▓▓ performed ▓▓▓▓.

Review Items

6. Which letter shows a kangaroo? H
7. Which letter shows a koala? F
8. Which letter shows a platypus? G

9. If you go east from Australia, what ocean do you go through? Pacific (Ocean)
10. If you go west from the United States, what ocean do you go through? Pacific (Ocean)
11. In what country are peacocks wild animals? India
12. What is a group of kangaroos called? mob
13. What is a baby kangaroo called? joey

14. What's the name of the large, beautiful bird of India with a colorful tail? peacock
15. How many meters long is that bird from its head to the end of its tail? 2 meters

Lesson 122   157

---

16. Which letter shows the stern? R
17. Which letter shows the hold? M
18. Which letter shows a deck? Q
19. Which letter shows the bow? P
20. Which letter shows a bulkhead? L

21. Write the letters of the 9 places that are in the United States.

[a.] Denver	[i.] New York City
b. Turkey	[j.] Texas
[c.] Chicago	[k.] San Francisco
d. China	[l.] Ohio
[e.] Alaska	[m.] California
f. Italy	n. Greece
[g.] Lake Michigan	o. Canada
h. Japan	p. Australia

158   *Lesson 122*

123

Name_____

Ⓐ The answers for items 2–9 should be spelled correctly.

1. A word that sounds the same as another word is called a
homonym

Write a homonym for each word below.

2. four for (fore)
3. ate eight
4. new knew
5. hear here
6. to two (too)
7. there their (they're)
8. rode road
9. won one

10. In the sentence below, **underline** each word that has a homonym.

She knew that he won four races.

Ⓑ **Story Items**

11. Is Hohoboho a real place or is it a make-believe place?
make-believe place

12. How did some words in the word bank get scars?
Idea: by fighting with each other

13. Do the words **run** and **eat** have scars? no
14. Why? Idea: because they weren't in fights

Lesson 123   41

The words in the first column had fights with words in the second column. Draw a line to connect the words that fought with each other.

right	their
15. here	for
16. there	write
17. two	hear
18. ate	to
19. four	eight

Review Items

Use these answers: • 100 pounds   • 150 pounds   • 500 pounds

20. About how much does a leopard weigh? 100 pounds
21. About how much weight can a leopard carry? 150 pounds
22. About how much does a chimpanzee weigh? 100 pounds
23. About how much force can a chimpanzee pull with? 500 pounds

24. How long is a football field? 100 yards
25. **Underline** 2 ways that a football team can move the ball down the field.

   • run   • slide   • pass   • bounce

GO TO PART D IN YOUR TEXTBOOK.

42   *Lesson 123*

D Number your paper from 1 through 12.
Review Items

1. Write the letters of all the words that belong to the
   jump family. *b, i, l, o, s*

2. Write the letters of all the words that belong to the
   ride family. *a, e, f, j, q*

a. ride	e. rode	i. jumps	m. hiding	q. riding
b. jumping	f. rider	j. rides	n. see	r. eats
c. hot	g. sitting	k. chair	o. jumped	s. jump
d. book	h. talked	l. jumper	p. flying	t. run

Some of Andrew's hang-times are shown on the
stopwatches.

3. Write the letter of the watch that shows his best
   hang-time. **B**

4. How many seconds are shown on that watch? **14**

5. Write the letter of the watch that shows his worst
   hang-time. **A**

6. How many seconds are shown on that watch? **6**

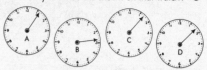

7. Write the letters of 3 ways that people traveled 2
   hundred years ago.
[a] by water	b. by jet	c. by train
[d] by walking	e. by car	[f] by horse

8. Is the United States [bigger] than most other countries
   or **smaller** than most other countries?

9. Which country is smaller, the [United States] or
   Canada?

---

10. What place does the **A** show? *United States*
11. What place does the **B** show? *Alaska*
12. What place does the **C** show? *Canada*

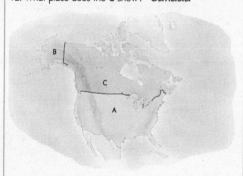

124

Name _____

Story Items

1. The words **there** and **their** were always fighting because they are the
   same in one way. Name that way.
   Idea: They sound the same.

2. What is different about **there** and **their**?
   Idea: spelling

3. How many other words sound the same as **three**? *none*

4. How many fights did the word **three** have? *none*

5. The word **one** had fights with another word. Write that word. Be
   sure to spell that word correctly. *won*

6. The word **four** had fights with another word. Write that word. Be
   sure to spell that word correctly. *for (fore)*

7. The word **eight** had fights with another word. Write that word. Be
   sure to spell that word correctly. *ate*

8. Write two words that the word **two** had fights with. Spell the words
   correctly. ① *to*   ② *too*

Review Items

9. Which animal is safer, a cow or an elephant? *elephant*

10. Why? *Idea: because it's bigger*

11. What do people keep in banks? *money*

12. A second is a unit of ▇▇.
    • weight   • length   • <u>time</u>   • distance

13. What is a group of kangaroos called? mob
14. What is a baby kangaroo called? joey
15. What is the only country that has wild kangaroos? Australia
16. How far can a kangaroo go in one jump? (over) 10 feet

17. Which letter shows a kangaroo? Y
18. Which letter shows a koala? Z

GO TO PART D IN YOUR TEXTBOOK.

D Number your paper from 1 through 16.

Skill Items

> Perhaps they will reply in a few days.
> 1. What word means **maybe**? perhaps
> 2. What word means **answer**? reply

Review Items

3. A word that sounds the same as another word is called a ▅▅▅. homonym

4. Find **S** on map 1. What place does the **S** show?
5. What's the name of place **R**? Pacific Ocean
6. Find **F** on map 2. What place does the **F** show?
7. What happened in place **F** about 3 thousand years ago?
8. What's the name of place **G**? Italy
9. What's the name of place **H**? Japan
10. What place does the **T** show? Australia

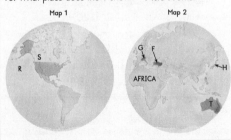

Map 1   Map 2

4. Canada
6. Turkey
7. Idea: the war between Greece and Troy

Copy words 11 through 16. After each word, write the letter of the word it fought with.

11. right	a. dew
12. there	b. write
13. knew	c. eight
14. road	d. new
15. do	e. their
16. ate	f. rode

11. right—b
12. there—e
13. knew—d
14. road—f
15. do—a
16. ate—c

125

Name _____

Story Items

1. The words **new** and **knew** had lots of fights because they are the same in one way. Name that way.
   Ideas: They sound the same; they're both homonyms.

2. Did the people in Hohoboho start talking very early in the morning?
   no

3. Why was the word bank calm early in the morning?
   Idea: because people weren't talking

4. Some words in the word bank wore earplugs. Tell why. Idea:
   because the word bank got so noisy

5. A change was made in the word bank so that words like **won** and **one** would stop fighting. The words were ▮▮▮▮.
   • spoken   • written   • drawn

6. Let's say someone in Hohoboho said, "It's over **there**." Which word would get the point, **there** or **their**? there

7. Let's say someone in Hohoboho said, "I have **two** dogs." Which word would get the point, **to, too, or two**? two

8. Were there any more fights in the word bank after the change was made? yes

Skill Items

9. Compare the word **eight** and the word **ate**. Remember, first tell how they're the same. Then tell how they're different.
   Ideas: They both sound the same; they're both homonyms.
   Eight tells about a number, but ate tells about
   something you do, etc.

Lesson 125   45

Review Items

10. Henry Ouch went for a vacation. He left San Francisco on a large ship. That ship went to Japan. Which direction did it go? west

11. How far was that trip? 5000 miles

12. What ocean did Henry cross? Pacific (Ocean)

13. The ship passed some islands. How did Henry know they were islands? Idea: They had water all the way around them.

14. Henry could see palm trees on some islands. He knew that the branches of a palm tree are called fronds

15. He also knew the name of the large hard things that grow on some palm trees. What are those things called? coconuts

16. When Henry got thirsty, he drank little drops of water that formed on the deck early in the morning. What are those drops called? dew

17. Henry did not drink water from the ocean. Why not? Idea: It makes you thirstier.

18. Henry did not like it when the temperature dropped because Henry's body worked like the bodies of other insects. Henry was cold -blooded.

19. Sometimes the temperature inside his body was higher than your normal temperature. What's your normal body temperature?
    98 degrees

20. Sometimes the temperature inside his body was lower than your normal temperature. When would the temperature inside his body get lower? Idea: when the temperature outside got colder

▰▰▰ GO TO PART D IN YOUR TEXTBOOK. ▰▰▰

46   Lesson 125

---

1. She paid the [correct] [amount].
2. [Perhaps] they will [reply] in a few days.

D Number your paper from 1 through 18.

Skill Items

Use the words in the box to write complete sentences.

reply	describe	difference	correct	attack
worst	behave	perhaps	single	amount

1. She paid the ▮▮▮ ▮▮▮.
2. ▮▮▮ they will ▮▮▮ in a few days.

Review Items

3. Did the first people who lived in caves cook their food? no

4. Did the people who lived in caves many years later cook their food? yes

5. What's the name of the large, beautiful bird of India with a colorful tail? peacock

6. How long is that bird from its head to the end of its tail? 2 meters

7. What do we call the part of a ship where the cargo is carried? hold

8. Name the country that is just north of the United States. Canada

9. How many seconds are in one minute? 60

176   Lesson 125

---

10. Which letter shows where Australia is? Z
11. Which letter shows where the United States is? T
12. Which letter shows where Canada is? P
13. Which letter shows where the Pacific Ocean is? S

Copy words 14 through 18. After each word, write the letter of the word it fought with.

14. for	a. hear
15. too	b. one
16. won	c. two
17. here	d. four
18. knew	e. new

14. for—d
15. too—c
16. won—b
17. here—a
18. knew—e

Lesson 125   177

161

Name _____

Story Items

1. New fights started as soon as the words were written on the screen. The words that fought were the same in one way. Name that way.
Idea: They were spelled the same.

2. How were they different from each other? **Ideas: They sounded different; they had different meanings.**

The words in the first column had fights with words in the second column. Draw a line to connect the words that fought with each other.

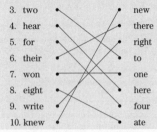

3. two — new
4. hear — there
5. for — right
6. their — to
7. won — one
8. eight — here
9. write — four
10. knew — ate

11. Let's say that someone in Hohoboho said, "Those dogs had a terrible **row**." The word that would get the point rhymes with ▮▮▮.

    • <u>how</u>   • no

12. Let's say that someone in Hohoboho said, "Do you **live** here?" The word that would get the point rhymes with ▮▮▮.

    • dive   • <u>give</u>

13. Someone in Hohoboho said, "Did you **read** this book?" The word that would get the point rhymes with ▮▮▮.

    • <u>need</u>   • bed

Lesson 126   47

---

14. Someone in Hohoboho said, "Please stand in the **bow** of the boat." The word that would get the point rhymes with ▮▮▮.

    • <u>how</u>   • no

15. Someone in Hohoboho said, "He uses a **bow** and arrow for hunting." The word that would get the point rhymes with ▮▮▮.

    • how   • <u>no</u>

Review Items

16. When a pond gets colder, which way does the temperature go?
down

17. A car gets hotter. So what do you know about the temperature of the car? **Idea: It goes up.**

18. Some clocks have a hand that moves fast. When that hand goes all the way around the clock, how much time has passed?
60 seconds

19. The hand that moves fast went around 6 times. How much time passed? **6 minutes**

20. In what country are peacocks wild animals? **India**

═══════ GO TO PART C IN YOUR TEXTBOOK. ═══════

48   *Lesson 126*

So there was a big change in the word bank. The words that sound the same didn't fight because they could look at the screen to see how the word was spelled. The word **two** didn't fight with the words that sounded the same. And the words that are spelled the same never had a problem because they listened to the voice. If the voice said, "That is a **live** fish," the sound of the word would tell who got the point. Most of the problems in the word bank were solved.

MORE NEXT TIME

───────────────────

C Number your paper from 1 through 18.

Skill Items

Write the word from the box that means the same thing as the underlined part of each sentence.

continued	couple	thawed	boiling
announcement	argument	enormous	comparison

1. The snow <u>melted</u> when the sun came out. **thawed**
2. The storm clouds were <u>very large</u>. **enormous**
3. The teacher's <u>message</u> told about our homework.
announcement

Lesson 126   181

Review Items

4. The names in one box tell about time. Write the letter of that box. **B**
5. The names in one box tell about length. Write the letter of that box. **A**

A	centimeter	inch	meter	mile	yard
B	week	year	second	month	minute	hour

6. How fast is truck A going? **20 miles per hour**
7. How fast is truck B going? **40 miles per hour**
8. Which truck is going faster? **B**

182   *Lesson 126*

---

9. Write the letter of the animal that is facing into the wind. **A**

10. Which direction is that animal facing? **south**

11. So what's the **name** of that wind? **south wind**

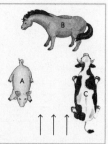

12. Which country is warmer, Canada or the United States?

13. Where do more people live, in Canada or in the United States?

Write a homonym for each word.
14. rode   **road**
15. write   **right**
16. eight   **ate**
17. new   **knew**
18. one   **won**

Lesson 126   **183**

Name _____

A

For each contraction below, write the two words that make up the contraction.

CONTRACTION	FIRST WORD	SECOND WORD
1. you'll	you	will
2. I've	I	have
3. he'll	he	will
4. shouldn't	should	not
5. we're	we	are
6. aren't	are	not

B   Story Items

7. The words **one** and **won** used to fight because they are the same in one way. Name that way. **Idea: They sound the same.**

8. Write two words that the word **two** used to have fights with. Spell the words correctly. **to, too**

9. A change was made in the word bank so that words like **one** and **won** would stop fighting. What was the change?
   Idea: They would appear on the screen.

10. Write the word that would fight with **tear** if the words were written.
   tear

11. If someone in Hohoboho says the word **you've**, two words get one point. Name those two words.
   you've, you

Lesson 127   **49**

---

12. Name the word that gets one-half point. **have**

13. If someone in Hohoboho says the word **wouldn't,** two words get one point. Name those two words.
   wouldn't, would

14. Name the word that gets one-half point. **not**

Write the letter or letters that are missing for each contraction.
15. couldn't **o**   17. she'll **wi**
16. we've **ha**   18. you're **a**

Review Items

19. **Underline** the 3 relatives of the word **talk.**
   • sits   • talked   • talking   • hopped   • walker   • talker

20. Let's say that someone in Hohoboho said, "I will **row** the boat across the lake." The word that would get the point rhymes with ▦.
   • how   • no

21. Let's say that someone in Hohoboho said, "I have a **live** bird in my room." The word that would get the point rhymes with ▦.
   • dive   • give

22. Let's say that someone in Hohoboho said, "Have you **read** this book?" The word that would get the point rhymes with ▦.
   • need   • bed

GO TO PART D IN YOUR TEXTBOOK.

D   Number your paper from 1 through 15.

Skill Items

Here's a rule: **Insects do not have bones.**
1. A beetle is an insect. So what else do you know about a beetle?
2. A worm is not an insect. So what else do you know about a worm? **Idea: nothing**
3. An ant is an insect. So what else do you know about an ant? **Idea: An ant does not have bones.**

Review Items
4. If you go east from Australia, what ocean do you go through? **Pacific (Ocean)**
5. A kangaroo is ▦ centimeters long when it is born. **3**
6. Big kangaroos grow to be as big as a ▦. **man**
7. A kangaroo that sits on a hill and warns the mob when trouble is coming is called a ▦. **lookout**
8. What does a male peacock spread when it shows off?
9. Which is more beautiful, a peacock's feathers or a peacock's voice?

1. Idea: A beetle does not have bones.
8. (its) tail feathers

163

10. Which letter shows the stern? **U**
11. Which letter shows the hold? **S**
12. Which letter shows a deck? **V**
13. Which letter shows the bow? **R**
14. Which letter shows a bulkhead? **T**

15. Boxers wear large mittens when they box. What are those mittens called? *boxing gloves*

Name _____

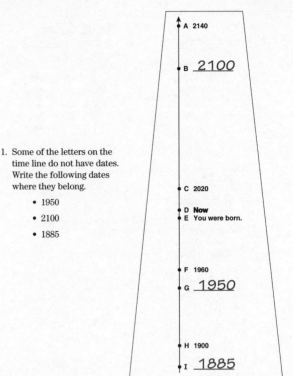

1. Some of the letters on the time line do not have dates. Write the following dates where they belong.
   - 1950
   - 2100
   - 1885

A 2140
B **2100**
C 2020
D **Now**
E You were born.
F 1960
G **1950**
H 1900
I **1885**

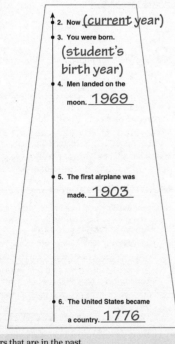

2. Now **(current year)**
3. You were born. **(student's birth year)**
4. Men landed on the moon. **1969**
5. The first airplane was made. **1903**
6. The United States became a country. **1776**

Write the years for the things shown on this time line.
- 1903
- 1969
- 1524
- 1776
- 2113

7. **Underline** the 5 years that are in the past.
   - 2009
   - **1871**
   - **1994**
   - 1990
   - 2990
   - **1490**
   - **690**
   - 3690

GO TO PART E IN YOUR TEXTBOOK.

E **Number your paper from 1 through 28.**

Passage B
1. If all buildings in a city are made of wood, what could happen?
2. In a large city, some buildings may be made of wood. What kind of buildings are those?
   - office buildings
   - stores
   - <u>houses</u>
   - barns
3. In a large city, some buildings are not made of wood. What kind of buildings are those?
   - <u>office buildings</u>
   - <u>stores</u>
   - houses
   - barns
4. Which city had a great fire that burned down most of the city? **Chicago**
5. In what year was that fire? **1871**
6. Taller buildings are made of steel, concrete, and brick because they are ▩▩▩.
   - taller
   - stronger
   - cheaper

Passage C
7. Are time machines **real** or **make-believe**?
8. A force is a ▩▩▩. **push**

1. Idea: Fire could spread and burn down the whole city.

9. Which picture shows the largest force? **D**
10. Which picture shows the smallest force? **C**

A B C D E

Skill Items

Write the word from the box that means the same thing as the underlined part of each sentence.

unpleasant	direct	except	announced
force	imagined	raw	frisky

11. The path between their houses was <u>straight</u>. **direct**
12. The hot weather was <u>not very nice</u>. **unpleasant**
13. Susan ate <u>uncooked</u> fish. **raw**

196   Lesson 128

Review Items
14. The temperature inside your body is about ▨▨ degrees when you are healthy. **98**
15. Most fevers don't go over ▨▨ degrees. **101**
16. Airplanes land at airports. Ships land at ▨▨. **harbors**
17. Airplanes are pulled by little trucks. Ships are pulled by ▨▨. **tugboats**
18. Airplanes unload at gates. Ships unload at ▨▨. **docks**

19. You would have the least amount of power if you pushed against one of the handles. Which handle is that? **H**
20. Which handle would give you the most power? **E**

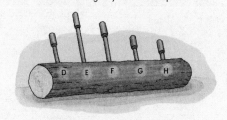

D E F G H

Lesson 128   197

---

21. Which is longer, a centimeter or a meter?
22. How many centimeters long is a meter? **100**

23. An arrow goes from the **R**. Which direction is that arrow going? **east**
24. An arrow goes from the **S**. Which direction is that arrow going? **north**
25. An arrow goes from the **T**. Which direction is that arrow going? **south**

26. How many ships sailed to Troy? **1 thousand**
27. How long did the war between Greece and Troy go on? **10 years**
28. If the Greek army could get a few men inside the wall of Troy, these men could ▨▨. **open the gate**

198   Lesson 128

129

Name _____

Story Items

1. Why were Eric and Tom on the mountain?
   - They were cutting down trees.
   - They were picking flowers.
   - <u>They were at a picnic.</u>

2. The time machine looked like a ▨▨.
   - giant pile
   - <u>giant pill</u>
   - giant clock

3. How did Tom feel when he saw the time machine?
   - happy
   - <u>scared</u>
   - sad
4. Did Eric feel the same way? **no**

5. In what year did Eric and Tom find the time machine? **(current year)**

6. What year was Thrig from? **2400**
7. That year is ▨▨.
   - in the past
   - <u>in the future</u>

8. Why couldn't Thrig go back to that year?
   - He was too lazy.
   - <u>He was too weak.</u>
   - He was too busy.

9. What did Eric do that closed the door of the time machine?
   - <u>sat down</u>
   - stood up
   - pulled on a handle
10. What did Eric do to make the time machine move in time?
   - sat down
   - stood up
   - <u>pulled on a handle</u>

Lesson 129   53

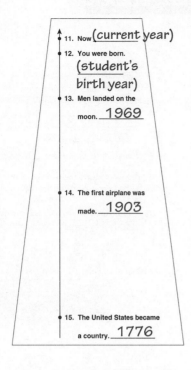

11. Now (current year)
12. You were born. (student's birth year)
13. Men landed on the moon. __1969__
14. The first airplane was made. __1903__
15. The United States became a country. __1776__

Review Items

Write the years for the things shown on this time line.

- 1903
- 1969
- 1524
- 1776

GO TO PART C IN YOUR TEXTBOOK.

C Number your paper from 1 through 22.

Skill Items

Here are 3 events that happened in the story. Write **beginning, middle,** or **end** for each event.
1. Tom felt a great force against his face and his chest. end
2. Eric and Tom were walking down a mountain with some boys and girls. beginning
3. A time machine landed on the side of the mountain. middle

The palace guards spoke different languages.
4. What's the name of the place where a king and queen live? palace
5. What word refers to the words that people in a country use to say things? languages
6. What word names the people who protect the palace? guards

Review Items

7. Which arrow shows the way the air will leave the jet engines? X
8. Which arrow shows the way the jet will move? W

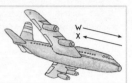

9. The biggest state in the United States is ▨▨▨.
10. The second biggest state in the United States is ▨▨▨.
11. Write the name of the state in the United States that is bigger than Japan.
   - Ohio
   - New York
   - Alaska
12. Write the letter of the plane that is in the warmest air. W
13. Write the letter of the plane that is in the coldest air. Z

	5 miles high
Z	4 miles high
Y	3 miles high
X	2 miles high
W	1 mile high

14. A force is a ▨▨▨. push
15. If all buildings in a city are made of wood, what could happen? Idea: The whole city could burn in a fire.
16. Taller buildings are made of steel and brick because they are ▨▨▨.
   - cheaper
   - taller
   - stronger
17. Which city had a great fire that burned down most of the city? Chicago
18. In what year was that fire? 1871

9. Alaska; 10. Texas

19. Which picture shows the largest force? C
20. Which picture shows the smallest force? A

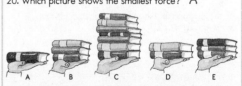

21. In a large city, some buildings are not made of wood. What kind of buildings are those?
   - office buildings
   - stores
   - houses
   - barns
22. In a large city, some buildings may be made of wood. What kind of buildings are those? houses

TEST 13 **130**

Number your paper from 1 through 33.

1. Boxers wear large mittens when they box. What are those mittens called? *boxing gloves*

2. A word that sounds the same as another word is called a ▢. *homonym*

3. Let's say that someone in Hohoboho said, "My friends got hurt in a **row.**" The word that would get the point rhymes with ▢.
   • ☐how☐   • no

4. Let's say that someone in Hohoboho said, "Do you **live** near her?" The word that would get the point rhymes with ▢.
   • dive   • ☐give☐

5. Let's say that someone in Hohoboho said, "I like to **read.**" The word that would get the point rhymes with ▢.
   • ☐need☐   • bed

> Write a homonym for each word.
> 6. dew   *do (due)*
> 7. to   *two (too)*
> 8. hear   *here*
> 9. new   *knew*
> 10. won   *one*
> 11. road   *rode*

TEXTBOOK

12. you are   13. we will   14. can not   15. I have

> For each contraction, write the two words that make up the contraction.
> 12. you're   13. we'll   14. can't   15. I've

16. A force is a ▢. The greater the force, the harder the ▢. *push; push*

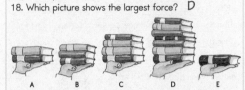

17. Which picture shows the smallest force?   *E*
18. Which picture shows the largest force?   *D*

A   B   C   D   E

19. In what year did Eric and Tom find the time machine?

> 20. What year was Thrig from?   *2400*
> 21. Is that year **in the past** or ☐**in the future?**☐

22. What do you do to close the door of the time machine?   *Idea: sit on the seat*
23. What do you do to make the time machine move in time?   *Idea: pull the handle*

19. *(current year)*

TEXTBOOK

26. *office buildings, stores*

24. If all buildings in a city are made of wood, what could happen?   *Idea: The whole city could burn.*
25. In a large city, some buildings may be made of wood. What kind of buildings are those?
   • office buildings   • stores   • ☐houses☐   • barns
26. In a large city, some buildings are not made of wood. What kind of buildings are those?

> 27. Which city had a great fire that burned down most of the city?   *Chicago*
> 28. In what year was that fire?   *1871*

29. Taller buildings are made of steel and brick because they are ▢.
   • taller   • ☐stronger☐   • cheaper

Skill Items

For each item, write the underlined word from the sentences in the box.

> She paid the <u>correct</u> <u>amount</u>.
> <u>Perhaps</u> they will <u>reply</u> in a few days.

30. What underlining means **answer?**   *reply*
31. What underlining means **right?**   *correct*
32. What underlining means **maybe?**   *perhaps*
33. What underlining tells **how much there is?**   *amount*

END OF TEST 13

WORKBOOK   **131**

Name _____

A

1. Look at the years in the list below. **Underline** the 4 years that are in the past.
   • <u>1920</u>   • <u>1996</u>   • <u>1790</u>
   • <u>1650</u>   • 2380   • 2560
2. What year did Eric and Tom start their trip? *(current year)* _____
3. What year was Thrig from? *2400* _____
4. Thrig was from a year in the ▢.
   • past   • <u>future</u>

B Review Items

5. The time machine took Eric and Tom to ▢.
   • New York
   • Japan
   • <u>San Francisco</u>
6. How did Eric and Tom find out where they were?
   • They asked 3 boys.
   • They listened to the radio.
   • <u>They found a newspaper.</u>

7. In what year did Tom and Eric see the San Francisco earthquake? <u>1906</u>

8. Where did Eric and Tom sleep?
   - in a hotel
   - <u>in a barn</u>
   - in the street

9. In 1906, most of the streets in San Francisco were ▊.
   - <u>dirt</u>
   - tar
   - brick

10. Most of the houses were made of ▊.
    - brick
    - glass
    - <u>wood</u>

11. The streetlights were ▊.
    - <u>not as bright</u>
    - brighter

12. **Underline** the 3 items that tell how people got from place to place.
    - <u>horses</u>
    - <u>bicycles</u>
    - vans
    - trucks
    - <u>wagons</u>
    - planes

13. Fires started when the ▊ lines broke.
    - water
    - <u>gas</u>
    - phone

14. What made the street crack?
    - a flood
    - a fire
    - <u>an earthquake</u>

15. What happened to Eric at the end of the story?
    <u>Idea: He fell into an earthquake crack.</u>

▬▬▬▬▬▬ GO TO PART D IN YOUR TEXTBOOK. ▬▬▬▬▬▬

D Number your paper from 1 through 21.

Skill Items

Use the words in the box to write complete sentences.

guards	amazing	languages	stretched	
palace	future	reply	flashed	perhaps

1. ▊ they will ▊ in a few days.
2. The ▊ ▊ spoke different ▊.

Write the word from the box that means the same thing as the underlined part of each sentence.

stern	finally	crouched	faded
	forever	buckle	bow

3. The <u>front</u> of the ship was damaged. *bow*
4. The smoke <u>slowly disappeared</u> in the gentle wind. *faded*
5. <u>At last</u>, he finished the book. *finally*

1. Perhaps they will reply in a few days.
2. The palace guards spoke different languages.

Review Items

c, f, h, k

6. Write the letters of the 4 names that tell about time.
7. Write the letters of the 4 names that tell about length or distance. *b, d, i, l*
8. Write the letter of the one name that tells about temperature. *g*
9. Write the letters of the 3 names that tell about speed.
   a. miles per hour *a, e, j*
   b. miles
   c. hours
   d. yards
   e. centimeters per second
   f. weeks
   g. degrees
   h. minutes
   i. inches
   j. yards per minute
   k. years
   l. centimeters

The arrow on the handle shows which way it turns.
10. Which arrow shows the way the log moves? *A*
11. Which arrow shows the way the vine moves? *D*

12. Write the letter of the sun you see early in the morning. *N*
13. Write the letter of the sun you see at sunset. *J*
14. Write the letter of the sun you see at noon. *L*

15. Airplanes land at airports. Ships land at ▨▨▨.
   • airports   • gates   • harbors
16. Airplanes are pulled by little trucks. Ships are pulled by ▨▨▨. little boats/ tugboats
17. Airplanes unload at gates. Ships unload at ▨▨▨.
   • docks   • gates   • harbors

18. Which picture shows the smallest force? B
19. Which picture shows the largest force? E

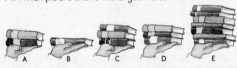

A   B   C   D   E

20. How many inches long is a yard? 36
21. About how many inches long is a meter? 39

Lesson 131   **219**

Name _____

A

1. In what year did Eric and Tom find the time machine? (current year)
2. What year was Thrig from? 2400
3. In what year did Eric fall into an earthquake crack? 1906

The time line shows events. Write the year for each event.
   • 2400   • 2100   • 1900   • 1906   • 2 thousand years ago
      • 5 thousand years ago   • 1776   • 1886

4. The year Thrig was from 2400
5. Now (current year)
6. You were born. (student's birth year)
7. Eric and Tom were in San Francisco. 1906

8. The United States became a country. 1776

9. Eric and Tom were in Egypt.
   5 thousand years ago

Lesson 132   **57**

B Story Items

10. Where did Eric and Tom go after leaving San Francisco?
   Egypt
11. Is San Francisco in the United States? yes
12. Is Egypt in the United States? no
13. When kings and queens of Egypt died, they were buried inside a ▨▨▨.
   • mummy   • pyramid   • palace
14. **Underline** the 2 things Tom took from the time machine.
   • handle   • clock   • flashlight   • scale
   • dial   • tape recorder   • camera

15. If you remember the things that happened in the story, you have learned some rules about the time machine. One rule tells about the handle of the time machine. If you pull the handle down, you move ▨▨▨ in time.

   • forward   • backward

16. Another rule has to do with the door of the time machine. When you sit down in the seat of the time machine, what happens to the door? Idea: It closes.

▨▨▨ GO TO PART E IN YOUR TEXTBOOK. ▨▨▨

58   *Lesson 132*

"What are pyramids for?" Eric asked.

Tom said, "When a king dies, they put him in a pyramid along with all of his slaves and his goats and everything else he owned."

Eric said, "Let's not leave the time machine now. We could take a nap. When it's dark, we'll go down to the city."

Tom and Eric slept. They woke up just as the sun was setting. Tom looked inside the time machine for a flashlight. He found one on a shelf. Next to it was a tiny tape recorder. He put the flashlight in one pocket and the tape recorder in the other.

Then Eric and Tom started down the mountain. They were very hungry. Down, down they went. They found a road at the bottom of the mountain. The road led into the city.

It was very quiet and very dark in the city. Tom took his flashlight out and was ready to turn it on when something happened.

MORE NEXT TIME

E Number your paper from 1 through 14.

1. Some buildings in Egypt are over ▨▨▨ years old.
   • 7 thousand   • 15 thousand   • 5 thousand
2. What is the name of the great river that runs through Egypt? Nile (River)

Lesson 132   **225**

3. Which letter shows where Turkey is? **B**
4. Which letter shows where Egypt is? **A**
5. Which letter shows where the Nile River is? **C**

Review Items

6. The temperature inside your body is about ▊ degrees when you are healthy. **98**
7. Most fevers don't go over ▊ degrees. **101**
8. Write the letters of the 4 years that are in the past.
   a. 1980   c. 2100   e. 1947
   b. 2010   d. 1897   f. 1994

9. Write the letters of the 9 places that are in the United States.
   a. Italy   f. Denver   k. Texas
   b. Ohio   g. San Francisco l. Lake Michigan
   c. China   h. Japan   m. Turkey
   d. Chicago   i. California   n. New York City
   e. Alaska   j. Australia   o. Canada
10. Write 3 years that are in the future. **Accept any 3 future years**
11. What is it called when the sun comes up?
    • sunrise   • sunset
12. What is it called when the sun goes down? **sunset**

13. You would have the least power if you pushed against one of the handles. Which handle is that? **H**
14. Which handle would give you the most amount of power? **J**

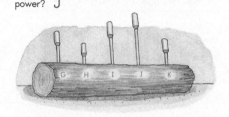

133

Name _____

A

The time line shows events. Write the year for each event.

1. The year Thrig was from **2400**

2. Now **(current year)**
3. You were born. **(student's birth year)**
4. Eric and Tom were in San Francisco. **1906**

5. The United States became a country. **1776**

6. Eric and Tom were in Egypt.
   5 thousand years ago

B Story Items

7. Just before the first soldier appeared, Tom took out his ▊.
   • watch   • radio   • tape recorder   • <u>flashlight</u>
8. Did the soldier speak English? **no**
9. At first, was the soldier friendly? **no**
10. Could Tom understand the soldier? **no**
11. What did the soldiers in Egypt think Tom was?
    • the sun   • <u>the sun god</u>   • a king
12. How did Tom try to show that he was a sun god?
    • <u>by shining a flashlight</u>   • by playing a tape recorder
           • by singing sun songs
13. Where did the soldier take Tom and Eric?
    • to the Nile   • <u>to the palace</u>   • in a pyramid
14. What year were Eric and Tom from? **(current year)**

Review Items

15. Write the letters of the 3 names that tell about distance or length.
    d, e, i
16. Write the letters of the 3 names that tell about time. **a, b, h**
17. Write the letter of the one name that tells about temperature. **f**
18. Write the letters of the 2 names that tell about speed. **c, g**
    a. weeks   d. miles   g. meters per week
    b. hours   e. centimeters   h. years
    c. miles per hour f. degrees   i. meters

GO TO PART D IN YOUR TEXTBOOK.

D Number your paper from 1 through 22.

Skill Items

Here are 3 events that happened in the story. Write **beginning, middle,** or **end** for each event.
1. A soldier led the boys to a palace. middle
2. Tom shined the flashlight on the old man's neck chain. end
3. A soldier pointed a sword at Tom. beginning

His argument convinced them to buy an appliance.
4. What word names a machine that's used around the house? appliance
5. What word means he **made somebody believe something?** convinced
6. What word refers to what he said to convince people? argument

Lesson 133   233

Review Items

7. Which letter shows where Italy is? W
8. Which letter shows where China is? Y
9. Which letter shows where Turkey is? X
10. Which letter shows where Japan is? Z
11. Is the United States shown on this map? No

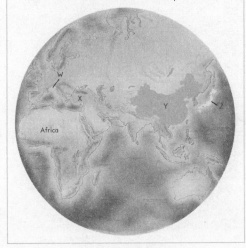

234   Lesson 133

---

12. A plane that flies from Italy to New York City goes in which direction? west
13. Some buildings in Egypt are over ▨▨ years old.
   • 20 thousand   • 5 thousand   • 8 thousand
14. When kings and queens of Egypt died, they were buried inside a ▨▨. pyramid
15. Write the letters of the 9 places that are in the United States.
   a. Denver   h. Japan
   b. Turkey   i. New York City
   c. Chicago   j. Texas
   d. China   k. San Francisco
   e. Alaska   l. Ohio
   f. Italy   m. California
   g. Lake Michigan   n. Egypt
16. A mile is a little more than ▨▨ feet. 5000

Lesson 133   235

---

17. What liquid does the **A** show? salt water
18. What liquid does the **B** show? crude oil
19. What liquid does the **C** show?
fresh water

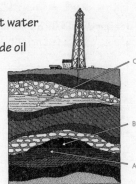

236   Lesson 133

TEXTBOOK

20. Which letter shows Turkey? A
21. Which letter shows Egypt? C
22. Which letter shows the Nile River? B

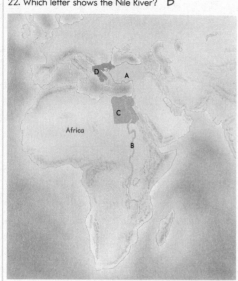

Lesson 133   **237**

WORKBOOK

134

Name _____

A

1. When a person makes an object for the first time, the person
   <u>invents</u> _____ the object.

2. The object is called ▓▓▓.
   • <u>an invention</u>   • an inventor   • an airplane

3. Most of the things that we use every day were invented after the
   year ▓▓▓.
   • <u>1800</u>   • 1900   • 2200

4. **Underline** the things that were invented after the year 1800.
   • shoes   • buildings   • <u>flashlights</u>   • doors
   • swords   • wagons   • <u>cars</u>

5. **Underline** the 5 things that were not invented by anybody.
   • chairs   • <u>horses</u>   • <u>flowers</u>   • <u>grass</u>   • planes
   • bottles   • <u>snakes</u>   • <u>spiders</u>   • rugs

B Story Items

6. The people in Egypt did not have cold milk because they didn't have
   ▓▓▓.
   • cows   • goats   • <u>refrigerators</u>

7. Why didn't the king believe that Tom was a sun god?
   • because the sun wasn't shining
   • because Tom was too young
   • <u>because the flashlight didn't work</u>

© SRA/McGraw-Hill. All rights reserved.   Lesson 134   **61**

WORKBOOK

Write the years for the things shown on this time line.

8. The year Thrig was from 2400 _____
9. Now (current year)
10. You were born. (student's birth year)
11. Eric and Tom were in San Francisco. 1906
12. The United States became a country. 1776
13. Eric and Tom were in Egypt.
    5 thousand years ago

14. What did the king do to the flashlight?
    • turned it on   • made it work   • <u>threw it on the floor</u>

15. What year were Eric and Tom from? (current year)

Review Item

16. **Underline** the 9 places that are in the United States.
    • <u>Texas</u>   • <u>Chicago</u>   • China
    • Egypt   • Japan   • <u>Lake Michigan</u>
    • <u>Alaska</u>   • Italy   • <u>San Francisco</u>
    • Turkey   • <u>Ohio</u>   • <u>New York City</u>
    • <u>California</u> • <u>Denver</u>   • Australia

═══════ GO TO PART D IN YOUR TEXTBOOK. ═══════

62   Lesson 134   © SRA/McGraw-Hill. All rights reserved.

TEXTBOOK

4. The palace guards spoke different languages.
5. His argument convinced them to buy an appliance.

D Number your paper from 1 through 22.

Skill Items

Write the word from the box that means the same thing as the underlined part of each sentence.

survived	damaged	lowered	rescued
woven	clomping	fixed	dull	center

1. Jane <u>saved</u> the child from the river. rescued
2. Tom <u>broke</u> the bicycle when he ran over the rock. damaged
3. She thinks that book is <u>boring</u>. dull

Use the words in the box to write complete sentences.

convinced	languages	modern	discovered	palace
argument	countries	dirty	guards	appliance

4. The ▓▓▓ ▓▓▓ spoke different ▓▓▓.
5. His ▓▓▓ ▓▓▓ them to buy an ▓▓▓.

Review Items

6. Airplanes land at airports. Ships land at ▓▓▓.
   • gates   • airports   • harbors
7. Airplanes are pulled by little trucks. Ships are pulled
   by ▓▓▓. little boats/tugboats
8. Airplanes unload at gates. Ships unload at ▓▓▓.
   • harbors   • docks   • gates

242   Lesson 134

172

TEXTBOOK

9. 32 degrees; 11. Idea: It's not frozen.

9. What is the temperature of the water in each jar?
10. Write the letter of each jar that is filled with ocean water. A, C, F
11. Jar C is filled with ocean water. How do you know?

32 degrees 32 degrees 32 degrees 32 degrees 32 degrees 32 degrees

12. Which is longer, a yard or a meter? meter
13. Which is longer, a centimeter or a meter? meter
14. How many centimeters are in a meter? 100

15. In 1906, most of the streets in San Francisco were made of ▮▮▮. • bricks • steel • dirt
16. The streetlights were ▮▮▮. • not as bright • brighter
17. Most of the houses were made of ▮▮▮. wood
18. Write the letters of the 3 items that tell how people got from place to place.

   a. airplanes   c. wagons   e. trucks
   b. bikes   d. horses   f. buses

19. During the San Francisco earthquake, fires started when the ▮▮▮ lines broke. gas
20. What made the street crack? earthquake

21. Where did Eric and Tom go after leaving San Francisco? Egypt
22. In Egypt, how did Tom try to show he was a sun god?
    Idea: by shining a flashlight

Lesson 134   **243**

WORKBOOK

Name _____

A

1. Write **north, south, east,** and **west** in the boxes to show the directions.
2. Make an **L** where Italy is.
3. Make an **E** where Egypt is.
4. Make a **C** where Greece is.
5. Make a **K** where Turkey is.
6. Greece is ▮▮▮ of Egypt.

   • north and west   • south and west   • south and east

7. Greece is __west__ _____ of Turkey.

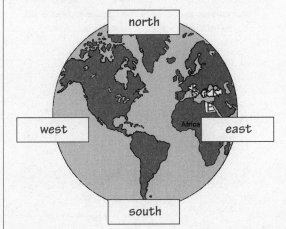

© SRA/McGraw-Hill. All rights reserved.   *Lesson 135*   **63**

WORKBOOK

B Story Items

8. What did Tom use in this story to make the king think he was a god?
   • flashlight   • radio   • tape recorder

9. Why didn't Tom use the flashlight?
   __Idea: It no longer worked.__

10. Name the river that flowed near the city in Egypt.
    __Nile (River)__

11. Which is the smarter way to move grain—by wagons or by raft?
    __raft__

12. Why didn't the people in Egypt use trucks to haul things?
    __Idea: Trucks were not invented yet.__

13. Eric and Tom saw some huge stones on rafts. What were the stones for? __Idea: to build a pyramid__

14. Did the handle of the time machine go **up** or **down** when the boys left Egypt? __up__

15. So did they go **forward** or **backward** in time?
    __forward__

▬▬▬▬ GO TO PART C IN YOUR TEXTBOOK. ▬▬▬▬

64   *Lesson 135*   © SRA/McGraw-Hill. All rights reserved.

TEXTBOOK

C Number your paper from 1 through 21.

Write the years for the things shown on this time line.

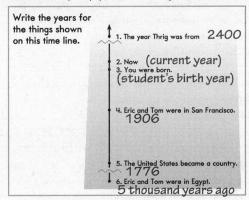

1. The year Thrig was from 2400
2. Now (current year)
3. You were born.
   (student's birth year)
4. Eric and Tom were in San Francisco.
   1906
5. The United States became a country.
   1776
6. Eric and Tom were in Egypt.
   5 thousand years ago

248   *Lesson 135*

173

Skill Items

Write the word from the box that means the same thing as the underlined part of each sentence.

ocean	always	pilot	attention	several
although	globe	galley	whole	

7. The plane's <u>kitchen</u> was very dirty. **galley**
8. He stayed home, <u>but</u> he wanted to go to the party. **although**
9. She gave me <u>more than two</u> books to read. **several**

Review Items

10. Write the letter that shows a tugboat. **B**
11. Write 2 letters that show ships.
12. Write 2 letters that show docks. **(Any 2): C, D, G**
11. **(Any 2): A, E, F**

Lesson 135 249

13. In what year did Tom and Eric see the San Francisco earthquake? **1906**
14. When kings and queens of Egypt died, they were buried inside a ▯. **pyramid**
15. Some buildings in Egypt are over ▯ years old.
    • 5 thousand   • 10 thousand   • 15 thousand
16. When a person makes an object for the first time, the person ▯ the object. **invents**
17. Write the letter of each thing that was not invented by somebody.

    a. television   f. trains
    b. flowers   g. bushes
    c. grass   h. cows
    d. toasters   i. tables
    e. spiders   j. dogs

18. Most of the things that we use every day were invented after the year ▯.
    • 2000   • 1900   • 1800
19. What is it called when the sun goes down?
    • sunrise   • sunset
20. What is it called when the sun comes up?
    • sunrise   • sunset
21. **Write the letter** of each thing that was invented after 1800.

    a. dishwashers   e. buildings   i. rafts
    b. cars   f. computers   j. flashlights
    c. doors   g. hats   k. swords
    d. pyramids   h. chairs

250   *Lesson 135*

Name _____

Ⓐ

1. Part of Greece went to war with **Troy**.
2. The war began because a queen from **Greece** ran away with a man from **Troy**.
3. ▯ ships went to war against Troy.
   • A hundred   • <u>A thousand</u>   • A million
4. How long did the war last? **10 years**
5. What kept the soldiers from getting inside Troy?
   Idea: wall around Troy
6. At last, the Greek army built a **(large wooden) horse**.
7. What was inside this object? **Idea: (Greek) soldiers**
8. What did the men do at night?
   • slept   • <u>opened the gate</u>   • rang a bell

Ⓑ Story Items

9. Where did the time machine take Eric and Tom after they left Egypt?
   • Turkey   • <u>Greece</u>   • Troy
10. Is Greece in the United States? **no**

11. What was the teacher in the story wearing?
    • a suit
    • <u>a robe</u>
    • a cape
12. The teacher wanted the students to argue so they would learn to ▯.
    • fight
    • <u>think clearly</u>
    • make long speeches
13. Where were the ships going? **to Troy**
14. At the end of the story, Eric and Tom left Greece. Which way did they move the handle in the time machine—up or down?
    down
15. So will they go **forward** in time or **backward** in time?
    backward
16. Will they go very far in time? **yes**

▰▰▰▰▰ GO TO PART D IN YOUR TEXTBOOK. ▰▰▰▰▰

Lesson 136 65

66   *Lesson 136*

TEXTBOOK

D Number your paper from 1 through 22.

Write the time for each event on the time line.

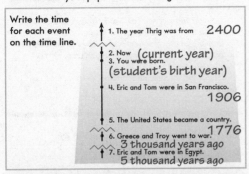

1. The year Thrig was from 2400
2. Now (current year)
3. You were born. (student's birth year)
4. Eric and Tom were in San Francisco. 1906
5. The United States became a country. 1776
6. Greece and Troy went to war. 3 thousand years ago
7. Eric and Tom were in Egypt. 5 thousand years ago

Skill Items

Write the word from the box that means the same thing as the underlined part of each sentence.

| completely | steel | supposed | lowered |
| fish | boiled | moist | buried | tadpoles |

8. She counted hundreds of <u>baby toads</u>. tadpoles
9. His clothes were <u>slightly wet</u> from the rain. moist
10. Jan's bedroom was <u>totally</u> clean. completely

Lesson 136   **255**

TEXTBOOK

11. Compare object A and object B. Remember, first tell how they're the same. Then tell how they're different.

Object A   Object B

Review Items

12. The temperature inside your body is about ▩ degrees when you are healthy. 98
13. Most fevers don't go over ▩ degrees. 101
14. A force is a ▩. push
15. In Egypt, how did Tom try to show that he was a sun god? Idea: by shining a flashlight
16. When a person makes an object for the first time, the person ▩ the object. invents
17. In Egypt, Eric and Tom saw some huge stones on rafts. What were the stones for? Idea: building a pyramid
18. Why didn't the people in Egypt use trucks to haul things? Idea: Trucks hadn't been invented yet.
11. Ideas: They are both horses/animals. They both have 4 legs/hooves, are brown, etc. A is a pony/small, but B is a draft horse/large.

256   *Lesson 136*

TEXTBOOK

19. Which letter shows where Italy is? S
20. Which letter shows where Egypt is? P
21. Which letter shows where Greece is? R
22. Which letter shows where Turkey is? Q

Lesson 136   **257**

WORKBOOK

137

Name _____

A

1. **Underline** 3 things that were true of humans 40 thousand years ago.

   * They lived in houses.
   * <u>They wore animal skins.</u>
   * They wore hats.
   * They were taller than people of today.
   * <u>They were shorter than people of today.</u>
   * They rode bikes.
   * <u>They lived in caves.</u>

B Story Items

2. The force on Eric and Tom was very great when they left Greece because the time machine ▩.
   * was broken
   * <u>went very far back in time</u>
   * was on a mountain

3. How far back in time were the boys in this story?
   * <u>40 thousand years</u>
   * 5 thousand years
   * 4 thousand years
   * 3 thousand years

4. **Underline** 3 kinds of animals the boys saw 40 thousand years ago.
   * lions
   * <u>saber-toothed tigers</u>
   * <u>horses</u>
   * bears
   * alligators
   * <u>mammoths</u>
   * cows

5. **Underline** 2 ways a mammoth was different from an elephant of today.
   * short tusks
   * <u>long tusks</u>
   * short hair
   * <u>long hair</u>

Lesson 137   **67**

6. **Underline** 2 ways a saber-toothed tiger was different from a tiger of today.

- no ears
- no teeth
- <u>long teeth</u>
- long tail
- <u>short tail</u>

7. The door of the time machine wouldn't close because
<u>Idea: It was bent.</u>

8. What scared the mammoth away? <u>humans</u>

9. Some humans ran toward the time machine. What were those humans wearing?

- shoes
- <u>animal skins</u>
- hats

10. What was Tom trying to do with the long branch?

- hit the humans
- <u>straighten the bent door</u>
- move the seat

Review Items

11. Which picture shows the largest force? <u>S</u>
12. Which picture shows the smallest force? <u>Q</u>

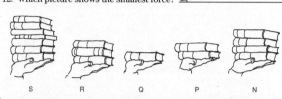

S R Q P N

GO TO PART D IN YOUR TEXTBOOK.

Two men were running toward the door. "Push on the door," Tom yelled. He was trying to bend the bottom of the door with the branch.

The men were only a few yards from the door now. Tom could smell them. "Push," Tom said. "Push."

"Blump." One of the men had thrown a rock and hit the side of the time machine. "Blump, blump, blump." More rocks.

One of the men grabbed the door. Tom could see his face and his teeth.

MORE NEXT TIME

D Number your paper from 1 through 24.

Story Items

Here are the names of the animals you read about: **mammoth, saber-toothed tiger, horse.** Write the name of each animal.

1. 2. 3.

1. horse 2. saber-toothed 3. mammoth
       tiger

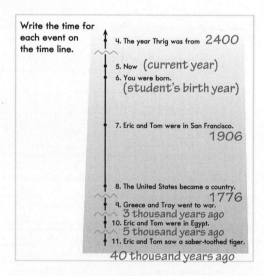

Write the time for each event on the time line.

4. The year Thrig was from 2400

5. Now (current year)
6. You were born.
 (student's birth year)

7. Eric and Tom were in San Francisco.
   1906

8. The United States became a country.
   1776
9. Greece and Troy went to war.
 3 thousand years ago
10. Eric and Tom were in Egypt.
 5 thousand years ago
11. Eric and Tom saw a saber-toothed tiger.
40 thousand years ago

Review Items

12. **Write the letters** of the 2 years that are in the future.

 a. 1980 c. 1890 <u>e.</u> 2090
 <u>b.</u> 2140 d. 1750 f. 1990

13. Write the letter of the one name that tells about temperature. g

14. Write the letters of the 2 names that tell about speed. h, j

15. Write the letters of the 4 names that tell about time.
b, c, f, i

16. Write the letters of the 4 names that tell about distance or length. a, d, e, k

  a. centimeters
  b. minutes
  c. years
  d. inches
  e. miles
  f. weeks
  g. degrees
  h. yards per month
  i. hours
  j. miles per hour
  k. meters

17. Three thousand years ago, part of Greece went to war with ▨▨▨. **Troy**
18. The war began because a queen from ▨▨▨ ran away with a man from Troy. **Greece**
19. ▨▨▨ ships went to war against Troy.
   • 5 thousand   • ☐ 1 thousand ☐   • 1 hundred
20. How long did the war last? **10 years**
21. During the war, what kept the soldiers from getting inside Troy? **Idea: the walls around Troy**
22. At last, the Greek army built a ▨▨▨. **(large wooden) horse**
23. What was inside this object? **Idea: men; (Greek) soldiers**
24. What did the men do at night? **opened the gate**

Lesson 137   **265**

Name _____

A

Write the time for each event shown on the time line.

   • 3 thousand years ago   • 4 thousand years in the future
             • 40 thousand years ago

1. Eric and Tom were in the city of the future.
   4 thousand years in the future
2. The year Thrig was from **2400**
3. Now **(current year)**
4. You were born. **(student's birth year)**
5. Eric and Tom were in San Francisco. **1906**
6. The United States became a country. **1776**
7. Greece and Troy went to war.
   3 thousand years ago
8. Eric and Tom were in Egypt.
   5 thousand years ago
9. Eric and Tom saw a saber-toothed tiger.
   40 thousand years ago

Lesson 138   **69**

B Story Items

10. Where did Eric and Tom go after they left the cave people?
    • San Francisco   • Turkey   • <u>city of the future</u>
11. About how many years from now were Tom and Eric in the city of the future?
    • 400 years   • 40 thousand years   • <u>4 thousand years</u>
12. Could all the people in the city understand Eric and Tom? **no**
13. Why could the old man understand them?
    • He studied old machines.
    • <u>He studied old languages.</u>
    • He studied old people.
14. The people in the city of the future did not fix their machines. What fixed their machines? **machines**
15. Eric and Tom couldn't get a machine that would help them work their time machine because their time machine was ▨▨▨.
    • too big   • <u>too old</u>   • too heavy
16. Why did the people of the future use such simple language?
    • <u>They didn't think much.</u>
    • They didn't have much time.
    • They didn't have any schools.
17. After Eric and Tom left the city of the future, they saw a ship. Was it a **modern ship** or was it an **old-time ship**?
    <u>old-time ship</u>

▬▬▬▬ GO TO PART D IN YOUR TEXTBOOK. ▬▬▬▬

D Number your paper from 1 through 21.

Skill Items

Write the word from the box that means the same thing as the underlined part of each sentence.

| humming | frost | frisky | rushing | announce |
| finally | human | rusty | moments | |

1. Many <u>people</u> were waiting for the train. **humans**
2. She watched the <u>playful</u> kittens at the pet shop. **frisky**
3. The water was <u>moving fast</u> over the rocks. **rushing**

Review Items
4. **Write the letter** of each thing that was invented after 1800.
   a. televisions   e. buildings   i. rafts
   b. cars   ☐f☐ computers   ☐j☐ flashlights
   c. doors   g. hats   k. swords
   ☐d☐ telephones   h. chairs

Lesson 138   **271**

---

5. Three thousand years ago, part of Greece went to war with ▮. *Troy*
6. How long did the war last? *10 years*
7. During the war between part of Greece and Troy, what kept the soldiers from getting inside Troy? *Idea: a wall around the city*
8. At last, the Greek army built a ▮. (large wooden) horse
9. What was inside this object?
10. What did the men in that object do at night? *opened the gate*

11. Write the letters of the 5 names that tell about time.
12. Write the letters of the 6 names that tell about distance or length. *g, i, j, l, m, n*
13. Write the letter of the one name that tells about temperature. *a*
14. Write the letters of the 3 names that tell about speed. *c, e, k*

a. degrees	i. miles
b. minutes	j. meters
c. inches per year	k. feet per second
d. years	l. inches
e. miles per hour	m. feet
f. weeks	n. yards
g. centimeters	o. days
h. hours	

9. Idea: men; (Greek) soldiers
11. b, d, f, h, o

272   Lesson 138

---

15. Write the letters of **3** things that were true of humans 40 thousand years ago.
   a. They were taller than people of today.
   b. They were shorter than people of today. ☑
   c. They lived in caves. ☑
   d. They wore hats.
   e. They wore animal skins. ☑
   f. They rode bikes.
   g. They lived in buildings.
   h. They lived in pyramids.
   i. They drove cars.

16. Write the letters that tell about a mammoth. *c, d*
17. Write the letters that tell about an elephant of today.
   a. short hair   c. long hair   *a, b*
   b. short tusks   d. long tusks

18. Write the letters that tell about a saber-toothed tiger. *a, e*
19. Write the letters that tell about a tiger of today. *c, f*
   a. short tail   c. long tail   e. long teeth
   b. no teeth   d. no ears   f. short teeth

20. During the San Francisco earthquake, fires started when the ▮ lines broke. *gas*
21. What made the street crack? *earthquake*

Lesson 138   273

139

Name _____
Story Items

1. Where did Eric and Tom go after leaving the city of the future?
   Spain
2. Who discovered America? *Columbus*
3. When did he discover America? *1492*
4. Is Spain in the United States? *no*
5. In what year were Eric and Tom in Spain? *1492*
6. Is the world round or flat? *round*
7. Did Columbus think the world was round or flat? *round*
8. Did the fat man think the world was round or flat? *flat*
9. The fat man thought that if Columbus sailed to America his ships would ▮.
   • go downhill
   • get caught in whirlpools
   • <u>sail off the edge of the earth</u>
10. What went into the time machine at the end of the story?
   (a white) dog
11. The fat man didn't like the dog because ▮.
   • the dog was white
   • <u>the dog bit a worker</u>
   • the dog ate wood

Lesson 139   71

Review Items

12. Write **north**, **south**, **east**, and **west** in the boxes to show the directions.
13. Greece is *west* _____ of Turkey.
14. Greece is ▮ of Egypt.
   • south and east   • south and west   • <u>north and west</u>

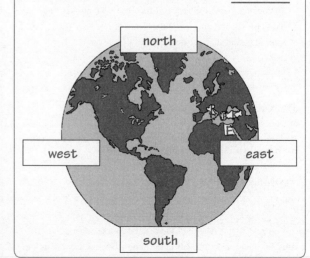

GO TO PART E IN YOUR TEXTBOOK.

72   Lesson 139

E Number your paper from 1 through 25.

Write the time for each event shown on the time line.
• 4 thousand years in the future
• 40 thousand years ago
• 3 thousand years ago

1. Eric and Tom were in the city of the future. **4 thousand years in the future**

2. The year Thrig was from **2400**

3. Now **(current year)**

4. You were born. **(student's birth year)**

5. Eric and Tom were in San Francisco. **1906**

6. The United States became a country. **1776**

7. Greece and Troy went to war. **3 thousand years ago**

8. Eric and Tom were in Egypt. **5 thousand years ago**

9. Eric and Tom saw a saber-toothed tiger. **40 thousand years ago**

10. Write the letters of 3 places that are in North America.
   a. Japan   c. Mexico   e. Canada
   b. the United States   d. Greece   f. Italy
11. Write the letters of 2 places that are in the United States.
   a. Japan   c. Italy   e. Ohio
   b. Mexico   d. San Francisco   f. Canada

Story Items
12. Let's say you saw a ship far out on the ocean. Would you be able to see the **whole ship** or just the top part?
13. Would you see more of the ship or **less** of the ship if the world was flat?

Review Items 15. **Idea: He studied old languages.**
14. Could all the people in the city of the future understand Eric and Tom? **no**
15. Why could the old man understand them?
16. The people in the city of the future did not fix their machines. What fixed their machines? **machines**
17. The people of the future used such a simple language because ▮▮▮▮.
   • They were very smart.
   • They didn't think much.
   • They didn't like people.

18. In 1906, most of the streets in San Francisco were made of ▮▮▮▮.
   • tar   • dirt   • brick
19. Most of the houses were made of ▮▮▮▮. **wood**
20. The streetlights were ▮▮▮▮.
   • not as bright   • brighter
21. Write the letters of the items that tell how people got from place to place.
   a. airplanes   c. wagons   e. trucks
   b. bikes   d. horses   f. buses

22. Which letter shows a horse from 40 thousand years ago? **K**
23. Which letter shows a saber-toothed tiger? **R**
24. Which letter shows a mammoth? **J**

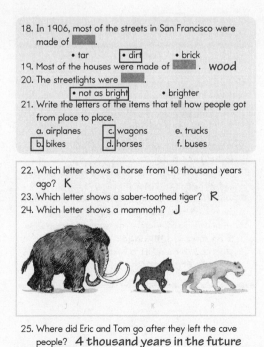

25. Where did Eric and Tom go after they left the cave people? **4 thousand years in the future**

TEST 14   140

Number your paper from 1 through 36.
1. Write the letters of the 3 years that are in the future.
   a. 2099   c. 1990   e. 2020   **a, e, f**
   b. 1888   d. 1699   f. 2220
2. Write the letters of the 5 names that tell about time. **a, b, e, i, n**
3. Write the letters of the 6 names that tell about distance or length. **c, d, f, h, k, m**
4. Write the letters of the 2 names that tell about speed. **j, l**
   a. days   h. feet
   b. minutes   i. hours
   c. centimeters   j. miles per hour
   d. inches   k. miles
   e. weeks   l. centimeters per day
   f. meters   m. yards
   g. degrees   n. years

5. Some buildings in Egypt are over ▮▮▮▮ years old.
   • 20 thousand   • 10 thousand   • 5 thousand
6. What is the name of the great river that runs through Egypt? **Nile (River)**
7. When kings and queens of Egypt died, they were buried inside a ▮▮▮▮. **pyramid**
8. When a person makes an object for the first time, the person ▮▮▮▮ the object. **invents**

9. Which letter shows where Turkey is? **B**
10. Which letter shows where Greece is? **C**
11. Which letter shows where Italy is? **E**
12. Which letter shows where Spain is? **A**
13. Which letter shows where Egypt is? **D**

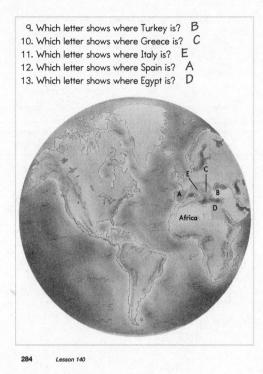

284   Lesson 140

14. **Write the letters** of the 5 things that were invented after 1800.

    a. pyramids   e. buildings   [i.] bicycles
    [b.] airplanes   f. clothing   [j.] flashlights
    c. doors   g. rafts   k. swords
    [d.] tape recorders [h.] movies

15. Three thousand years ago, part of Greece went to war with ▆▆▆. **Troy**
16. The war began because a queen from ▆▆▆ ran away with a man from ▆▆▆. **Greece, Troy**
17. ▆▆▆ ships went to war with Troy.
    • 5 hundred   • [1 thousand]   • 2 thousand
18. How long did the war last? **10 years**

19. Write the letters that tell about a mammoth.
    [a.] long tusks   c. short tusks
    [b.] long hair   d. short hair
20. Write the letters that tell about a saber-toothed tiger.
    a. no ears   c. no teeth   [e.] long teeth
    b. long tail   [d.] short tail
21. Write the letters of the 9 places that are in the United States.
    a. Italy   [f.] Denver   [k.] Lake Michigan
    b. Turkey   [g.] Ohio   [l.] New York
    [c.] Chicago   [h.] California   m. Egypt
    d. China   [i.] Texas   n. Spain
    [e.] Alaska   [j.] San Francisco   o. Greece

Lesson 140   285

22. **4000 years in the future**
(Accept current year + 4000.)

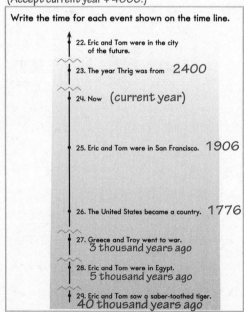

Write the time for each event shown on the time line.

22. Eric and Tom were in the city of the future.
23. The year Thrig was from   **2400**
24. Now   **(current year)**
25. Eric and Tom were in San Francisco.   **1906**
26. The United States became a country.   **1776**
27. Greece and Troy went to war.   **3 thousand years ago**
28. Eric and Tom were in Egypt.   **5 thousand years ago**
29. Eric and Tom saw a saber-toothed tiger.   **40 thousand years ago**

286   Lesson 140

30. Is the world [round] or flat?
31. Did Columbus think that the world was [round] or flat?

Skill Items

For each item, write the underlined word from the sentences in the box.

> The palace guards spoke different languages.
> His argument convinced them to buy an appliance.

32. What underlining names the place where a king and queen live? **palace**
33. What underlining means he made somebody believe something? **convinced**
34. What underlining names a machine that's used around the house? **appliance**
35. What underlining refers to the words that people use to say things? **languages**
36. What underlining refers to what he said to convince people? **argument**

END OF TEST 14

Lesson 140   287

WORKBOOK

Name _____

141

A

Write the time for each event shown on the time line.

1. Eric and Tom were in the city of the future.
   4 thousand years in the future

2. The year Thrig was from **2400**

3. Now **(current year)**

4. You were born. **(student's birth year)**

5. Eric and Tom were in San Francisco. **1906**

6. The United States became a country. **1776**

7. Columbus discovered America. **1492**

8. Greece and Troy went to war.
   3 thousand years ago

9. Eric and Tom were in Egypt.
   5 thousand years ago

10. Eric and Tom saw a saber-toothed tiger.
    40 thousand years ago

WORKBOOK

B Story Items

11. Who did the dog like—Eric or Tom? **Eric**

12. The fat man ran away from the time machine because he was ████.

    • hungry   • <u>frightened</u>   • in a hurry

13. Eric wanted to take the dog with them in the time machine because he was afraid that the soldiers would ████.

    • <u>hurt the dog</u>   • hurt the fat man
    • steal the time machine

14. Which way did Tom move the handle when they left Spain?
    down

15. Did he move the handle in the right direction? **no**

16. Did Eric and Tom go forward in time or backward in time?
    backward (in time)

17. The boys saw a ship when the door of the time machine opened. What kind of ship was it?

    • a Greek ship
    • a ship that Columbus sailed
    • a <u>Viking ship</u>

GO TO PART D IN YOUR TEXTBOOK.

TEXTBOOK

D Number your paper from 1 through 23.

Story Items

Tell about the dog that Tom and Eric found in Spain.
1. Write one word that tells how fat the dog was. **skinny**
2. Write one word that tells about the color of the dog. **white**
3. Write one word that tells about the size of the dog. **large**

small	large	middle-sized	white
black	spotted	fat	skinny

Skill Items

The army was soundly defeated near the village.
4. What word means **beaten**? **defeated**
5. What word means **small town**? **village**
6. What word means **completely** or **really**? **soundly**

Review Items
7. **Write the letters** of the 4 places that are in the United States.
   a. Turkey   e. Chicago   h. Denver
   b. China   f. Ohio   i. Alaska
   c. Mexico   g. Japan   j. Canada
   d. Italy

TEXTBOOK

8. Which picture shows the smallest force? **A**
9. Which picture shows the largest force? **C**

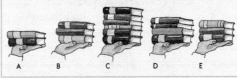

A   B   C   D   E

10. Write the letters of the 3 places that are in North America.
    a. Mexico   d. Canada   f. Spain
    b. Italy   e. Japan   g. United States
    c. China

11. Let's say you saw a ship far out on the ocean. Would you be able to see the **whole ship** or just the **top part**?

12. Would you see **more** of the ship or **less** of the ship if the world was flat?

13. What is it called when the sun comes up?
    • sunset   • **sunrise**

14. What is it called when the sun goes down?
    • **sunset**   • sunrise

15. Who discovered America? **Columbus**
16. When did he discover America? **1492**

17. Is the world round or **flat**?
18. Did Columbus think that the world was round or **flat**?

19. Which letter shows Italy? **T**
20. Which letter shows Egypt? **R**
21. Which letter shows the Nile River? **S**

22. In what year did Eric fall into a crack in the earth? **1906**
23. A mile is a little more than ▓ feet. **5000**

Name _____

Story Items

1. Tom and Eric found a dog in Spain. Write **3** things that tell what the dog looked like. **Ideas (any 3): large, white, skinny, dirty**

2. Which way did Tom move the handle when they left Spain? **down**

3. Did he move the handle in the right direction? **no**

4. Did the boys go **forward** in time or **backward** in time? **backward**

5. After the boys left Spain, they saw a ship when the door of the time machine opened. What kind of ship was it? **Viking ship**

6. In what year were Eric and Tom in the Land of the Vikings? **1000**

Here are some things the Vikings said:
- Su urf.
- (Ul fas e mern.)

7. **Circle** the words that mean **Come with me**.
8. **Underline** the words that mean **I like that**.

9. Why couldn't Eric and Tom understand what the Vikings said?
   - They didn't speak.
   - Their language was different.
   - They talked too fast.

10. **Underline 2** things that tell what the Vikings wore.
    - animal skins
    - glasses
    - helmets
    - slippers

11. Why did the Vikings like Tom and Eric's dog?
    - It beat their best dog.
    - It was white.
    - It was hungry.

12. The boys were eating inside the large building. How many windows were in that building? **Idea: none**

13. What did the Vikings use to eat their meat? **Idea: hands**

14. Which direction do you go to get from Italy to the Land of the Vikings? **north**

Review Item

15. **Underline 3** things that were true of humans 40 thousand years ago.
    a. They wore hats.
    b. They were shorter than people of today.
    c. They lived in caves.
    d. They drove cars.
    e. They lived in pyramids.
    f. They rode bikes.
    g. They were taller than people of today.
    h. They wore animal skins.

GO TO PART D IN YOUR TEXTBOOK.

D Number your paper from 1 through 23.

1. Which letter shows where the Land of the Vikings is? **K**
2. Which letter shows where Italy is? **A**
3. Which letter shows where Spain is? **T**
4. Which letter shows where Greece is? **C**
5. Which letter shows where Turkey is? **U**
6. Which letter shows where Egypt is? **P**
7. Which letter shows where San Francisco is? **R**

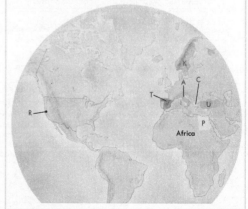

8. Who sailed across the ocean first, the |Vikings| or Columbus?
9. Copy 2 words that tell what the winters were like where the Vikings lived.
   • short   • cool   • |cold| • |long| • sunny

Skill Items

Use the words in the box to write complete sentences.

| probably | defeated | attacked | appliance | argument |
| village | valley | convinced | soundly | studied |

10. His ▭ ▭ them to buy an ▭.
11. The army was ▭ ▭ near the ▭.

Write the word from the box that means the same thing as the underlined part of each sentence.

| lowered | future | jungle | buried |
| survived | blade | tumbled |

12. The clothes <u>turned over and over</u> in the dryer.   *tumbled*
13. Many strange plants live in the <u>warm, wet forest</u>.   *jungle*
14. Our dog <u>lived through</u> her illness.   *survived*

10. His |argument| |convinced| them to buy an |appliance|.
11. The army was |soundly| |defeated| near the |village|.

302   Lesson 142

Review Items

15. Where did the time machine take Eric and Tom after they left Egypt?
    • |Greece| • San Francisco   • City of the Future
16. What was the teacher in the story wearing? *a robe*

    Idea: wall around Troy
17. During the war between part of Greece and Troy, what kept the soldiers from getting inside Troy?
18. At last, the Greek army built a ▭. *(large wooden)*
19. What was inside this object?   *horse*
20. What did the men do at night?

21. How far back in time were Eric and Tom when they saw animals that no longer live on earth?
    • 40 thousand years in the future
    • 4 thousand years ago   • |40 thousand years ago|

22. **Write the letters** of 3 animals the boys saw 40 thousand years ago.
    |a.| saber-toothed tiger   e. alligator
    b. bear   f. pig
    c. lion   g. cow
    |d.| horse |h.| mammoth

23. When did Columbus discover America? *1492*
19. *Ideas: men; (Greek) soldiers*
20. *Idea: opened the gate*

Lesson 142   303

143

Name _____

A

1. What year were Eric and Tom from? *(current year)*
2. About how many years in our future is the city of the future? *4 thousand years (in the future)*
3. What year was Thrig from? *2400*
4. In what year were Eric and Tom in San Francisco? *1906*
5. In what year did Columbus discover America? *1492*
6. In what year were Eric and Tom in the Land of the Vikings? *1000*
7. How far back in time were Eric and Tom when they were in Greece? *3 thousand years (ago)*
8. How far back in time were Eric and Tom when they were in Egypt? *5 thousand years (ago)*
9. How far back in time were Eric and Tom when they saw the cave people? *40 thousand years (ago)*

B **Story Items**

10. Tom and Eric ate inside a large building. How many windows were in that building? *Idea: none*
11. The Vikings from the other village wore ▭.
    • leg bands   • head bands   • <u>arm bands</u>
12. What did Tom use to stop the fighting?
    • <u>tape recorder</u>   • radio   • flashlight
13. Tom said he was the god of *sounds*

Lesson 141   77

---

14. Which way did Tom move the handle when the boys left the Land of the Vikings? *up*
15. Did they go forward in time or back in time? *forward*
16. What season was it when the door of the time machine opened? *winter*
17. What was Tom looking for when he left the time machine?
    • <u>people</u>   • animals   • snow
18. What did Tom hear when he was in the grove?
    • Vikings   • <u>bells</u>   • people
19. Why did Tom get lost on his way back to the time machine? *Idea: heavy snow*

GO TO PART D IN YOUR TEXTBOOK.

Review Items

20. Write the letters of the 9 places that are in the United States. *e, g, i, j, k, l, n, p, s*

21. The United States is one country in North America. Write the letters of the 2 other countries that are in North America. *c, f*

    a. Japan   h. Greece   n. Denver
    b. Turkey   i. New York City   o. Spain
    c. Canada   j. Texas   p. California
    d. Land of the Vikings k. San Francisco   q. China
    e. Alaska   l. Ohio   r. Italy
    f. Mexico   m. Egypt   s. Chicago
    g. Lake Michigan

78   Lesson 141

But then Tom heard something. It sounded like a bell, very far away. So he ran through the trees toward the sound of the bell. He still couldn't see anything. And he was getting very cold. "I'd better get back to the time machine," he said to himself. He started to run back. The snow was coming down much harder now. Big fluffy flakes filled the air.

Tom ran back through the trees. Then he stopped and looked. He could not see the time machine. He called out, "Eric!" Then he listened. No answer. Tom was lost. The cold was cutting into his fingers and ears.

MORE NEXT TIME

D Number your paper from 1 through 19.

Story Items

Here are some things the Vikings said:
   a. Su urf.   b. Ul fas e mern.   c. Left ingra.

1. Write the letter of the words that mean **I like that.** *a*

2. Write the letter of the words that mean **Danger, danger.** *c*

3. Write the letter of the words that mean **come with me.** *b*

4. Why did the Vikings like Tom and Eric's dog? Ideas: **because it was a good fighter; because it was mean**

Lesson 143   309

Skill Items

5. Compare object A and object B. Remember, first tell how they're the same. Then tell how they're different.

Object A   Object B

Review Items

6. Which arrow shows the way the air will leave the jet engines? M

7. Which arrow shows the way the jet will move? N

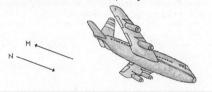

5. Ideas: **They're both trucks; they're both red; they're both vehicles; A is full, but B is empty; A has a flat tire, but B doesn't; A is short/rounded but B isn't.**

310   Lesson 143

---

8. When a person makes an object for the first time, the person ▭ the object. **invents**

9. Which letter shows where Italy is? K
10. Which letter shows where Egypt is? L
11. Which letter shows where Greece is? M
12. Which letter shows where Turkey is? J
13. Which letter shows where Spain is? N
14. Which letter shows where the Land of the Vikings is? O

Lesson 143   311

---

15. Who sailed across the ocean first, the ▭Vikings▭ or Columbus?

a, c, h, k, n

16. Write the letters of the 5 names that tell about time.

17. Write the letter of the one name that tells about temperature. *g*

18. Write the letters of the 6 names that tell about distance or length. *b, d, e, f, i, l*

19. Write the letters of the 2 names that tell about speed. *j, m*

   a. minutes   f. miles   k. hours
   b. centimeters   g. degrees   l. meters
   c. years   h. weeks   m. feet per minute
   d. inches   i. feet   n. days
   e. yards   j. miles per hour

SPECIAL PROJECT

A story that tells about a real person and that reports things that are true is called a **biography.** You may be able to find biographies of several Vikings. One is Leif Ericson; another is Eric the Red.

Look for a biography about one of these men and write three important things about his life.

312   Lesson 143

WORKBOOK

Name _____

A

1. The United States used to be part of ▨▨.

    • Spain   • England   • Italy

2. When the United States announced that it was a country, England went to war with the United States. Who was the leader of the United States Army during the war?

    • George Wilson   • Abe Lincoln
    • George Washington

3. Which country won the war? the United States

4. Who was the first president of the United States?
   George Washington

5. Who is the president of the United States today?
   (current president)

B Story Items

6. In the Land of the Vikings, what did Tom use to stop the fighting?
   tape recorder

7. After leaving the Land of the Vikings, did the boys go **forward** in time or **backward** in time? forward

8. What was Tom looking for when he left the time machine?

    • people   • food   • warm clothes

Lesson 141   79

WORKBOOK

9. Why did Tom get lost on his way back to the time machine?
   Idea: It was snowing hard.

10. In what year were Eric and Tom in Concord? 1777

11. Is Concord in the United States? yes

12. When Eric and Tom were in Concord, the United States was at war. Which country was winning that war in 1777?
    England

13. Who led Tom and Robert to Eric? the (white) dog

14. Tom and Eric could understand the people in Concord. Tell why.
    Idea: They spoke English.

15. The English soldiers were looking for spies. What would they do to spies that they found? Idea: shoot them

16. The English soldiers were shooting at Tom, Eric, and Robert because the soldiers thought that they were shooting at ▨▨.

    • Vikings   • an enemy   • friends

17. The English soldiers wore ▨▨ coats.

    • long   • warm   • red

══════ GO TO PART D IN YOUR TEXTBOOK. ══════

80   Lesson 141

TEXTBOOK

D Number your paper from 1 through 22.

Story Items

1. Which letter shows where San Francisco is? C
2. Which letter shows where Egypt is? B
3. Which letter shows where Greece is? F
4. Which letter shows where the Land of the Vikings is? A
5. Which letter shows where Concord is? E
6. Which letter shows where Spain is? D

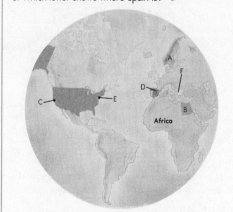

Lesson 144   319

TEXTBOOK

Review Items

7. How many legs does an insect have? 6
8. How many legs does a fly have? 6
9. How many legs does a bee have? 6
10. How many legs does a spider have? 8
11. How many parts does a fly's body have? 3
12. How many parts does a spider's body have? 2
13. In Egypt, Eric and Tom saw some huge stones on rafts. What were the stones for? pyramids
14. Why didn't the people in Egypt use trucks to haul things? Idea: Trucks hadn't been invented yet.

15. Write the letters that tell about a mammoth.
    [a.] long hair   c. short hair
    [b.] long tusks   d. short tusks
16. Write the letters that tell about an elephant of today.
    a. long hair   [c.] short hair
    b. long tusks   [d.] short tusks

17. Write the letters that tell about a saber-toothed tiger.
    [a.] long teeth   c. no teeth   e. no ears
    [b.] short tail   d. long tail   f. short teeth
18. Write the letters that tell about a tiger of today.
    a. long teeth   c. no teeth   e. no ears
    b. short tail   [d.] long tail   [f.] short teeth

320   Lesson 144

19. When did Columbus discover America? **1492**
20. In what year did the United States become a country? **1776**

21. Let's say you saw a ship far out on the ocean. Would you be able to see the **whole ship** or just the top part?
22. Would you see more of the ship or less of the ship if the world was flat?

SPECIAL PROJECT

You have learned what a biography is. There are biographies of George Washington.

Find a biography about George Washington and write three important things about his life. Don't write about anything that you've already read about in your textbook.

Lesson 144 **321**

Name _____

A

Write the time for each event shown on the time line.

1. Eric and Tom were in the city of the future.
   4 thousand years in the future
2. The year Thrig was from **2400**
3. Now **(current year)**
4. You were born. **(student's birth year)**
5. Eric and Tom were in San Francisco. **1906**
6. Eric and Tom were in Concord. **1777**
7. The United States became a country. **1776**
8. Columbus discovered America. **1492**
9. Eric and Tom were in the land of the Vikings. **1000**
10. Greece and Troy went to war.
    3 thousand years ago
11. Eric and Tom were in Egypt.
    5 thousand years ago
12. Eric and Tom saw a saber-toothed tiger.
    40 thousand years ago

Lesson 145 **81**

B Story Items

13. Who led Eric, Tom, and Robert to the time machine?
    the (white) dog
14. Robert decided not to go with Eric and Tom. What was he going to do?
    • join the English army   • join Washington's army
                • become president
15. The door of the time machine wouldn't close because something was frozen. What was frozen? **the seat**
16. What was inside the door on the dashboard?
    • a tape recorder   • a microphone   • a flashlight
17. Did Tom and Eric tell the other kids where they got the dog?
    no
18. What did Tom and Eric name the dog? **Columbus**

━━━━━━ GO TO PART D IN YOUR TEXTBOOK. ━━━━━━

D Number your paper from 1 through 20.
Review Items

The speedometers are in two different cars.

A   B
Miles per hour   Miles per hour

1. How fast is car A going? **30 miles per hour**
2. How fast is car B going? **45 miles per hour**
3. Which car is going faster? **B**

4. When the temperature goes up, the number of ▨ gets bigger.
   • miles   • degrees   • hours   • miles per hour

5. When the United States announced that it was a country, England went to war with the United States. Who was the leader of the United States army during the war? **George Washington**
6. Which country won the war? **United States**
7. Which country was winning that war in 1777? **England**

8. Who was the first president of the United States?
9. Who is the president of the United States today?

8. **George Washington**
9. **(current president)**

Lesson 145 **329**

Write the letter that shows where each place is.

10. Italy **H**
11. Egypt **I**
12. Greece **K**
13. Turkey **J**
14. Spain **A**
15. Land of the Vikings **G**

16. Concord **B**
17. San Francisco **D**
18. Canada **E**
19. United States **F**
20. Mexico **C**

End-of-Program Test

Number your paper from 1 through 30.

1. Who sailed across the ocean first, the Vikings or Columbus?

2. When the United States announced that it was a country, England went to war with the United States. Who was the leader of the United States army during the war? *George Washington*
3. Which country won the war? *United States*
4. Which country was winning that war in 1777? *England*

5. Who was the first president of the United States?
6. Who is the president of the United States today?
7. In what year did the United States become a country?

5. *George Washington*
6. *(current president)*
7. *1776*

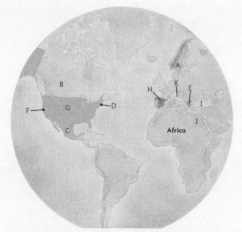

8. Which letter shows where Greece is? **E**
9. Which letter shows where Turkey is? **I**
10. Which letter shows where Spain is? **H**
11. Which letter shows where the Land of Vikings is? **A**
12. Which letter shows where Concord is? **D**
13. Which letter shows where Canada is? **B**
14. Which letter shows where Mexico is? **C**

Write the time for each event shown on the time line.

15. Eric and Tom were in the city of the future. *4 thousand years in the future*
16. Now *(current year)*
17. You were born. *(student's birth year*
18. Eric and Tom were in San Francisco. *1906*
19. Eric and Tom were in Concord. *1777*
20. The United States became a country. *1776*
21. Columbus discovered America. *1492*
22. Eric and Tom were in the Land of the Vikings. *1000*
23. Greece and Troy went to war. *3 thousand years ago*
24. Eric and Tom were in Egypt. *5 thousand years ago*
25. Eric and Tom saw a saber-toothed tiger. *40 thousand years ago*

Skill Items

For each item, write the underlined word or words from the sentences in the box.

> The army was <u>soundly</u> <u>defeated</u> near the <u>village</u>.
> His <u>argument</u> <u>convinced</u> them to buy an <u>appliance</u>.

26. What underlining means **beaten**? *defeated*
27. What underlining refers to what he said to convince people? *argument*
28. What underlining means a **small town**? *village*
29. What underlining means **completely** or **really**? *soundly*
30. What underlining means he made somebody believe something? *convinced*

Student's preference for 1–5

Special Items
1. Below is a list of some of the stories you read in this program. Write the letters of your **2 favorite** stories.
   a. Tina the apple tree saves the forest.
   b. Joe Williams gets a new job.
   c. Aunt Fanny learns how to share.
   d. Goad the toad escapes from the Browns.
   e. Nancy learns about being tiny.
   f. Herman the fly flies around the world.
   g. Linda and Kathy survive on an island.
   h. Bertha uses her nose.
   i. Andrew Dexter learns about being super strong.
   j. Toby the kangaroo finds his father.
   k. Eric and Tom travel in a time machine.
   l. The word bank solves its problems.
2. Below is a list of some of the characters you read about in this program. Write the letters of your **3 favorite** characters.
   a. Aunt Fanny   h. Maria Sanchez the investigator
   b. Goad the toad   i. Achilles
   c. Nancy   j. Andrew Dexter
   d. Herman the fly   k. Toby the kangaroo
   e. Linda   l. Eric
   f. Kathy   m. Tom
   g. Bertha Turner
3. What place that you read about would you like to learn more about?
4. What did you like most about this program?
5. What did you like least about this program?